Nooksack Place Names

Nooksack Place Names
Geography, Culture, and Language

Allan Richardson and Brent Galloway

UBCPress · Vancouver · Toronto

Online audio and visual supplementary materials can be accessed through http://hdl.handle.net/2429/34111.

20 19 18 17 16 15 14 13 12   5 4 3

Printed in Canada on FSC-certified ancient-forest-free paper (100% post-consumer recycled) that is processed chlorine- and acid-free.

Library and Archives Canada Cataloguing in Publication

Richardson, Allan

Nooksack place names : geography, culture, and language / Allan Richardson and Brent Galloway.

Includes bibliographical references and index.
Also issued in electronic format.
ISBN 978-0-7748-2045-5 (bound); ISBN 978-0-7748-2046-2 (pbk.)

1. Nooksack Indians – History. 2. Salishan languages – Semantics. 3. Salishan languages – Phonology. 4. Names, Geographical – Social aspects – British Columbia. 5. Names, Geographical – Social aspects – Washington (State). I. Galloway, Brent Douglas II. Title.

E99.N84R53 2011   971.1004'9794   C2011-905143-5

e-book ISBNs: 978-0-7748-2047-9 (pdf); 978-0-7748-2048-6 (epub)

Canadä

UBC Press gratefully acknowledges the financial support for our publishing program of the Government of Canada (through the Canada Book Fund), the Canada Council for the Arts, and the British Columbia Arts Council.

This book has been published with the help of a grant from the Canadian Federation for the Humanities and Social Sciences, through the Aid to Scholarly Publications Program, using funds provided by the Social Sciences and Humanities Research Council of Canada. The Nooksack Tribal Council also kindly provided assistance for the publication of this book.

UBC Press
The University of British Columbia
2029 West Mall
Vancouver, BC V6T 1Z2
www.ubcpress.ca

Noxwsá7aq Temíxw Pókw

Nooksack Place Name Book

Lhiyá kwes tse7ít xwhítsolh ilh ta Noxwsá7aq Temíxw tolí7 slhiyólh yestí7ixwólh.
This here now is truly the history of the Nooksack Place Names from our late elders.

Án7ma híkwt-as-kwm tíya s7aháynit ilh ta mókw'wát.
It'll be very important work for everyone.

Ílholh ay ná7an kwóxwenalikw Selhám Líche7tsen qe sqw'ó7 ta Selhám Lawéchten.
The authors were Mr. Allan Richardson along with Dr. Brent Galloway.

S7aháynitas tíya Noxwsá7aq Temíxw Pókw tamatl'ótl'em qex̲ syilánem, yalh as-híq'-as
They worked on this Nooksack Place book for many years, finally it's completed.

Stl'í7-chalh kwes tson as7ísta tíya, "Yalh kwómalh as-hóy" ilh ta Selhám Líche7tsen qe Selhám Lawéchten kwes ay aháynitas tíya án7ma híkw syáyos.
We want to say like this to Mr. Richardson and Dr. Galloway, "thank you" for working on this very important project.

Ílh-olh-chalh kw ay wo7-aháyan-as tíya aslhq'ílnoxw ilh ta Lhéchalosemáwtxw-chalh.
We are already using this information for our Lhéchalosem class.

Íma ílh-olh-chalh kw ay wo7-aháyan-as tíya aslhq'ílnoxw ilh ta qalát ay welhtáchtxw-as welhnímelh xwhítsolh qe welhnímelh asláq'alhsólh.
Also, we are already using this information for reclaiming our history and our culture.

Tl'ósmas-kwom tse7ít-as tíya Pókw ay kwóxwen txwyátl' slhiyólh sníchichim ilh ta Noxwsá7aq Stí7ti7ixw.
Then so truly this book will help in the return of our language to the Nooksack People.

Tl'ósmas yalh óla málaq-chalh welhnímelh yestí7ixwólh ay t'ónoxwtewálhen-as.
Then so now we will never forget our late elders' teachings.

Syélpx̲en ta ánats tolí7 ta Noxwsá7aq
George Adams, from Nooksack

Contents

Illustrations

Maps

Photographs

Acknowledgments

FIRST AND FOREMOST, WE would like to thank the elders of the Nooksack Tribe, whose attention, memory, and caring made this research possible, by preserving traditional knowledge and passing it on to us. All those we worked with have passed on now (except Martha Castillo and Carol MacWilliams), but this work is a tribute to their memory. This includes especially George Swanaset, Sindick Jimmy and his wife, Susan, Mrs. Louisa (Johnson) George, Esther Fidele, Mrs. Ella Reid, and Mrs. Alice (Cline) Hunt. Also helpful were the other members of the Halkomelem Workshop of the Nooksack Tribe: Martha Castillo, George Cline, Martha Cline, Norma Cline, Mamie Cooper, Mabel Hicks, Carol MacWilliams, Ernie Paul, Helen Paul, Alice ("Jojo") Reid, Bill ("Elder") Roberts, Matilda Sampson, Philomena Solomon, Dan Swanaset, Elizabeth Jane Swanaset, Maria Villanueva, Clara Williams, Ollie Williams, and Walt Williams. We hope their families and descendants will see their names and their contributions here. We would also like to thank George Adams (Syélpx̱en), the first fluent speaker of Nooksack in the 21st century, for his invaluable help. More about him in the Introduction.

Both of us began working with the elders in 1974, assisted by the Nooksack Tribe (both tribal government and non-elder members) and, beginning in January 1975, by Coqualeetza Education Training Centre in Sardis, British Columbia, where Brent Galloway began work to help revitalize the Halkomelem language, a sister language to the Nooksack language. The latter work included working once a week with the Nooksack elders on restoration of the Halkomelem language and what they remembered of the Nooksack language.

In August 1979, we designed a joint research project on Nooksack place names, combining ethnohistorical and linguistic approaches. It was approved by the Nooksack Tribe and funded by the Melville and Elizabeth Jacobs Research Fund.

We gratefully acknowledge the support of both organizations as well as the support of the Nooksack elders and the Social Sciences and Humanities Research Council of Canada. Sabbaticals granted by Whatcom Community College enabled Allan Richardson to conduct extensive archival research in 1989 and 1997, and to do additional research and writing in 2005. Assistance in converting maps to digital format was provided by Brooke Farrell and Kara Roberts, students at Western Washington University in Bellingham. Six-month sabbaticals granted by the First Nations University of Canada in the last two decades allowed Galloway time to work extensively on the Nooksack language as well as Halkomelem. Grants from the National Endowment for the Humanities also enabled Galloway to do this research, assisted by research assistants Darren Okemaysim, the late Mary Wilde, and Mrs. Sonja van Eijk. We would like to acknowledge their assistance and that of the NEH, which made possible the digitization onto CDs of all the extant tapes of the Nooksack language and all of Galloway's tapes of Upriver Halkomelem. It also made possible the typing into computer files of all the 6,000 or so file cards of Paul Fetzer, who worked with the Nooksack language for two years prior to his untimely death in 1952.

We gratefully acknowledge grants from the Social Sciences and Humanities Research Council of Canada for First Dictionaries of Upriver Halkomelem and Nooksack, with articles on theoretical and descriptive semantics (1998-2001 grant), for Morphology and Syntax of Nooksack (2004 grant), and for an On-line Classified Word List of Nooksack Language (2006 grant) (now nearly complete on writely.com); and from both the Melville and Elizabeth Jacobs Research Fund and the Humanities Research Institute at the University of Regina for completion of the On-line Classified Word List of Nooksack Language. Also see Galloway 1992, 1996b, 2007, 2008; Galloway et al. 2004a, 2004b; and Adams et al. 2005. All helped in the analysis of the Nooksack language terms in this book.

Besides these organizations and individuals, we would also like to acknowledge with deep thanks M. Terry Thompson, Dr. Laurence C. Thompson, Dr. Pamela T. Amoss, Dr. Barbara Efrat, and the late Dr. Wayne Suttles, all of whom provided their help, tapes, and field notes upon which much of our work is based.

The first full-length manuscript of this book was completed in December 2005. We would like to thank the Nooksack Indian Tribe, its members, and tribal employees for supporting our efforts since then to have this book published. We first contacted Darcy Cullen, acquisitions editor at UBC Press, in August 2008, and she has been a tireless advocate in seeing the book through the review and publication process. We also would like to thank Anna Eberhard Friedlander, production editor, Eric Leinberger, cartographer, and the two unnamed reviewers for their efforts in turning our rough manuscript into a finished book.

This book has been published with the help of a grant from the Canadian Federation for the Humanities and Social Sciences, through the Aid to Scholarly Publications Program, using funds provided by the Social Sciences and Humanities Research Council of Canada.

Nooksack Phonemes and Orthographic Conventions

Key to Nooksack Phonemes

Lhéchelesem or Nooksack orthography	Lhéchelesem or Nooksack phonemes	Lhéchelesem or Nooksack orthography	Lhéchelesem or Nooksack phonemes
<a>	æ	<qw>	q^{w}
<ch>	č	<qw’>	q$’^{w}$
<ch’>	č’	<s>	s
<e>	ə	<sh>	š
<h>	h	<t>	t
<i>	i	<t’>	t’
<k>	(k)	<th>	(θ)
<k’>	(k’)	<th’>	(θ’)
<kw>	k^{w}	<tl’>	ƛ’
<kw’>	k$’^{w}$	<ts>	c
<l>	l	<ts’>	c’
<lh>	ɬ	<u>	[u] (allophone of /o/)
<m>	m	<w>	w
<n>	n	<x>	(x^{y})
<o>	o	<x̲>	x̣
<o̲>	(a)	<xw>	x^{w}
<p>	p	<x̲w>	x̣^{w}
<p’>	p’	<y>	y
<q>	q	<7>	ʔ
<q’>	q’	<´>	´

Orthographic Conventions

We use the non-technical writing systems developed by Galloway and others as much as possible, but use phonetic alphabets when source materials or linguistic accuracy make it necessary. Nooksack, Halkomelem, Samish, and Kwakw'ala are written in the practical orthography outlined in the key provided above (Halkomelem's < ´ > and < ` > are high-tone and mid-tone phonemes instead of stresses; its practical orthography also uses apostrophe instead of <7> for glottal stop; Galloway's Samish practical orthography also adds <ng> for the /ŋ/ phoneme in that language).

Lushootseed, Northern Straits, and Thompson words are written in the International Phonetic Alphabet (Americanist IPA) (with citation to where to find a key to those [e.g., *Handbook of North American Indians* 7: 12, 17]); where a cited passage uses an orthography for any of the above languages that is different from those above, the original orthography from that source is maintained. Bracketed expressions of terms in the practical orthography used in the text will be added within quoted passages.

Part 1
About This Book and Its Sources

1
Introduction

About This Book

THIS BOOK IS AN exciting voyage into the language, culture, and history of the Nooksack indigenous people, generally known to themselves and others as the Nooksack Indians. Since it is the term preferred by the people themselves, we will use "Indian" rather than "Native American" or "First Nation." (The Nooksack Tribe, in all its signs, e-sites, and literature, refers to itself as the Nooksack Indian Tribe.) By reading the results of our 35 years of work, finding the places on the maps, looking at the photographs of these places, and listening to material in the online audio and photo supplement (which provides an elder's recorded pronunciations of all of the place names, along with several hundred colour images; accessed through http://hdl.handle.net/2429/34111), you will get a feel for the richness and strength of the Nooksack people's connection to the land. Although a few of the place names refer to places outside of Nooksack territory, most refer to Nooksack traditional lands.

Our task from the beginning has been to preserve as much of the ancient knowledge as we could; to locate, visit, and document every named Nooksack place; and to discover the authentic literal meanings of the names through ethnohistorical research (Allan Richardson) and linguistic analysis (Brent Galloway). The work has been a fascinating combination of collaboration with a wonderful group of Nooksack elders, digging into historical records, and travel to all the named rivers, creeks, villages, mountains, and other sites of the Nooksack people. We think you will be drawn into the subject as we have been.

Although the last fluent speaker of Nooksack, Sindick Jimmy, died in 1977, and the last partial speaker, Alice Hunt, died in 2004, George Adams has been fluent since 2002, after studying the compact discs that Galloway's research assistant, Sonja van Eijk, made from all the original tapes of field work by earlier linguists. Galloway has himself become partially fluent, and he and Adams exchange e-mails and phone calls in Nooksack without needing to use English. In the last four years or so, Adams (Syélpx̲en) has also been teaching classes in Nooksack, and so more people of all ages are gaining some beginning fluency in the language. (The Nooksack language is called Lhéchelesem. "Lh" is like a blown voiceless "l," "e" is like the sound in "nut," and "ch" is as in "church," while the accent shows the vowel pronounced the loudest.) Adams is also captain of the Nooksack canoes that each year travel on a journey with canoes from many other tribes of British Columbia and Washington. His pronunciation of all the place names can be heard in the online audiovisual supplement. Adams is the first fluent speaker of Nooksack or Lhéchelesem since the death of Sindick Jimmy in 1977. He has written the first conversational lessons in Lhéchelesem and used them in teaching the language for several years. Galloway has developed lessons in literacy and a four-year course in Lhéchelsem (completed in 2010). These materials are already being used by George Adams in teaching Nooksack language intern teachers the language and teaching techniques. Adams has also developed a number of curriculum materials in Lhechelesem; he uses "Lhéchalosem" as the language name, rather than "Lhéchelesem," which is the language name with a slight Halkomelem accent and the only way Galloway and Richardson heard the language name pronounced. Richardson has been teaching the anthropology, ethnohistory, and ethnobotany of the Nooksack Tribe in anthropology courses at Whatcom Community College in Bellingham, Washington, for the past 30 years or so, and some of his students have been Nooksacks.

This is an exciting time to be a Nooksack!

This book should be of interest to people in a number of diverse fields. There is much here for students of anthropology, geography, linguistics, history, oral history, law (land claims), natural resource management, ecology, and botany. We wrote it so that the reader need not be a professional specialist in these fields, and so that the average inhabitant of British Columbia and Washington state should find it quite accessible as well as technically accurate. First Nations people outside the area may also find it useful as a model.

It is a book about a nearly extinct Native language, the people who spoke this language, and their knowledge of the land they lived on. Such knowledge includes traditional uses and how these have changed over time, as well as the Native language names for the places in their traditional lands, what these names mean literally, and the stories behind them. Place names give a fascinating insight into another culture or an earlier phase of our own culture. For example, the place name "Oxford" is clearly *ox-ford* and names a location where oxen were able to ford or cross a small river in England. Its widely known significance, however, is not for the place as a crossing but for its association with the famous

Photo 1 *Nooksack elders in the Halkomelem Workshop at the Nooksack Tribal Center, Deming, WA, 30 March 1978. Front row, left to right: Maria Villanueva, Carol MacWilliams, Helen Paul. Second row (seated), left to right: Susan Jimmy, Frank Reid, Dan Swanaset, Mamie Cooper, Louisa George. Third row, left to right: Alice Hunt, Norma Cline, Elizabeth Swanaset, Mabel Hicks, Martha Cline. Back row, left to right: Brent Galloway, Ernie Paul, Alice "Jojo" Reid, and George Cline.* (Photo courtesy of the Nooksack Indian Tribe)

scholarly institution. Similarly, a linguist can analyze place names in Northwest Coast Indian languages, and an anthropologist-historian can discuss their significance. It is on this basis that we have studied Nooksack place names.

In 1974, Richardson began research on Nooksack traditional villages and fishing sites as a temporary employee of the education and planning departments of the Nooksack Tribe. In the course of this work, he interviewed a number of elders and made two field trips. In December of that year, his report on this research was published by the tribe (Richardson 1974), and he helped prepare maps and other materials (Nooksack Indian Tribe 1974). In 1975 and 1976, he did research for the tribe on Nooksack Indian homesteading and completed a detailed report (Richardson 1976) (a much abbreviated version of this report is Richardson 1979). The homesteading research showed a continuity of occupation from the traditional villages of the early 19th century to the present day.

In 1974, Galloway began weekly linguistic research with a group of Nooksack elders at the request of the tribe. This group, shown in Photo 1, had decided to concentrate on the Halkomelem language (the Indian language spoken by most members), and called itself the Halkomelem Workshop. Galloway recorded some Nooksack place names and words when these were remembered by Sindick Jimmy and others during 1974-77, but concentrated on Halkomelem until May 1979, when he began eliciting Nooksack place names from the group, stimulated by field notes of earlier researchers Wayne Suttles, Percival Jeffcott, and Allan Richardson.

In August 1979, Richardson and Galloway designed a joint research project on Nooksack place names, combining ethnohistorical and linguistic approaches. It was approved by the Nooksack Tribe and funded by the Melville and Elizabeth Jacobs Research Fund. We gratefully acknowledge the support of both organizations as well as the support of the Nooksack elders and the Canada Council (a Social Sciences and Humanities Research Council of Canada grant enabled Galloway to complete the phonological and morphological analysis [Galloway 1982, 1983a, 1983b, 1984a, 1984b, 1985, 1988, 1993b, 1997]). In 1983, we completed a 63-page report on our work for the 18th International Conference on Salishan Languages, published as Galloway and Richardson 1983. While this report circulated for many years, we continued with our research, expanding the work to complete this book.

Sabbaticals granted by Whatcom Community College enabled Richardson to conduct extensive archival research in 1989 and 1997, and to do additional research and writing in 2005. Sabbaticals granted by the First Nations University of Canada in 1998-99, 2002, and 2006 aided in Galloway's completion of the work to date on Nooksack, as did self-funded field trips to meet with Richardson and Adams during the summers in these periods.

One of our goals was to visit each site with the tribal elders and to locate and photograph the sites with both slides and black-and-white prints. We made 21 field trips between November 1979 and October 1981, visiting and photographing about 135 out of 142 places known at the time. We were able to utilize manuscript material and maps from the 1857-62 International Boundary Survey, which included the entire Nooksack territory; we visited and photographed these sites and tried to re-elicit the Nooksack names. We also utilized ethnographic and linguistic field notes of Paul Fetzer and Wayne Suttles, as well as manuscript materials of Percival Jeffcott and tapes of Oliver Wells, Barbara Efrat, Laurence Thompson, and Pamela Amoss. Their work preserved much of the knowledge of George Swanaset and Sindick Jimmy, the last speakers of Nooksack who learned it as their first language – audio and written records that have been essential keys to our work on place names. Galloway and the Nooksack Tribe have copies of all this previous work by linguists and anthropologists. We also made tape recordings of all the place names we could still elicit. Copies of

Photo 2 *Nooksack elders, left to right: Louisa George, Helen Paul, Esther Fidele, and Ernie Paul at the viewpoint at the end of Glacier Creek Road, with place 108 Sháwaq, Church Mountain, in the background. 3 September 1980.* (Photo by B. Galloway)

our field notes, tapes, and photos are on file with the Jacobs Fund Collection and the Nooksack Tribe.

An essential goal over the many years of this project has been to preserve a record of the language and cultural traditions for the Nooksack people. The foremost authorities have been the Nooksack elders whose knowledge forms the core of the content of this book. The written and tape-recorded records of George Swanaset (b. 1871, d. ca. 1960) and Sindick Jimmy (b. ca. 1907, d. 1977) were the most important primary sources. The most direct contributions were by members of the Halkomelem Workshop from 1979 to 1981: George Cline, Esther Fidele (d. ca. 1990), Louisa George (b. ca. 1906, d. 1988), Alice Hunt (b. ca. 1912, d. 2004), Ernie Paul and his wife, Helen Paul (d. ca. 1990), four of whom are shown in Photo 2. Esther and Louisa were partial speakers of Lhéchelesem, and their linguistic contributions will be frequently cited. All of the elders shared their knowledge of traditional and historical use of the places, and helped locate the places in the field.

Other elders in the Halkomelem Workshop between 1974 and 1981 also contributed useful information. The place of origin of the Indian names (tribes or villages) are given in parentheses in what follows. The whole group included Martha Castillo, or Ts'etósiya (Shxwháy, or "Skway," name); George Cline, or Lex̱é:ym (Nooksack name); Martha Cline, or Siyamelhót (Tzeachten name); Norma Cline, or Thxwólemòt (Tzeachten name); Mamie Cooper, or Ts'átsesemíya (Musqueam name); Esther Fidele, or Sthṓnelh (Nooksack name); Louisa George, or Tsisxwíselh or Tsisyúyud (Skagit name); Mabel Hicks, or Slól'met (Deroche name); Alice Hunt, or Gyi'x̱démqe (Cape Mudge Kwakw'ala name), Soyó:lhéwet, or Siyá'me (named after Agnes James); Sindick Jimmy, or X̱á:x̱wemelh; Susan Jimmy, or Chúchowelwet (Yakweakwioose name, originally from Squamish); Ernie Paul, or Gwítsideb (Skagit name); Helen Paul, or Ts'etósiya (Shxwháy, or "Skway," name); Ella Reid, or X̱ó:lelh; Bill Roberts, or Snúlhem'qen (Nooksack name); Matilda Sampson, or Iyésemqel (Stó:lō name); Philomena Solomon (she did not remember her Indian name); Dan Swanaset, or Selhámeten (Nooksack name); Elizabeth Jane Swanaset, or Lísepet (based on her English name); Maria Villanueva, or Siyémchesót (Yakweakwioose name); Clara Williams or Iyálh (Soowahlie name); Ollie Williams, or Swolesót (Soowahlie name); Walt Williams, or Dedíchbed (Skagit name taken from the English "Dutchman").

Of all the elders mentioned, George Swanaset was the most fluent speaker of Nooksack according to Fetzer, who worked with him in 1950-51; he was taped by Pamela Amoss in 1956 and by Wayne Suttles as late as 1958. George was an influential elder in the Nooksack Tribe. He held tribal office and helped the tribe recover its tribal status. He is shown in Photo 3 with two other important elders of the 1950s, Lottie Tom and Agnes James. Fetzer (1951b) gives George's biography in an unpublished paper, "Nooksack Enculturation: a Preliminary Consideration":

> Mr. Swanaset, 79, came to the Nooksacks when he was about six years old. His mother, a Sumas commoner, separated from his father, a Langley-Tsawassen High-Born, and married John skʷá·kʷa, the Headman at sčá·wɩxʷxʸɩn and one of the three leaders of the kʷɛ́·nɛč band. When George was in his early twenties, his step-father died and his mother married his deceased step-father's brother, Jim ləqʷəlqé·nəm (called "Kelly"). The family of skʷá·kʷa and ləqʷəlqé·nəm does not seem to have attained true High-Born rank, but, as in the case of Mrs. Tom's paternal line, was in the process of becoming High-Born. For both brothers were Headmen of their single-house villages, and both of them occupied positions of undeniable importance in most of the chief activities of their band and of the Tribe as a whole. George Swanaset, then, is High-Born by birth only through his father's line. (His father's mother's brothers were the great "chiefs" of the Tsawassen, the youngest of whom gave the last potlatch held in that Tribe.)

Photo 3 *Nooksack elders George Swanaset, Agnes James, and Lottie Tom (seated) in the 1950s.* (P.R. Jeffcott Collection, no. 1351)

As a lad of seven or eight, George attended the Methodist school at kʷɛ́·nɛč and at sčá·wɩxʷxʸɩn, then on to Tulalip, and finally, in his twenties, to Haskell, where he stayed for a year.

Upon returning from Haskell, George married Sarah, the daughter of té·nɩs George and the grand daughter of səɬɛ́·mɛtɛn (called, "Lynden Jim"). Now Lynden Jim was to the northwestern Nooksack band má·maqʷəm, what Charlie ɛdɛ́·s was to its southern band, the foremost High-Born leader. He is the only Nooksack of whom I have an account who gave two potlatches, one in 1886 and one in 1912. Thus by marrying his grand daughter, George gained both a substantial dowry and the recognition of being a Nooksack High-Born. The fact that he was the only Nooksack with more than an elementary school education added to his prestige and influence.

From Sarah, George had one child, Dan, who lives with his second wife, Jane, on his father's farm.

After Sarah, George married Susan, who bore him two children, both of whom died as infants. Susan died shortly thereafter.

After Susan, George married Louisa, a nuxʷá·ha-Samish, and she bore one child, Georgina. When the child was but a year old, Louisa separated from George and married Charley Anderson, a Skagit. While George publicly regards Georgina as his daughter, they maintain no father-daughter relations, and she comes to visit him for a few minutes only once every several years.

In his youth, George lived in three different Tribal bands, and, in each case, in a traditional smokehouse. His early alliance with the Methodist Church proscribed his participation in the power-quest. And although his mother was a famous šiwɩ´·n (seer) and his father-in-law was a practicing Shaman, he never attempted to acquire either of these powers. His attitude was, and is, that long ago, before his birth, people did acquire guardian spirit and Shamanistic powers, but since the arrival of the White Man, all of the old assortment of persons who claimed and claim to possess the protection of one of these supernatural forces are fakers, or "bull-shitters," as he puts it. He still believes that some people can manipulate the skwədí·lič (soul-detector) and that there are genuine šiwɩ´·n (seers), but none of these are to be found among the Nooksacks.

Upon the death of James Antone, the younger brother of Mrs. Agnes James and the first "chief" of the united bands of the Nooksack, George Swanaset became "chief." He was elected to this position, in 1920, for two reasons: (1) he was the best educated male member of the Tribe – and this was of prime importance at a time when the Nooksacks were preparing their first brief against the US Government in an attempt to gain a recovery for the lands and food-quest rights expropriated by the Government and individual Whites; (2) Many of the other eligible Tribal leaders were afraid to accept the "chieftainship," because of the work of Charlie sɛqó·ə, a practicing Shaman, who had been run-around when James Antone was elected to be the first "chief," and who was highly covetous of this position. sɛqó·ə, it was claimed, had caused the death of Antone and would kill, by intrusive magic, anyone who dared to fill his role. George, who has always been critical of modern Shamans accepted sɛqó·ə's challenge.

After the Nooksack claim was rejected by the Government in 1926, and at a time when George was in Yakima racing his thoroughbred horses, a cabal of anti-Swanaset leaders voted to remove him from office, and elected the ranking representative of a minor High-Born family, Sam George, to the "chieftainship" of the Tribe. In 1929, Sam George died and the Tribe adopted its present system of formal organization, abolishing the position of "chief." But even today, George Swanaset's influence in the Tribe remains undiminished, if it has not increased over the years. For only two months ago, six of the seven offices in the Tribal Organization were filled by persons amenable to the Swanaset logic, last year's Tribal Chairman, an anti-Swanaset spokesman, being overturned on a unanimous ballot. In this, Mrs. Agnes James, the paternal aunt of that gentleman, joined the Swanaset forces and spoke to her assembled Tribesmen against her nephew's followers and policies.

Mr. Swanaset's memory, in terms of both its clarity and temporal depth, is second only to that of Mrs. James. In fact, he is the only Nooksack alive who can yet speak the Nooksack tongue with ease and fluidity. The aforenamed informants [Mrs. Lottie Tom, Mrs. Agnes James, and Mrs. Josephine George] can understand their natal language, when spoken by him, but they cannot themselves say more than a few simple sentences or remember a few place-names or labels for some common household objects. For when they "were coming to their senses," the Lower Fraser dialect of hɛlq'ɔmé·nəm had already completed its conquest of the Nooksack Tribe, leaving only a handful of intransigents[?] who continued to speak Nooksack among themselves ...

The name Swanaset is an Europeanization of the name of one of the two Tsawassen culture-heroes, swá·nıs. [George Swanaset's name as he gave it on recordings was <Swó̲leset> [swáləsət] or <Swó̲lestsut>[swáləscut]].

[The references to "commoner" and "High-Born" refer to a class system present in traditional Nooksack society and that of neighbouring tribes. There were three classes: the High-Born (hereditary leaders and their families, <selhám> in the Nooksack language and <siyá:m> in Upriver Halkomelem, and other lower-ranked, respected families); commoners (all other free Native people of the tribe); and slaves (prisoners captured during conflicts, usually from other

Photo 4 *Nooksack elders, from left: Jack Jimmy, Mary Tuchanon, Mariah Johnny, and Louisa George. Photo taken in the 1930s at place 80 Spálhx̱en, Johnson Island longhouse.* (Nooksack Indian Tribe 1974)

Photo 5 *Nooksack elder and language consultant Louisa George at the viewpoint at the end of Glacier Creek Road. 3 September 1980.* (Photo by B. Galloway)

tribes, and their descendants, called <skw’iyóts> in Lhéchelesem, the Nooksack language, and <skw’íyeth> in Upriver Halkomelem). A detailed study of this class system is presented by Wayne Suttles in his article “Private Knowledge, Morality, and Social Classes among the Coast Salish,” originally published in 1958. In his words, “Coast Salish society consisted of three classes: a large upper class of good people, a smaller lower class of worthless people, and a still smaller class of slaves” (Suttles 1987, 11).

There are also references to origins like Langley-Tsawassen and nux^{w}á·ha-Samish. These refer to village and/or language or dialect of the parents; for example, one parent from Langley and the other from Tsawwassen, both locations in British Columbia, or one parent from nux^{w}á·ha (Nuwhaha, a Skagit Lushootseed-speaking group now included in the Upper Skagit Tribe, who lived in an area immediately south of the Nooksack) and another parent of Samish origin (a dialect of the Northern Straits language and the people who spoke it).]

A linguistic field notebook of Laurence C. Thompson (1966-69) notes about George Swanaset’s speech that “there are some features of GS’s speech as recorded on tape and in the Thorsen-Amoss notes that suggest GS substituted some Chilliwack phonemes for those of Nooksack – notably /Θ, Θ’/ for /c, c’/, perhaps also /á/ for /ó/.” (In our practical orthography, these would be <th, th’> for <ts, ts’> and <ó̲> for <ó>, respectively.) This is something that Galloway has found to be true and determined to be an Upriver Halkomelem accent to Swanaset’s Nooksack.

In the same notebook, Thompson adds information on Esther Fidele (EF), Louisa George (LG; shown in her youth in Photo 4 and in her later years in Photo 5), and other speakers of Nooksack:

> Esther Fidele, in Bellingham, heard Nooksack until her grandfather died (after she was already grown). It seems likely that she understands the language well (LG thinks she probably remembers Nooksack better than LG) ... Jim Kelly had a brother, Long John, whose son (Jack Johnny) was Esther Fidele’s father.
>
> Sindick Jimmy’s mother’s father spoke Nooksack (his name was Robert sʔalcaldeəb). SJ’s mother = Lizzie, who married Jack Jimmy (half Skagit, half Nooksack). Lizzie’s mother was part Sumas (or thereabouts), and she spoke Chilliwack (or similar dialect). SJ learned some Nooksack from his grandfather but otherwise had little opportunity to learn the language.
>
> For LG’s background, see Skagit Notebook # , [sic; number omitted in original source] p. 602. It should be noted that LG, although she had relatively little opportunity to learn Nooksack, did hear the language a good deal when she was a child; she certainly understands it well. More important, she is the kind of informant who usually initiates the pronunciation of other dialects, rather than

> substituting sounds from her own – so her information on Nooksack, in so far as it goes, is in some ways more accurate than that of informants who spoke it with substitution of Halkomelem pronunciations.
>
> It seems quite clear from examination of the earlier collected material (by Pamela Thorsen Amoss, Jimmy G. Harris, and Paul Fetzer) and from working through considerable material with LG that none of these informants (LG, SJ, GS) really had anything approaching native control of the language. Both SJ and GS spoke a Halkomelem dialect (presumably Chilliwack) and it seems evident that both frequently substituted Halkomelem elements for original Nooksack ones.

Although the conclusion of the last sentence seems accurate for George Swanaset, as tape-recorded and transcribed, it was true only of Sindick Jimmy (SJ) in the earliest tapes and transcriptions. Sindick's wife was a very fluent speaker of Chilliwack Halkomelem, and through this and through work with linguists, in later tapes and transcriptions he lost his Halkomelem accent. Sindick also knew some Skagit, and this and conversation with Louisa George probably also contributed to the loss of his Halkomelem accent. Of course, speaking with George Swanaset would have stimulated or reinforced the Halkomelem accent.

The other elder we worked with who knew some Nooksack was Alice (Cline) Hunt (b. ca. 1912, d. 2004), shown with Esther Fidele in Photo 6. Here's a brief biographical note that Galloway wrote for her memorial:

> I met her in summer of 1974 when I began work with the Halkomelem Workshop at the Nooksack Tribal Offices. This was a great group of elders and younger people, all interested in preserving what they knew of the Halkomelem language and in learning more themselves. Alice was one of the most enthused and faithful, and she had a great way of looking sideways at you with a twinkle in her eye and asking questions. Her knowledge of Halkomelem was extensive, but she was always modest in wanting to learn more.
>
> As the Workshops proceeded over the next few years, the elders met twice a year with the Stó:lō elders who also met weekly to work with me on the Halkomelem language and with others to preserve the culture. At the Workshop each person with an Indian name brought it out and we spelled it and learned it; those who didn't have a formal Indian name, worked out a Halkomelem pronunciation of their other name and used that. Alice actually had three Indian names: Gyix̱démqe (a Cape Mudge, B.C. Kwakw'ala name), Soyó:lhéwet, and Siyá'me (formerly Agnes James's name).
>
> As the Workshop proceeded, Alice and also Louisa George suggested they call me Lawéchten, the Nooksack name of an Indian doctor, Charlie Lewiston, who

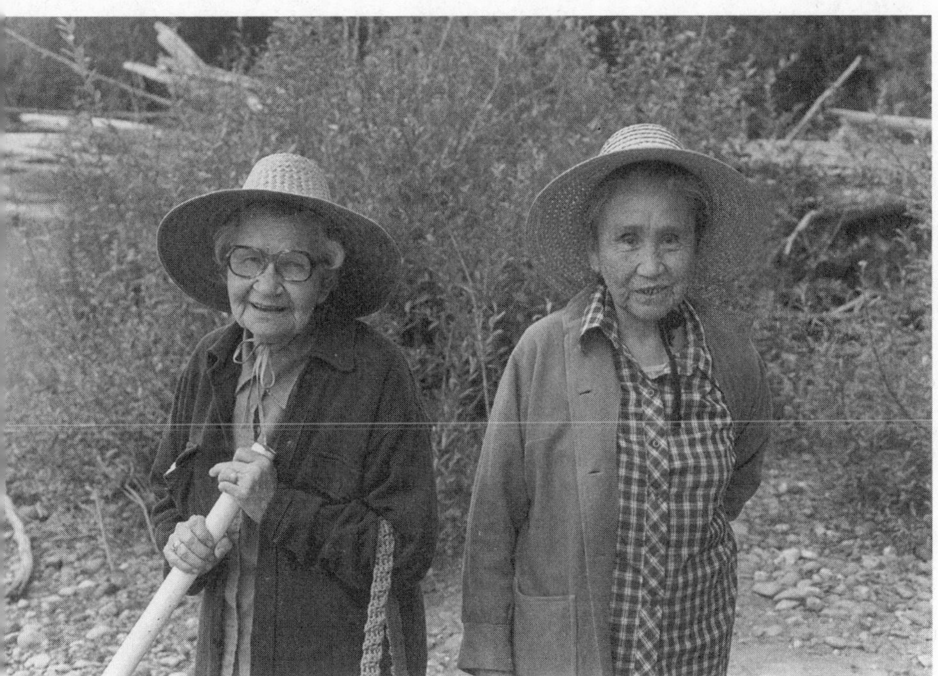

Photo 6 *Nooksack elders Alice Hunt (left) and Esther Fidele (right) at place 73 Scháw7shen* (trail coming to river/beach)*, village on the east bank of the Nooksack River about two miles upriver from Everson, known as "Jim Kelly's place." 14 August 1980.* (Photo by B. Galloway)

travelled around trying to help people, as I travelled between Chilliwack and the Stó:lō people and the Nooksacks. In 1977 at a gathering Oct. 9, 1977 at the longhouse in Chehalis, B.C., she and Louisa George did a formal naming ceremony and gave me that name. Others were being named at the same time (Shirley Leon and others) and the ceremony was done with blankets, witnesses, and a Lushootseed speaker arranged by Louisa George. Ever since I have felt like I was an adopted son of Alice and Louisa.

Alice and Louisa, along with Esther Fidele and several other Nooksack elders, also participated in the work Allan Richardson and I did to document all the Nooksack place names. We had many delightful trips driving and hiking all over Nooksack territory, taking colored slides and black and white photos. We recorded some of our trips too on audio tape ...

When I left Coqualeetza Education Training Centre in Chilliwack in 1980 and passed on the coordination of the Halq'eméylem program to elder Amelia Douglas, I continued meeting with the Nooksacks and the Halkomelem Workshop. Eventually, in 1984 I moved to Victoria and the distance was too great for

> more than visits every year or two. In 1988 I was hired as a professor and had to move to Regina, Saskatchewan. I return every few years to visit the Nooksack elders group and the Stó:lō elders group. Alice was always with the Nooksack elders group till she moved to Bellingham.
>
> The last visit I paid to see Alice was when she was in a Rest Home in Bellingham. I went there with Catalina Renteria, coordinator of the Nooksack Tribe's Halkomelem program. We found Alice in good spirits, teaching the staff Halkomelem words and greetings. We had a great visit and with her permission made a video tape of her speaking some conversational Halkomelem with me and Catalina and her giving some words and phrases. That has been used in the Nooksack Tribe's Halkomelem language program, as it was a digital camera and the film can be viewed on computer and can help teach younger students the language.
>
> As we worked together in the Halkomelem Workshop, we found an old Methodist Hymnal with hymns translated into Halkomelem by Rev. Tate and some elders. I got a modern hymnal and we were able to revive several of them, with the help of elders like Louisa George and Alice Hunt, who still knew how to sing them. When one of the elders passed away who had helped, we sang, Shall We Gather at the River, in Halkomelem at the funeral. We also sang it at a gathering put on by Vi Hilbert [Violet Georgina (Swanaset) Hilbert, daughter of George Swanaset; her Nooksack name was Qw'estániya7] near Seattle. Alice was one of the singers and had a beautiful voice.

In May 2002, Galloway donated to the Nooksack Tribe CD copies of almost all the extant tapes of the Nooksack language made by Amoss, Thompson, and Efrat (as well as quite a few of Halkomelem that he himself had made). We invited to the ceremony all those who had worked with the Nooksack language and were still alive (Laurence Thompson, Pamela Amoss, Barbara Efrat, and Galloway's research assistant, who had digitized and copied the tapes to CDs, Sonja van Eijk). The Thompsons and Efrat could not make it, but the others came. George Adams (Syélpx̲en), a grandson of Philomena Solomon and a speaker of Lummi, was the master of ceremonies. The day before, he and Galloway discussed what "work" would be done. He asked if Galloway had learned any Nooksack; Galloway showed him a page of Nooksack that Sonja van Eijk had asked him to bring, which had Nooksack words and sentences appropriate to a gathering and which we hoped to use, if appropriate. Adams took a copy home and the next day gave the first speech in the Nooksack language in 30 years. The whole tribe was invited to the ceremony of bringing back the Nooksack language, and we were stood up with blankets over us and over the CDs, and the latter were formally given to the tribe. Ever since, Adams and Galloway (with occasional help from Catalina Renteria) have been working to transcribe them and learn from them. Adams has done most of the work and has now become relatively fluent in the language. The three of them speak together in the language and exchange e-mails in it (often with no English) whenever they can.

In 2000, Renteria set up a Halkomelem language program for the Nooksack Tribe and taught and coordinated it. Adams became the Nooksack language specialist with the Nooksack Tribe in 2002, and joined us in 2005 in our effort to complete this work, helping us discover etymologies and pronouncing all the place names in a digital recording that can be found in the online Audio and Photo Supplement. We hope that this book and other materials from the place names study will be of practical use to the Nooksack community as well as a contribution to scholarship. We also want to share with a broader public what we have learned about the Nooksack people, their language, and their connection to the land.

The Nooksack People

The Nooksack Indians are one of many groups encompassed by the broad terms "Salish" or "Coast Salish." The Nooksack spoke a distinct Salishan language known as Nooksack, or Lhéchelesem, which in the 19th century was spoken only by them. In the early 19th century, they lived in 13 or more winter villages on or near the Nooksack River and its tributaries, the Sumas River, and Lake Whatcom, centred on present-day Whatcom County, Washington. At that time, they were both a geographic grouping and a speech community, but not the political entity that they formed in the mid-19th century and that continues to the present.

In 1857, the Nooksack population, excluding persons living at Lake Whatcom, was officially estimated at 450 (Fitzhugh 1858, 326). Smallpox and other epidemics had decimated Native populations prior to this time. Boyd (1990, 136) estimates a pre-1774 Nooksack population of 1,067. Richardson (1979, 8-9), using ethnographic data on the number of occupied houses, estimates a population of 863 in 1820, and 1,125 or more before 1800. The population declined further in the late 19th century, then began increasing in the 20th century. The members of the Nooksack Tribe today (approximately 2,000 in 2009) are the direct descendants of the Nooksack Indians identified as living in the Nooksack River drainage in the middle of the 19th century.

Nooksack territory, within which they had direct access to resources, extended into Skagit County to the south, into British Columbia to the north, and from Bellingham Bay in the west to the area around Mt. Baker in the east. Map 1 shows the approximate territories of the Nooksack and adjacent groups in 1820.

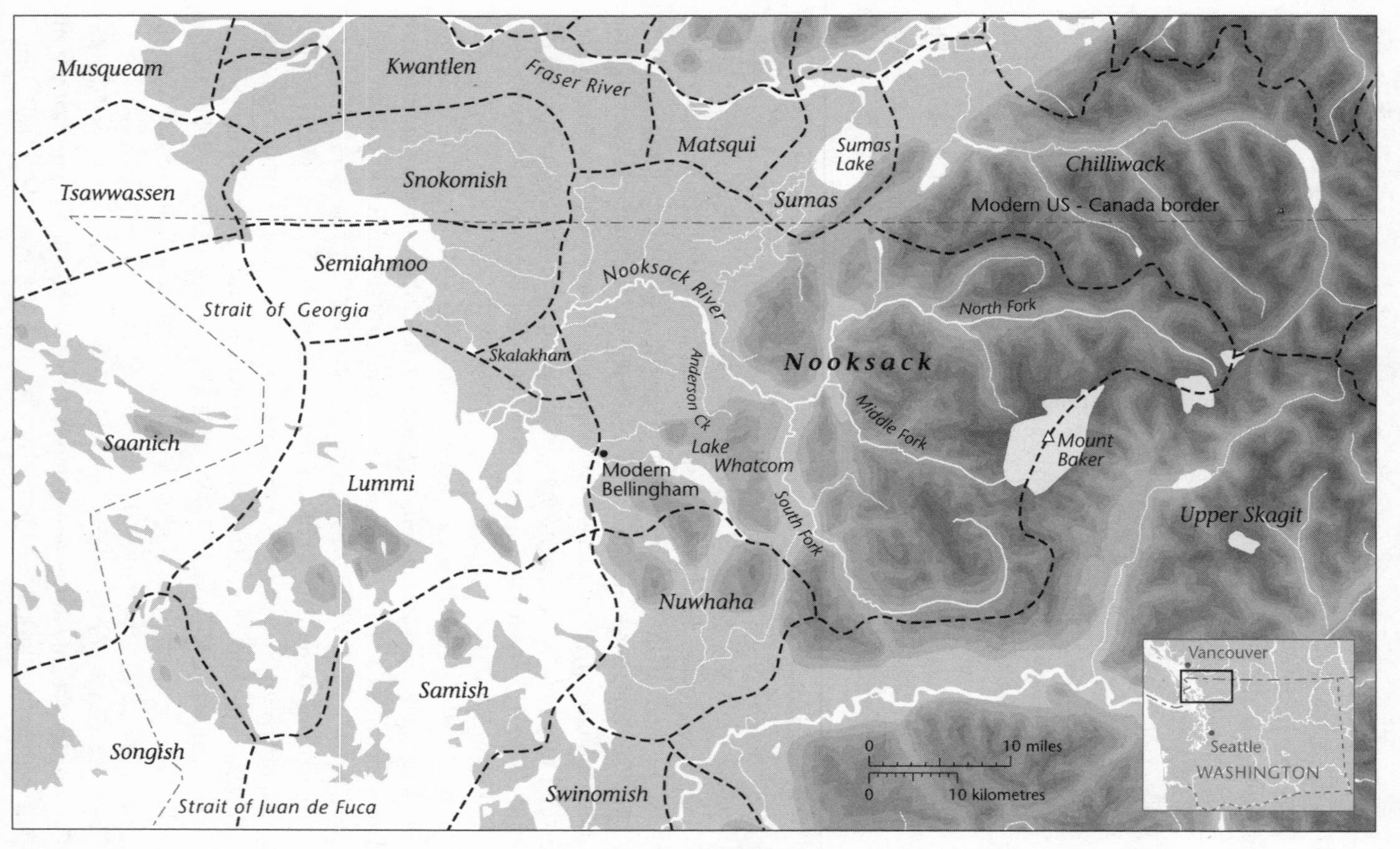

Map 1 *Territory of the Nooksack and adjacent groups, ca. 1820.* (Adapted from Amoss 1978, 2, after Richardson 1977)

This is the earliest date for which we feel confident in defining these areas based on historical and ethnographic records. Also, a specific date needs to be stated for maps such as this, since group territories were undergoing many changes in the early historical period between the first disease epidemics of the 1780s and the treaty negotiations of the 1850s. For example, in 1820 the Skalakhan, or Sq'eláx̲en, were a small remnant population located on a prairie on the southeast bank of the Nooksack River near modern Ferndale, Washington. (This location is discussed further under place name 1 in Chapter 4.) By the 1850s, the Sq'eláx̲en group no longer existed, although individuals of Sq'eláx̲en descent have been noted in the Nooksack and Lummi tribes. Some time before 1820, the Sq'eláx̲en occupied the mouths of the Nooksack River and controlled the surrounding saltwater areas, including Lummi Bay and much of Bellingham Bay (Curtis 1913, 25-30; Suttles 1954, 51-52). The Nooksack were surrounded by neighbouring groups, as shown on Map 1. Despite appearances, the lines on the map do not represent rigid boundaries since the areas used by adjacent groups often overlapped. For example, use of Chuckanut Bay south of Bellingham was shared by the Lummi, Samish, Nuwhaha, and Nooksack. Overlapping lines might better represent the shared use but would make the map rather difficult to interpret. Brian Thom (2005, 2009) presents a challenge to the representation of tribal territories on maps such as Map 1 that will be explored further under "Place Names, Land Ownership, and Territory" in Chapter 6. We conclude that within joint-use areas, as in the primary Nooksack area, a strong sense of territory is reinforced by the distribution of Nooksack place names.

How resources were accessed is an aspect of territoriality that has implications for the use of many of the names to be discussed individually and in detail in Chapter 4. Among the Coast Salish peoples, resources were not open for the taking by all, but neither were members of other groups rigidly excluded, even in cases where specific resources were owned and inherited within kin groups (Kennedy 2007; see also "Place Names, Land Ownership, and Territory" in Chapter 6). Richardson's study of ownership and control of resources on the traditional Northwest Coast (1982) found that among the Coast Salish, three patterns can be seen: (1) direct access to resources in sites owned by kin groups, (2) free use of resources in community-owned and joint-use areas, and (3) access to resources in areas controlled by other groups based on ties of descent or marriage.

The Nooksack people directly controlled the Nooksack River and its watershed from near its mouth to its headwaters surrounding Mt. Baker, plus most of the Sumas River drainage south of the present International Boundary. There was separate kin group (family) ownership of root digging plots at Nuxwsá7aq (see place name 78 in Chapter 4), the place which gave its name to the river and the people. Non-Nooksack people could use the resources in the Nooksack area if they shared descent from Nooksack ancestors or if they were tied to living Nooksack families by marriage. Joint-use areas occurred at the edges of Nooksack territory, including the upper North Fork, shared with the Chilliwack; the upper South Fork, also used by Skagit River people; and Lake Whatcom, with a mixed Nooksack and Nuwhaha village. All of the saltwater areas used by the Nooksack were also used by other groups. Access to resources controlled by other groups was important, although perhaps not essential to survival. On the basis of shared descent or marriage ties, most Nooksacks could traditionally have fished on the Fraser, Skagit, and Samish Rivers. Similarly, the resources of Sumas Lake were available to the Nooksack, even though it was located outside Nooksack territory. Places named in the Nooksack language are concentrated in the primary Nooksack area and the joint-use areas. Only a few are located in areas directly controlled by other groups.

Today, the Nooksack people live predominantly in the area where the place names are concentrated, an area that they directly controlled two centuries ago. The modern city of Bellingham, where many Nooksack people live, includes several named places in a former joint-use area. Nooksack occupation of the area where their language was spoken in the 19th century has been continuous to the present, although the terms of occupation have changed, as can be seen in a brief historical review.

The Nooksack were one of many Indian groups that were party to the Point Elliott Treaty of 1855, in which title to the land of much of western Washington was exchanged for recognition of fishing, hunting, and gathering rights and a guarantee of certain government services. The Nooksack were not granted a reservation. They were expected to move to the Lummi Reservation, but few did. In 1873 and 1874, attempts were made to move the Nooksack to the reservation, but it became clear that they would not move without military force and it was recommended that the Nooksack Indians be allowed to remain in the Nooksack Valley (Richardson 1977; 1979, 10-11). Following this, Nooksacks were able to gain legal title to small portions of their traditional lands, including many of the village sites, by filing homestead claims on them. In 1874, only the lower, downriver Lynden and Everson areas had been surveyed, and seven homestead claim applications were made at this time. These included the claims of James Seclamatan (Lynden Jim, Selhámetan, who is shown in Photo 7), surrounding place 27 Sqwehálich, and of George Olooseus (Welósiws), surrounding place 54 Kwánech. These first homesteads received five-year restricted-patents under the provisions of an act of Congress passed on 3 March 1875. None of these lands are in Indian ownership today, except for the two tribal cemeteries

Photo 7 *Lynden Jim (Selhámetan), an important Nooksack leader of the late 19th century. His 1874 homestead included the site of place 27 Sqwehálich, and in 1890 he donated land for the Stickney Home mission school.* (P.R. Jeffcott Collection, no. 1347)

on Northwood Road. As upriver areas were surveyed, 30 additional homestead claims were filed, and 29 trust titles were eventually granted to 3,847 acres under provisions of the Indian Homestead Act of 1884 (Richardson 1977). These trust homesteads included many villages and other sites that will be discussed in Chapter 4, such as place 74 X̲elx̲ál7altxw on the John Suchanon (Long Johnny) homestead, place 80 Spálhx̲en on the Johnson homestead, place 84 Yex̲sáy on the Sampson Santla homestead, and place 92 Nuxw7íyem on the Charley Adass homestead. These lands have since been administered by the Bureau of Indian Affairs and some 2,400 acres remain in trust today, although much of this is of little economic use due to complex multiple heirship.

In just a few decades, Nooksack settlement was transformed from traditional villages of cedar plank longhouses to homesteads on a Euro-American model. The Nooksack held secure title, as individuals, to a very small fraction of their traditional lands, which had been almost entirely held in common. Despite the change in land ownership, and despite their now living on small homestead farms, there were many continuities with the traditional past. The homesteads were all within a short distance of the traditional villages, which had also been small and scattered. After homesteading, and well into the 20th century, the Nooksack continued to depend heavily for food on fishing, hunting, and gathering at traditional places named in Lhéchelesem.

Since the Nooksack were not granted a separate reservation, they were no longer recognized as a tribe by the Bureau of Indian Affairs, yet they continued to function as a tribe. In 1926, they met under the leadership of George Swanaset to join in the *Duwamish et al. v. United States of America* (79 C. Cls. 530) case before the US Court of Claims. In 1935, the Nooksack tribe voted to accept the Indian Reorganization Act, but was not permitted to organize under the act since it was not a recognized tribe. In the 1950s, the tribe, under the leadership of Joe Louie, pursued a land claim case with the Indian Claims Commission (ICC), which decided in 1955 that the Nooksack were indeed a tribe of Indians whose lands had been taken without compensation, but that they only "exclusively occupied and used" a small portion of their traditional territory (Indian Claims Commission, Docket No. 46). It was further decided that the value of the lands at the time of the Point Elliott Treaty was $0.65 per acre, and that only this amount would be paid. A payment of $43,383 for 80,000 acres of the 400,000 acres claimed was provided by Congress in 1965. The 400,000-acre claim approximates the Nooksack territory shown in Map 1 and includes a large majority of the places named in the Nooksack language that are south of the US-Canada boundary. The land claim money was distributed in equal portions on a per-capita basis to each recognized descendant of the Nooksack tribe of 1855.

In the 1960s, the tribe had a Community Action Program and launched an effort to gain federal recognition. In 1970, it gained title to four buildings on an acre of land; this became the Nooksack Reservation and is the location of the present tribal centre. In 1973, full federal recognition was granted. The following year, the Nooksack Tribe joined the *United States v. Washington*, 384 F.Supp. 312 (W.D. Wash. 1974), case as a treaty tribe with fishing rights for enrolled members. In 2009, there were about 2,000 enrolled members of the tribe, about half of whom lived on or near Nooksack trust lands.

A major focus of Nooksack tribal programs today is land and resources, with special emphasis on fishing. Fishing in the Nooksack River and saltwater areas is an important source of income and food for many families, as well as a source of cultural pride and identity. The tribal fisheries program regulates fishing and works to enhance fish runs and protect the environment that the fish depend on. The tribe works closely with local, state, and federal agencies to review proposed developments, timber harvests, and other environmental disturbances, and to evaluate their impact on water quality, fisheries, and cultural sites. All of this is taking place in the area where the Nooksacks' ancestors lived, and often at places named in Lhéchelesem. Knowledge of traditional uses of these places is an essential element of modern resource management.

A second major area of concern for the Nooksack Tribe today is cultural survival and education. To promote cultural survival, the tribe has begun an inventory of cultural sites of historical and continuing importance. Protection of these sites will preserve links to the traditional past and enable the continued practice of the traditional religion. This study of place names is an integral part of the Nooksack cultural and educational programs.

Nooksack Linguistic Boundaries

The Nooksack people with their distinct language were bounded by speakers of at least three other Salishan languages. In the mid-19th century, speakers of Lushootseed (with Skagit as the most northerly dialect) occupied areas to the south of the Nooksack, speakers of Northern Straits (for example, the Lummi and Samish dialects) lived to the west, and speakers of Halkomelem (Upriver and Downriver dialects) lived to the north. The mountainous area to the east was used by speakers of various languages, including Thompson, an Interior Salish language also known as Nlaka'pamux. The 1820 territory of the Nooksack shown in Map 1 approximates the area of the Nooksack language, Lhéchelesem, but with some clarification needed.

The Lake Whatcom basin was occupied by a group that was bilingual Nooksack-Lushootseed (cf. Suttles 1954, 52) and only loosely associated with other Nooksack speakers. The area marked "Skalakhan" in Map 1 was occupied by the remnants of the Sq'eláx̱en /sq'əlǽx̣ən/ group, which had previously had villages at both mouths of the Nooksack River and controlled the surrounding area. The smaller upriver Sq'eláx̱en area was later used by the Nooksack and includes several Nooksack place names, but the language spoken by the Sq'eláx̱en has not been determined.

In the upper Sumas River drainage near the present International Boundary was a bilingual Nooksack-Halkomelem community. This group, sometimes referred to as the "Nooksack-Sumas" (Paul Fetzer field notes), had strong ties with other Nooksack villages and with the Sumas Stó:lō. To the east of the upper Sumas and western Chilliwack areas is Cultus Lake, British Columbia, which also apparently had a bilingual Nooksack-Halkomelem village. There are various reports from both Nooksack and Stó:lō people of Lhéchelesem-speaking people and also a place name in Lhéchelesem at Cultus Lake. This should not be considered a social or political extension of the Nooksack, but rather an indication of an earlier wider spread of the Lhéchelesem language. There is evidence (cf. Duff 1952, 43; Galloway 1977, xviii; Galloway 1993a, 6-7; Maud et al. 1981; Wells 1987; and especially Galloway 1985) of an earlier, more extensive use of Lhéchelesem in the upper Chilliwack River area in addition to that at Cultus Lake. Marian Smith (1950) also hypothesized a much greater extent of Lhéchelesem in the prehistoric past.

What is clear is that by the mid-19th century, Lhéchelesem was spoken almost exclusively within the Nooksack River drainage and by groups now known as the Nooksack. Bilingual groups occupied its northern and southern borders, and intermarriage with Upriver Halkomelem speakers had already made much, if not most, of the Nooksack territory bilingual in Nooksack and Halkomelem. Intermarriage with Skagits had also introduced bilingualism in Nooksack and Skagit in southern parts of the Nooksack territory. With the introduction of English, all three Indian languages lost ground proportionately until the last fluent speaker of Nooksack (Sindick Jimmy) died in 1977. Upriver Halkomelem is the Indian language now most remembered, with a few individuals also remembering Skagit. At present, few people understand any Nooksack and only one person speaks the language fluently (George Adams), having learned it from tapes and written notes. A few others can speak some words and sentences and have some increasing fluency.

The Nooksack Language: Phonemes and Orthography

The Nooksack language is called <Lhéchelesem> [ɬə́čələsəm] /ɬə́čələsəm/, perhaps a Halkomelemized version of *<Lhéchalosem> *[ɬə́čælosəm] */ɬə́čælosəm/ (see place 29 in Chapter 4). Spellings of words in phonetic transcription are enclosed in square brackets; the phonemic versions are enclosed in slashes, and the spellings in the orthographies of Halq'eméylem and Lhéchelesem are enclosed in angle brackets.

The ethnographic name for the people is Nooksack <Nuxwsá7aq> [nʊxʷsǽʔæq ~ nuxʷsǽʔæq] /noxʷsǽʔæq/ (see place 78 in Chapter 4). Lhéchelesem has the following phonemes: /p, t, (k), kʷ, q, qʷ, ʔ, p', t', k'ʷ, q', q'ʷ, c, č, (θ'), c', č', ƛ', (θ), s, š, (xʸ), ɬ, xʷ, x̣, x̣ʷ, h, m, n, y, l, w, I, æ, ə, (a), o, ´/ (see Galloway 1983a). Symbols in parentheses in the list are in borrowings or Halkomelem-influenced pronunciations. In the broad phonetic transcriptions, quoted aspiration of obstruents (predictable) is omitted. Neighbouring and influential Upriver Halkomelem is called <Halq'eméylem> [hælq'əméyləm] /hɛlq'əmɛ́yləm/ by its speakers. The ethnographic name for Halkomelem speakers (of both Upriver and Downriver dialects) is Stalo (/stá·lo/ or, as the people themselves now orthographically prefer, <Stó:lō>). A phonemic orthography, a slight variant of the Upriver Halq'eméylem or Stó:lō orthography, has recently been developed for Lhéchelesem (reported in Galloway et al. 2004a), and is used throughout this book. The phonetic transcription equivalent of the orthographic symbol for each Nooksack phoneme is given in the Key to Nooksack Phonemes on page xvii. For more information on the Nooksack language, see the sources cited under "About This Book" above.

The chapters that follow will discuss the sources and their interpretation; present a list of Nooksack place names with discussions of their linguistic form, meaning, and location; and examine semantic naming patterns, features named, and typical problems in locating the sites.

2
Major Sources and Their Interpretation

Northwest Boundary Survey, 1857-62

THE RECORDS PRODUCED IN conjunction with the survey of the boundary between the United States and Canada from 1857 to 1862 have provided an important supplement to the usual and more personal records of anthropologists and linguists. The Boundary Survey records include extensive documentation of Indian use of areas near the boundary, details of Indian culture, descriptions of the involvement of Indian people with the work of the survey, and many place names in the Native languages. A brief background sketch about the survey will place these records in historical context.

In 1818, the 49th parallel of latitude was established as the boundary between British North America and the United States from the Great Lakes area to the Rocky Mountains; west of the Rockies, the Oregon Country from Spanish California to Russian Alaska was open for joint use by the British and Americans. In 1846, the Treaty of Washington extended the US-Canada land boundary along the 49th parallel from the Rocky Mountains to the Strait of Georgia. Since a parallel of latitude is an imaginary line, no one knew exactly where the boundary was on the ground. The beginning of settlement, and especially the discovery of gold on the Thompson River in 1856, made a boundary survey necessary (Stanley 1970, 8). Separate boundary commissions were established by the American and British governments and sent to the Pacific coast to begin marking the boundary. The survey teams of the two countries worked independently in the field, the American team from 1857 to 1861 and the British from 1858 to 1862, then later agreed on a final boundary location. The US-Canada boundary of today is the line surveyed between 1857 and 1862. Even though later surveys with more advanced instruments have placed the 49th parallel of latitude more accurately, the International Boundary has not been moved.

The Northwest Boundary Survey generated many published accounts and a considerable volume of unpublished material. The published reports and maps and the formal official documents have very few place names in the Native languages or much about the Native peoples. We cite just one published report (Baker 1900) and one official map ("Map of Western Section," in Cartographic Series 66). The field materials, textual and cartographic, of the United States Northwest Boundary Survey held at the US National Archives have been by far the most useful. Following consideration of the British records, the American records that we have used will be covered in more detail.

Preserved British records are limited almost entirely to official correspondence and formal records. The British survey teams in the field certainly generated a volume of field notes and maps comparable to that of the Americans, but six weeks of searching by Allan Richardson in 1997 and the work of other scholars have turned up almost nothing. After the final maps and related documents were signed by the officials of the two governments in 1869, the field materials were apparently destroyed. The final meeting of the Joint Commission on the Land Boundary was held on 7 May 1869 and agreement was reached on all surveyed points and maps of the land boundary. Following this, the British commissioner, Colonel J.S. Hawkins, Royal Engineers, wrote to the Foreign Office regarding disposition of records, stating that "Anderson" should sort the materials and that "the useless papers should be destroyed" (J.S. Hawkins to Foreign Office, 5 June 1869, FO 5/1468). In another letter regarding the officers of the survey, Hawkins included "Lieut S. Anderson R.E. – Asst. Surveyor, and Secretary after the return of the Commission to England" (Hawkins to Foreign Office, 7 June 1869, FO 5/1468). In July 1869, Anderson wrote that the astronomical and surveying records would be handed over to the Astronomer Royal, selected records would be bound in books, and that "the other records of the Commission being now useless will be destroyed according to Colonel Hawkins' wishes" (S. Anderson to Foreign Office, 22 July 1869, FO 5/1468).

One published account of the US Northwest Boundary Survey (Baker 1900) gives a small selection of Native language place names with their elevations, latitudes, and longitudes. Although all the names are also found in the unpublished records, Baker does provide the locations and some transcriptions of the place names not found elsewhere. The unpublished records related to the Northwest Boundary Survey are for the most part in the US National Archives in Record Group 76 (RG 76), the Records of Boundary and Claims Commissions and Arbitrations. Textual and cartographic records are now all located at the new archives building in College Park, Maryland. To describe the records used in this study of Nooksack place names, we will first consider the most formal maps and reports, then conclude with the rough field materials.

Many maps were prepared for future publication but few were actually published. Cartographic Series 66, "Maps Signed by United States and British Commissioners, 1857-62," includes "Map of Western Section" published by the US Boundary Survey Office in 1866. This map has several place names in the Nooksack area that reinforce the unpublished records.

Cartographic Series 68, "Miscellaneous Maps, 1857-63," includes manuscript maps being prepared for publication. One of these is a large topographical map extending from longitude 120°50′ to 123°20′ W and from 48°40′ to 49°25′ N, roughly bounded by the Fraser River (to the north, to Hope), the upper Skagit River (to the east), Mt. Baker and Lake Whatcom (to the south), and the mainland shore (to the west). This map (RG 76, Series 68, Folder 1, Map 1) shows 244 Indian place names, of which about 55 are Nooksack. The map has some distortions, especially on the southern end, but in general is fairly accurate. It also shows numerous Indian trails. The place names on it were recorded by George Gibbs, a superior linguist of his day. We worked from high-quality copies and both of us have examined the original at the National Archives. A portion of this map, centred on the Nooksack area, is reproduced here as Map 2.

We were first made aware of another document in the National Archives through the courtesy of Randy Bouchard, and then realized that it coordinated directly with the map. This document, in the handwriting of George Gibbs, is entitled "Indian Nomenclature" and is located with the textual records in Entry 223 (E 223), "List of Indian Words, n.d." (Gibbs 1857-61). It lists 248 Indian place names on the first nine pages, of which 63 are additional to those on the map; the rest are identical, with a few minor variants, to those on the map. The map also has 54 place names that are not on the list. The advantage of the list is that it begins with a phonetic key to the orthography Gibbs used, and it gives in words the location of each place name and the characteristics of most – river, village, mountain, bay, bluff, and so on.

As mentioned, the quality of the linguistic transcriptions was very high for its day. For example, Galloway, working with the elders, was able to make accurate modern transcriptions from most of the Northwest Boundary Survey transcriptions, and with that find etymologies for many of them. George Gibbs was the most accurate. Considering the lack of recent Nooksack speakers (one fluent, six or seven partial or fragmentary speakers), much of our work would not have been possible if the transcriptions had been similar in quality to the usual government documents of the day.

Our opinion is that many informants about Nooksack place names provided their information to intermediate Indian guides such as Teosaluk (probably <Tiyóseleq>), who was, we believe, a Thompson Indian (Nooksack <s7ómena> Thompson Indian [WS:GS]), not a Nooksack, but who could certainly repeat

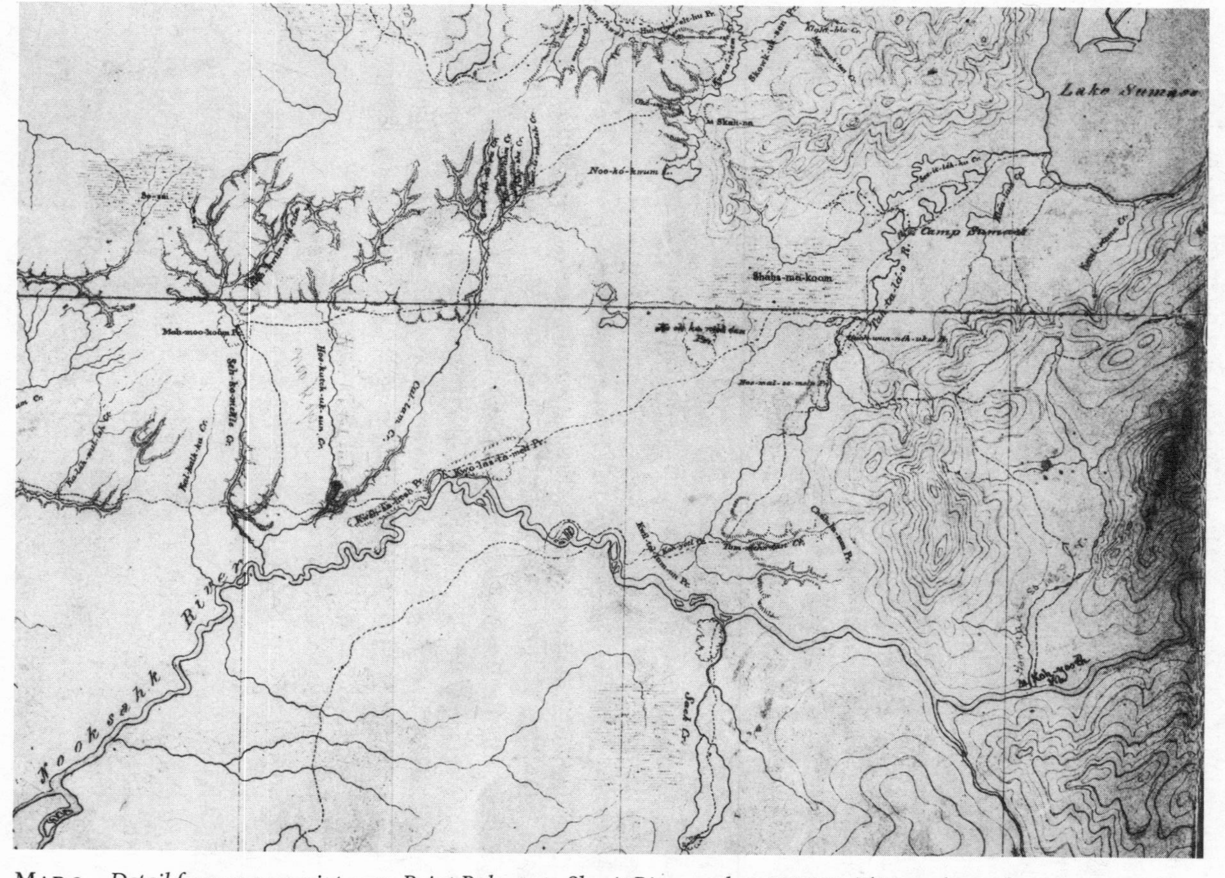

MAP 2 *Detail from manuscript map, Point Roberts to Skagit River, scale 1:120,000. This is a large, formal map without date or title, and with handwritten additions.* (United States Northwest Boundary Survey, RG 76, Series 68, Folder 1, Map 1)

Nooksack place names accurately. We have noted occasional inaccuracies of location and map drawing – to be expected since the Boundary Survey did not have our modern topographic and satellite mapping techniques – but the work is otherwise generally of very high quality as well. The surveyors used state-of-the-art equipment and good personnel, and the quality of most locations on the maps was excellent for their day, otherwise they would not have correlated so well with the locations we got from the Nooksack elders of the 1970s. This confirms that the surveyors' application of toponyms to place and geographic extent were both fairly accurate. There is no better confirmation of this than the study we have completed with the help of all the extant tape recordings and written recordings of the Nooksack language as well as the elders of the 1970s.

Several members of the Boundary Survey completed reports on their field work. These are grouped at the National Archives in Entry 196 (E 196), "Reports on Surveys, 1857-66." For the Nooksack area, the reports on the reconnaissance trips of G. Clinton Gardner and Henry Custer are the most valuable. Gardner was the assistant astronomer and surveyor, while Custer was listed as a topographer (United States Congress 1869). Although number three in the hierarchy, Gardner appears to have been the most important person in the day-to-day work of the survey. He also took charge of the first reconnaissance of new areas, including two trips to the Nooksack area soon after the arrival of the US Boundary Commission at Camp Simiahmoo, located at present-day White Rock, BC. Custer did follow-up reconnaissance to determine access routes to less accessible portions of the boundary, and to gather data for maps. In their reports on this work, they described in detail their route of travel, Indian settlements, and their encounters with Indian people.

The following excerpts give a sense of the work of the Boundary Survey, interaction with the Nooksack Indians and other Native people, and the historical value of the field reports. Spelling and punctuation are as in the originals. Gardner's report (1857a), describes travel from Bellingham Bay up the Nooksack River with a stop at prairies in the Lynden area, then overland travel from near Everson to the Sumas area:

Camp Semiahmoo N.W. Bdy. Survey
September 3rd 1857

Lieut. John G. Parke
Chief Asstr. & Surveyor N.W.B.S.
Sir,

I have the honor to submit the following report of the reconnaissance of the country east of this Camp, made pursuant to your instructions with the party consisting of the following persons: Mr. Herbst Mr. Custer and Mr. Peabody – Harris and Jim (an indian boy)

We left this place on the 24th of Aug. in the boat belonging to the survey and arrived at Bellingham Bay that night, by the passage through the mouth of the Lummi river. The Lummi empties by one channel into Bellingham Bay and by two channels into a small bay formed by Sandy Point with the main land; the most southern of which was the route travelled. The passage is difficult and can only be made at high tide.

On the morning of the 25th Mr. Peabody made a selection of seven Indians from those that are found in the vicinity of Bellingham Bay and hired two canoes, so by half past one o'clock we were en route up the river. Before starting I sent the crew, of three men, in the boat back to this Camp with all the letters that were at Bellingham Bay for different members of the survey. After travelling five miles and passing one Indian village we came to the large drift that obstructs canoe passage. The Indians have cut a trail around it and laid cross timbers to enable them to haul their canoes over: so a portage of about six hundred yards was easily made and we encamped at the end of it for the night. The Indians living on the river are different bands of the Nook-sahk tribe and call it the Nook-sahk river – the different channels through which it empties itself they call the Lummi river. The timber and underbrush are very dense on its banks, on account of which, we were unable to observe for our position.

On the 26th we continued our journey in two other canoes which were obtained above the drift, and after travelling about six miles and passing two Indian villages we came to a second drift, around which the river had cut a channel. Finding our force not sufficient I hired an additional Indian making in all nine Indians in our party: After travelling during the day about twenty miles we came to the upper portion of the Nook-sahk Prairie: this Prairie extends for some miles almost parallel to the river on its north bank and appears to be very fertile soil ...

On the 27th after travelling about thirteen miles we came to the point where the trail leaves the river just above a large Indian village. Here we left our canoes and packed the Indians for the trip across to the Soo-mass Prairie. After travelling four miles over quite a good foot path through dense timber and underbrush we encamped for the night a short distance beyond an unoccupied Indian hut.

Henry Custer, although officially listed as a topographer, is referred to by himself and others as just "assistant." He was an immigrant to the United States from German-speaking Switzerland (Beckey 2003, 147), so his English spelling and usage is often unusual. Even so, his reports give more detail and a better feel for the land and the Native people. Also, Indian place names are carefully recorded and located on preliminary field maps, such as the one reproduced here as Map 3. The following is an excerpt from his report on "Reconnaissance of the Country between Camp Simiahmoo and Sumass Prairie ... April 7, 1858" (Custer 1858a). The route of travel (shown on Map 3) is overland from Drayton Harbor, crossing Bertrand Creek, then Fishtrap Creek, to reach the same "Nooksahk Prairie" visited with Gardner in 1857.

> The trail here is very good, through green timber with little underbrush. Cheerfully everybody proceeded on, at 9^h AM, we crosse a large Tributary of the Séh-ku-mich, the Noo-Kópe coming from the north, after crossing this Stream the ground began to rise, and continued so, until the trail lead to a considerable eminence. The ridge on which we are here now is cut through by a large Creek the Kwoo-laām, wich flows in a cañon, about 50 or 60′ deep and 200 or 300 yards wide. This creek is crossed by the trail wich has now a Northeast direct. Here one of the Indians killed a pheasant, a very pleasant addition to the small variety of our supplies.
>
> About 11 AM we found ourselves on the boarders of the lower Nook-sahk prairie, about 15-16 miles from Camp Simiahmoo. I proceeded for about ¾ of a mile further up the Prairie and encamped on the boarders of a slough leading to the River nearby. We were not long in Camp before some Indians of the Nooksahk tribe living on the boarders of the River came to gratify their curiosity and to see the strangers. They compared very favorably with our Saltwater Indians they were well formed and intelligent looking fellows, and some of their women quite handsome. Very soon barter begun, they brought potatoes of wich they had plenty, I bought some to add to our supplies.

In June 1858, Custer surveyed and mapped the coastline south from Semiahmoo, including the mouths of the Lummi/Nooksack River and Bellingham Bay. After reaching the town of Whatcom, he travelled to Lake Whatcom for further reconnaissance and then went overland to the Nooksack River. This last route north from the Agate Bay area, passing Squalicum Lake and following Anderson Creek downstream, he describes as follows (Custer 1858b):

> *June 20* I had engaged the services of our lake Indian, as guide and paker and early this morning we proceeded on our way. The trail proved to be a very rough and indistinct one difficult & tiresome to follow: its direction was almost due north, through a low breack of the mountains surrounding the lake. At noon we reached a small lacke the headwaters of the Nocallachum creek emptiing in the sound near Whatcomb. From here the trail leads over undulating country densely timbered, we crosse the Sack creek, a small stream coming from the Southeast & some of its tributaries several times. At last after a most fatigueing march of

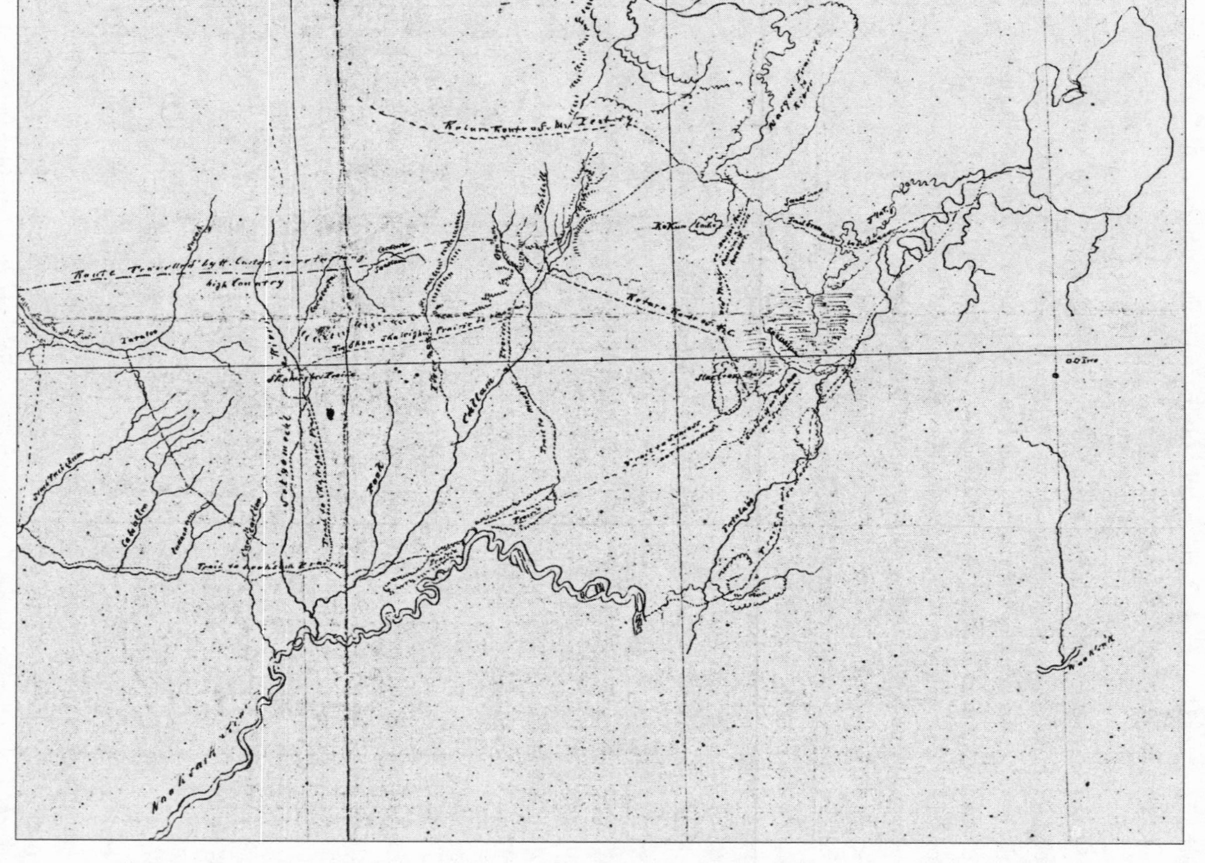

MAP 3 *The area between Semiahmoo and Sumas based on reconnaissances of 1857 and early 1858, especially the route of Henry Custer in March-April 1858.* (United States Northwest Boundary Survey, RG 76, Series 69, Map 23)

> 15 miles we reached a little prairie on the boarders of the Nooksahk river, near by the Sak creek empties into the Nooksahk, and on its banks we selected our camp. Numerous Indians were here occupied to cultivate their potatoe fields, & certainly the exidingly rich soil of the prairie promised rich crops. The prairie is only of small area, perhaps ½ mile long and 300-400 y wide & covered with an immense growht of ferns, through which we had difficulty to break our way. We were soon surrounded by a circle of curious Indians, to whom our esploits were duly made interessting by their fellow tribesman our talkative Nooksahk Indian. Everything however went on in perfect peace & quitness.

This last location is the place named Nuxwsá7aq (see place 78 in Chapter 4), meaning 'always bracken fern roots' in Lhéchelesem, the original Nooksack language. This specific place name is the source of the word "Nooksack," already with a wider geographic use in 1858.

Another important group of materials from the US National Archives consists of the bound field notebooks in Entry 201 (E 201), "Topographic Notes, 1857," and Entry 202 (E 202), "Reconnaissance Books, 1857-63." These are the immediate, in-the-field records of the explorations later written up in the reports. Place names were recorded in the field and sketches made of areas while still in the field. Henry Custer appears to have been the best at recording these details.

Finally, we come to the field maps grouped under Cartographic Series 69, "Field Maps, 1857-62." These reinforce and expand on the field reports and field notebooks. Many are referred to in the discussion of the specific place names in Chapter 4. Two unusual maps, Maps 26 and 27 in the US National Archives Series 69, drawn by Teosaluk, a "Samana" Indian, will be discussed here, with Map 26 reproduced here as Map 4. These maps, with 66 Indian names, have some details and spellings that all of the other maps lack, although the scale and placement are badly off in places. Gibbs labelled features on the map in Halkomelem, Nooksack, and probably Thompson. Teosaluk's tribal and linguistic affiliation was probably Thompson; "Samana" is the Nooksack and Halkomelem name for the Thompson people (Nooksack <s7ómena> [sʔámənɛ] [WS:GS, see "Field Notes" below] /sʔámənæ/, Upriver Halkomelem <s'ómél:a> /sʔámə́l·ɛ/). Teosaluk's main information concerned the eastern boundaries of Stó:lō and Nooksack territory, the mountainous inland areas, especially east of Mt. Baker. Baker (1900, 45) reports a Samana village on the Chilliwack River, 24 miles above (upriver from) the Chilliwack Depot and 2 miles above the mouth of Senehsay (Slesse) Creek. This was 12¾ miles east of the nearest Stó:lō village (Soowahlie <Th'ewálí> /Θ'əwɛ́lí/) and quite isolated. Teosaluk may have come from this group. Henry Custer (1866) wrote the following of him on page 4 of a 49-page report (spellings are his):

> One of the Indians in my employ (Jhiusoloc) a Samona Chief, had the most extended geographical knowledge of any Indian ever had to deal with. By request he made me a map of the extend of country he was well acquainted with, it was Bounded by the Fraser River to the North, by the Skagit River to the East, by some tributary of this river to the South, and by the Nookhsahk + Chiloweyeuk Rivers to the West. Within these limits his knowledge of the country was most minute + reliable. The map he made of it, although in the most primitive style, was remarkable for its oreitness [rightness?] + completeness. In this way we gained most of our first knowledge of the country as also many of the names of its mountains, smaller streams + lakes.

Some of the names on this map clearly appear to be Thompson ("Wil-la-kul-sa-háist," "Nuch-nái-cheen," "N'mes-téh-tam," "Hoz-a-méen"), but further study by those knowledgable in Thompson is necessary to sort out the details and crucial in discovering the eastern boundaries of Stó:lō, Nooksack, and Skagit territories and the southern and western boundaries of Thompson territory in BC and Washington, although place names can occur beyond territorial boundaries, as in cases such as the Nooksack name for Sumas Lake or the Lummi name for Mt. Baker (see "Place Names, Land Ownership, and Territory" in Chapter 6).

By comparing the various archival documents with topographical maps of Washington and British Columbia, it has been possible to locate most of the named items fairly precisely. Comparing the spellings of Gibbs with transcriptions in other sources has resulted in the identification of well over a hundred so far with modern attestations of Nooksack and Halkomelem names, and half a dozen with modern attestations of Semiahmoo or Lummi names. This provides a key to aid in the phonetic interpretation of the remaining names. Gibbs shows neither glottalization nor glottal stop, but glottal stop and semi-vowels between vowels can sometimes be inferred from his syllabification by hyphens in each word. Labialization is usually shown, by various means such as "kw," "wh," "hw," "qu," "hoo," "ko," "ku," and so on. Stress is shown for most names, on either the map, the list, or both. Postvelars are not shown directly, but "k" followed by a consonant or a non-rounded vowel (in the absence of /k/ and /k'/ in Halkomelem and Nooksack) indicates /q/, /q'/, or /x̣/. Further, because /i/ is [iᵊ] before postvelars in Halkomelem and Nooksack, combinations like "éh-a-kw" or "éh-u-kw" often indicate [iᵊqʷ] or [iᵊq'ʷ] or [iᵊx̣ʷ]. /xʸ/ is shown for Halkomelem by "sh" and rarely by "ch"; /x̣/ is shown also by "ch" or "h"; /č/ or /č'/ is shown by

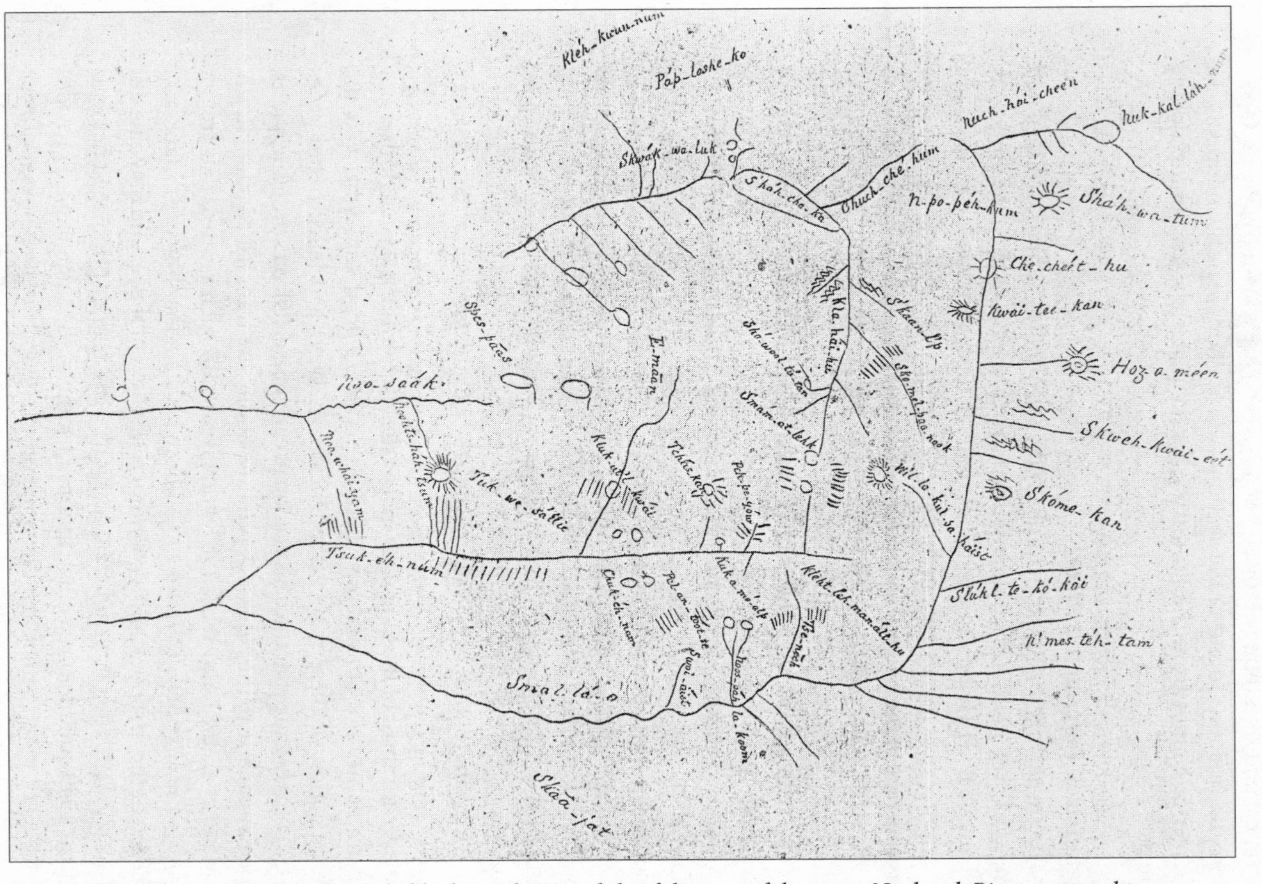

MAP 4 *Sketch map, not to scale, probably drawn by Teosaluk, of the area of the upper Nooksack River eastward to the upper Skagit River.* (United States Northwest Boundary Survey, RG 76, Series 69, Map 26)

"tch"; /ɬ/ or /ƛ'/ are shown by "kl" and "tl," while /ɬ/ is also shown by "lh" or sometimes "sh." Vowels are indicated fairly accurately by eight symbols or digraphs, and diphthongs (vowel + semi-vowel) are shown by five digraphs. More discussion is found in the section "A Few Phonological Comments" in Chapter 3. Names from the Boundary Survey materials are cited in double quotes.

Materials of Percival R. Jeffcott

The following materials were helpful: (1) the self-published *Nooksack Tales and Trails* (Jeffcott 1949); (2) an unpublished manuscript entitled "The Nooksack Indians: A Brief History of the Tribe" (Jeffcott 1964, 95 pages with map); and (3) an interview of P.R. Jeffcott by Oliver N. Wells on 12 July 1965. The latter exists on tape in the Linguistics Division of the Royal British Columbia Museum in Victoria, BC, copies of which remain with the family as well. There is also a manuscript transcription of this interview (Maud et al. 1981, 587-604g), cited here as Wells-Jeffcott, sometimes abbreviated as OW-PJ. Parts of this manuscript were published in Wells 1987.

Nooksack Tales and Trails provides abundant ethnographic and historical information about Nooksack places, and on pages 54-57 there is a list of 37 Nooksack place names, 8 Lummi place names, 7 Halkomelem place names, and 4 Semiahmoo place names. These are largely from August Martin, Mrs. Lottie Tom, and Boundary Survey records. Jeffcott's transcription is far worse than that of Gibbs (for example, "Tom-whik-sen" [Boundary Survey], "Clam-quis-ksun – gooseberries; the Lummi's name for Gooseberry Point" [Jeffcott 1949], /t'ǽmx^{w}iqsən/ [Suttles 1951], which would be <T'ámxwiqsen> in the Nooksack orthography). Jeffcott's chief virtue, however, is in the literal meanings that he provides for most of the names, as well as the ethnohistorical background and 7 place names not attested anywhere else. Wells-Jeffcott somewhat aids the interpretation of these names phonetically, as Wells had Jeffcott read pages 54-57 entirely and pronounce his version of each name; Jeffcott's pronunciations, though not close to the Nooksack pronunciations, are transcribed phonetically in Maud et al. 1981 and Wells 1987, and give details such as stress that are not indicated in his spelled versions. (Galloway was a co-author with Maud and Weeden of the first book and a co-editor with them of the second book; he did all the phonetic and phonemic transcriptions.) This transcription, together with Jeffcott 1949 and modern transcriptions of some of the same names, provides a partial key to the names that are found only in Jeffcott 1949. Nooksack forms written by Jeffcott will be cited in double quotes as syllabified by him.

Jeffcott 1964, especially pages 1-10 (Chapter 1, "The Nooksack's Habitat"), amplifies Jeffcott 1949, providing some new information and two new place names. The spelling and translations of names given in Jeffcott 1949 remain the same.

Field Notes

Through Wayne Suttles and Pamela Amoss we have copies of Paul Fetzer's ethnographic and linguistic field notes on the Nooksack from 1950 and 1951. Fetzer's field notes were taken directly on file slips and kept in file boxes. Brent Galloway presently has the linguistic notes; the ethnographic notes were in the possession of Wayne Suttles at the time of his death in 2005. Fetzer worked with Mrs. Lottie Tom (then 81, of Nooksack and Sumas parentage), George Swanaset (79, Nooksack-Langley), Josephine George (73, Nooksack-Sumas, wife of Louis George), Louis George (73 or 74, Nooksack-Matsqui), and Mrs. Agnes (Antone) James (77, Nooksack-Matsqui). (Sumas, Matsqui, and Langley are adjacent Halkomelem-speaking areas in BC.) All but Josephine George are part of the group shown in Photo 8, and Lottie Tom is shown by herself in Photo 9. Place names from identified people are cited with their initials preceded by the initials of the field worker. Fetzer was trained in linguistics and anthropology at the University of Washington, and his transcriptions are in the IPA (International Phonetic Alphabet). His version of the IPA is a slightly older version than the Americanist version most widely used in North America since 1960. Unfortunately, he died in 1952. His transcriptions and ethnographic information are quite helpful though variable, as early field work often is. He usually heard velars rather than postvelars and wrote vowel clusters and long lax vowels, neither of which are likely present in Nooksack.

Wayne Suttles provided us with parts of his field notes containing Nooksack place names, work dating from 1949 to 1952 and 1958. This includes material from interviews in 1949 and 1951 with August Martin (who later moved to Lummi), George Swanaset in 1950 and 1958, and Agnes James in 1952. In one case, Suttles re-elicited many of Fetzer's place names with Swanaset, using Fetzer's notes. The material with Swanaset and James is especially good, and more accurate than Fetzer's. These will be cited as either "Suttles field notes" or as a reference to a specific interview; where the speaker is more important than the individual interview, the initials WS:GS will stand for "George Swanaset (Wayne Suttles transcription)."

Linguistic field notes and tapes of the Nooksack language made by Pamela Amoss, Laurence Thompson, and Barbara Efrat were made available to Galloway and George Adams, who each completed extensive analysis of them (begun by Galloway under Social Sciences and Humanities Research Council of Canada grant no. 410-82-0913). These materials proved to be helpful in interpreting the Nooksack place names and their etymologies. Further analysis is ongoing

Photo 8 *Nooksack Board of Elders in the 1950s. Front row: Mariah Johnny, Grandma Roberts, Agnes James, George Swanaset, Lottie Tom, Louis George. Back row: Louisa George, Clara Williams, Helen Paul, Sindick Jimmy, David Johnson, Bill Sampson, Ella Reid, Walter Williams. The names of the two children are unknown.* (Nooksack Indian Tribe 1974)

(as linguists specializing in a language usually continue doing this for the rest of their lives), but is resulting in very few additional corrections, all of them minor (one or two such corrections per year initially, but none for several years now).

The Nooksacks who provided this recorded information were George Swanaset, Sindick Jimmy, and Louisa George. We make only rudimentary use of this material in this book; a more complete linguistic analysis of some of the place names may be possible later. One tape in particular, an interview with Sindick Jimmy by Barbara Efrat on 24 November 1970, contains a valuable discussion and texts regarding a number of Nooksack place names.

In the course of the project and before it, both of us took ethnographic and linguistic field notes (Richardson's notes were more ethnohistorical, Galloway's more linguistic), and of course these are the basis for any transcriptions not

PHOTO 9 *Nooksack elder Lottie Tom spinning wool in the 1950s. Original caption: "Lottie Tom, Nooksack Indian Spinning for Siwash Socks."* (P.R. Jeffcott Collection, no. 1355)

attributed to the Boundary Survey, Jeffcott, Suttles, Fetzer, and so on. Richardson has also published several papers on Nooksack ethnohistory and ethnogeography that include information on place names, and these are listed in the References.

Papers by Paul Fetzer

Through Wayne Suttles and Pamela Amoss we have copies of two unpublished graduate papers by Paul Fetzer: "The First Draft of Some Preliminary Considerations on the Subject of Territory and Sovereignty among the Nooksack and Their Neighbors" (Fetzer 1951a) and "Nooksack Enculturation: A Preliminary Consideration" (Fetzer 1951b). The former includes a discussion of Nooksack boundaries as perceived by the Nooksacks and their neighbours. The latter contains, among other things, a list of 30 Nooksack villages and camps, a discussion of how these grouped into bands, and a discussion of the genealogies and biographies of Fetzer's main Nooksack informants, Lottie Tom, Agnes James, Josephine George, and George Swanaset.

Tapes of Oliver Wells

Besides the 1965 Wells-Jeffcott interview, another tape made by Oliver Wells (cited as Wells 1966) is relevant to this study: his interview of 11 September 1966 with Mr. and Mrs. J.W. Kelleher and their daughter, Irene. A copy of this tape is in the Galloway Collection of the Northwest Linguistic Collection of the University of Washington. Mr. Kelleher, then 94, was the son of a white man and Madeline Jobe, a Nooksack. He was raised in Mission, BC, and lived most of his life in the Sumas-Mission-Abbotsford area of British Columbia. Wells brought *Nooksack Tales and Trails* (Jeffcott 1949) to the interview and went through pages 54-57, discussing each place name. In the tape, Kelleher pronounces and discusses each name that he can read or remember; in fact, he pronounces several of the names correctly and comes closer than Jeffcott does with a number of others. He also gives a number of Halkomelem words and several Nooksack words correctly (including glottalization). The full transcript is found on pages 850-900 in Maud et al. 1981, and a partial transcript is found in Wells 1987. Galloway performed the phonetic transcription found in these two sources.

Recently Published Maps

To locate the named places, we made extensive use of recently published maps. This was essential to finding our way to the places on our field trips, documenting the locations for their protection, and enabling us to produce our own maps of the place names. Complete sets of topographic maps on both sides of the border were of course invaluable: in BC, both 1:100,000 and 1:50,000 sets; in Washington, both 1:62,500 (15′) and 1:24,000 (7.5′) sets. We also used a number of commercial maps, such as the Official Road Map of Western Whatcom County by the Whatcom County Engineering Department and the Road Map of the Fraser Valley, Vancouver to Hope, by Dominion Map Ltd. Further discussion of the use of maps in place names research is included under "Methodological Insights" in Chapter 6.

Part 2
Nooksack Place Names

3
Introduction and Phonological Comments

Introduction

AT THE BEGINNING OF the historical period, speakers of the Nooksack language inhabited western Whatcom County, Washington, especially areas drained by the Nooksack River and its tributaries, the North Fork, Middle Fork, and South Fork. Many of the named places are also in areas used outside the Nooksack drainage. All of the named places and other significant locations without known names are shown by number on Map 5, which includes the names for places not included on the detail maps (Maps 6, 7, 9, 10, 12, and 15). All of the places are covered in detail in the numerically ordered list that comprises Chapter 4. The sequence begins at the head of the Nooksack River delta below Ferndale, then proceeds upriver to the northeast and east, with side trips up tributaries and trails to other sites but always back to Nooksack River and continuing upriver. Every effort has been made to list associated places together.

A major excursion after place 54 Kwánech at Everson heads east to the town of Nooksack, then northeast on the Sumas River (downriver) to Sumas Lake. We then return to sites on the Nooksack River, again heading upriver, now southeast. Reaching the Deming area, the list touches the South Fork Nooksack River, then the Middle Fork and a tributary, then heads up the North Fork. It goes up the North Fork and its tributaries and mountains to Mt. Shuksan, then breaks to return to place 125 Ts'éq at Acme and to proceed up the South Fork, with side trips up its tributaries to the Twin Sisters Range. It leaves the Nooksack drainage north of Wickersham, going to Lake Whatcom, nearby places, and several places along the saltwater shoreline of Whatcom County. The list concludes with three attested place names whose locations are uncertain or unknown, and three that may show a Nooksack substratum in Chilliwack territory.

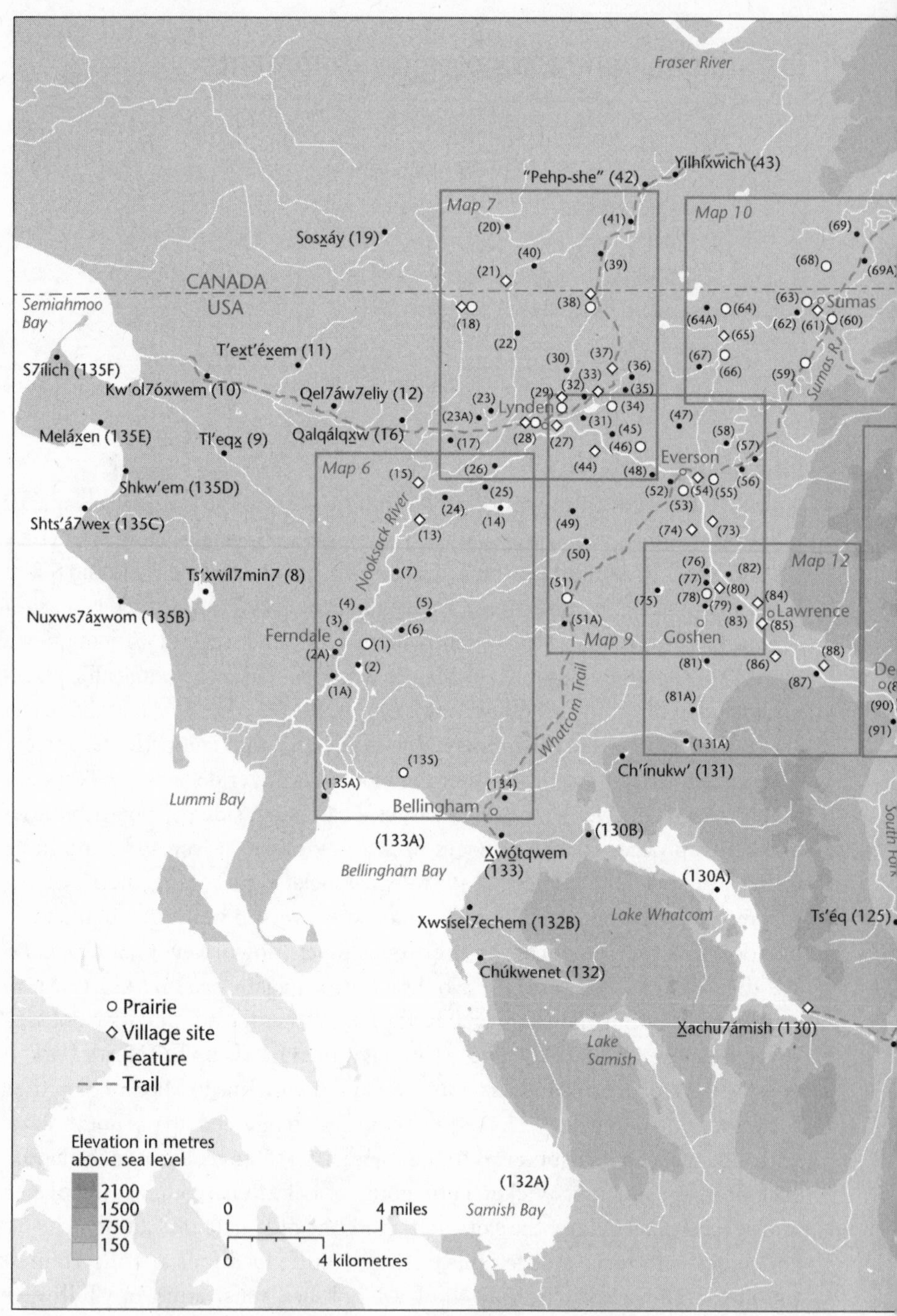

Map 5 *Nooksack place names.* (Adapted from Richardson and Galloway 2007)

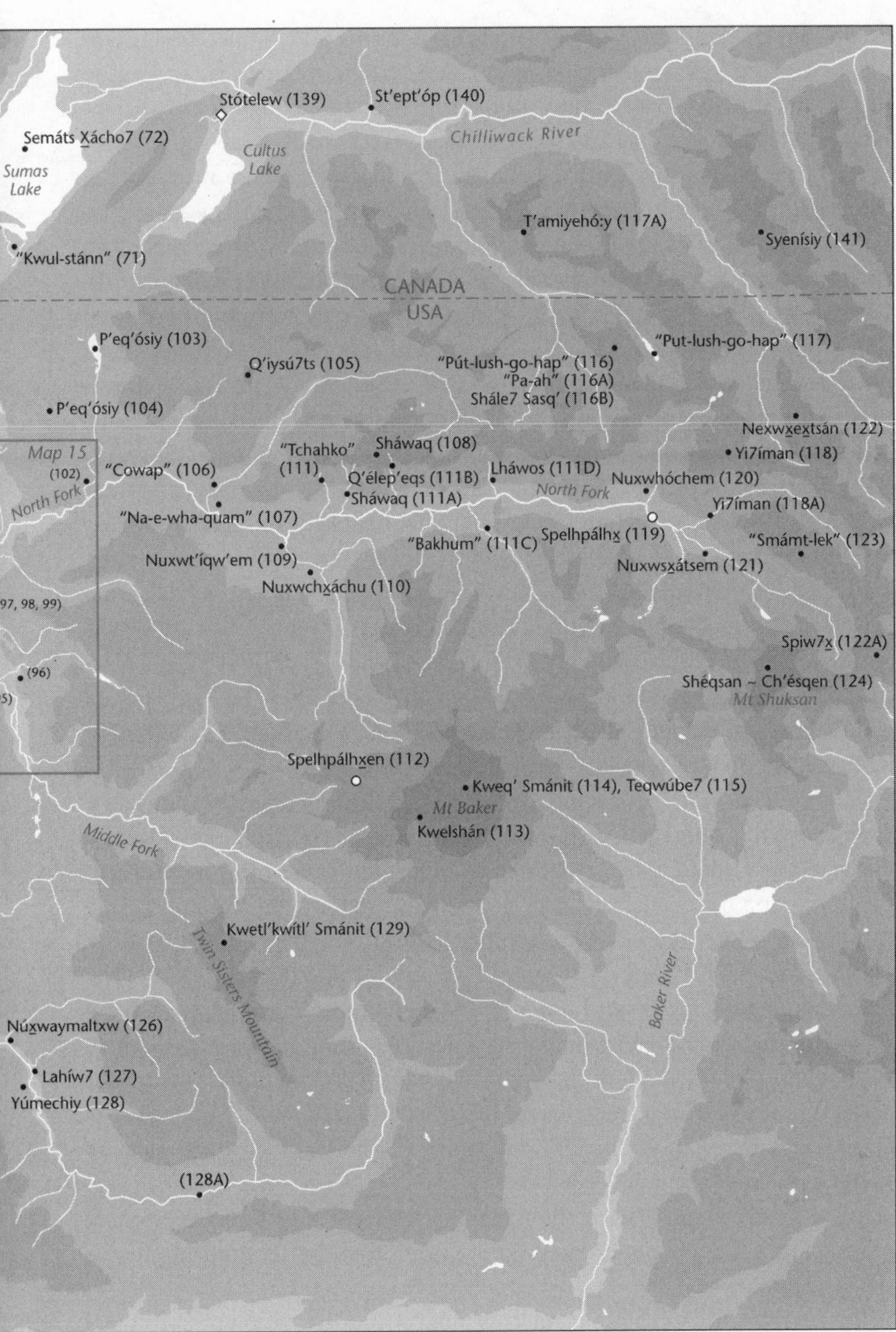

Stótelew (139)
St'ept'óp (140)
Semáts X̲ácho7 (72)
Sumas Lake
Cultus Lake
Chilliwack River
T'amiyehó:y (117A)
Syenísiy (141)
"Kwul-stánn" (71)
CANADA
USA
P'eq'ósiy (103)
Q'iysú7ts (105)
"Pút-lush-go-hap" (116)
"Pa-ah" (116A)
Shále7 Sasq' (116B)
"Put-lush-go-hap" (117)
P'eq'ósiy (104)
Nexwx̲ex̲tsán (122)
Map 15
(102)
North Fork
"Cowap" (106)
"Tchahko" (111)
Sháwaq (108)
Q'élep'eqs (111B)
Sháwaq (111A)
Lháwos (111D)
North Fork
Nuxwhóchem (120)
Yi7íman (118)
Yi7íman (118A)
"Na-e-wha-quam" (107)
"Bakhum" (111C)
Spelhpálhx̲ (119)
"Smámt-lek" (123)
Nuxwt'íqw'em (109)
Nuxwsx̲átsem (121)
Nuxwchx̲áchu (110)
(97, 98, 99)
(96)
Spiw7x̲ (122A)
Shéqsan ~ Ch'ésqen (124)
Mt Shuksan
Spelhpálhx̲en (112)
Kweq' Smánit (114), Teqwúbe7 (115)
Mt Baker
Kwelshán (113)
Middle Fork
Kwetl'kwítl' Smánit (129)
Twin Sisters Mountain
Baker River
Núx̲waymaltxw (126)
Lahíw7 (127)
Yúmechiy (128)
(128A)

After a reference number, each place name is given in the Nooksack language practical orthography unless the form is not certain, followed by an English identifying statement. Next, each place name is analyzed linguistically beginning with the name in the Nooksack language practical orthography (Galloway et al. 2004a), then in standardized phonetic orthography, where attested, then the initials of the linguist and those of the Native speaker. Phonetic transcriptions without initials are by Brent Galloway where there was agreement in pronunciation by all Native speakers available, namely, Sindick Jimmy (SJ), Louisa George (LG), and Esther Fidele (EF). Variant transcriptions are given only where they may be correct; where our transcription is confirmed by all other transcriptions, the others are omitted. If no phonetic transcription is available, the place name is given in double quotes (as syllabified in the original sources) in the only other orthographies it is attested in (Boundary Survey = BS, Jeffcott 1949 and 1964 = PJ, Paul Fetzer map = PFM, and one name transcribed by Percival Jeffcott and quoted at the Tennant Lake Interpretive Center = PJ-TL). Other initials used include: AJ for Agnes James, a fluent speaker; PA for Pamela Amoss, the linguist; GC for George Cline, one of the last partial speakers; AM for August Martin, a Nooksack speaker interviewed by Wayne Suttles and Paul Fetzer; BE for Barbara Efrat, the linguist; HP for Helen Paul, daughter of the most fluent speaker of Nooksack after 1977 (Louisa George); and AC for Amy Cooper, fluent in Upriver Halkomelem. Pages xiii and 7-8 list all the elders we worked with.

This is followed by the segmented phonemic form or probable phonemic form where this could be ascertained. Where the form is either certain or most likely, it is in boldface. This is followed by a gloss of the meanings of each segment where possible, italicized, then by comments on the phonetic or phonemic form of the name. We are using another linguistic tradition in the analysis, placing hyphens between morphemes in the phonemic forms quoted of the place names and, in the same order, in the literal meanings of each affix and root of the place name – for example, "/yúmech-iy/ *spring salmon-place,*" where the first morpheme (the root) means *spring salmon* and the suffix /-iy/ means *place.* Where a literal meaning for the place name is certain or most likely, it is given in boldface. More general comments on phonological interpretation are found in the next section.

Angle brackets are used to show Nooksack practical orthography, square brackets indicate phonetic transcription, and slashes surround phonemic transcriptions.

The coverage of each place name concludes with a discussion of traditional and historical use, historical documentation, more specific location, present access, and current land use.

Abbreviations Used in Place-Name Entries

Linguists and Native Speakers
(cited as Linguist:Speaker, e.g., WS:GS)

Linguists and other interviewers		*Native speakers and other interviewees*	
AR	Allan Richardson	AC	Amy Cooper
BE	Barbara Efrat	AH	Alice Hunt
BG	Brent Galloway	AJ	Agnes James
GA	George Adams	AM	August Martin
LT	Laurence Thompson	EF	Esther Fidele
OW	Oliver Wells	GA	George Adams
PA	Pamela Amoss	GC	George Cline
PF	Paul Fetzer	GS	George Swanaset
WS	Wayne Suttles	HP	Helen Paul
		LG	Louis George (with PF or WS)
		LG	Louisa George (with BE, BG, GA, or LT)
		LT	Lottie Tom
		SJ	Sindick Jimmy

Other sources for word forms

BS	Boundary Survey
BS-Cuṣter	Custer in Boundary Survey materials
BS-Teosaluk	Teosaluk in Boundary Survey materials
NKF	Fetzer Linguistic Field Notes (e.g., NKF1.1 = Fetzer's Linguistic Field Notes, file card box 1, card 1)
OW-PJ	Oliver Wells interview of Percival Jeffcott (also abbreviated as Wells-Jeffcott)
PAC	Pamela Amoss file cards (e.g., PAC101 = Pamela Amoss file cards, card 101)
PFM	Paul Fetzer Map (unpublished)
PJ	Percival Jeffcott

Other abbreviations and linguistic notation

< >	practical orthography	lit.	literally
[ ]	phonetic transcription	N	north (E = east, NE = northeast, etc.)
/ /	phonemic transcription	poss.	possibly
~	varies with	prob.	probably
bet.	between	R.	river
Cr.	creek	s-o	someone
IPA	International Phonetic Alphabet	s-th	something
L.	lake	vill.	village

A key to the contents of each entry is below.

Format of Each Place-Name Entry

Place #. Nooksack place name English identification/description. **Map #**

> **<Nooksack practical orthography>** [phonetic transcription] (Linguist:Speaker), /phonemic form/, etymology. ***Most certain gloss on meaning*** or *less certain gloss*. Further comments on forms of the name and glosses.

Discussion of traditional and historical use of the place and name; explanation of historical documentation; more specific description of location; present access to site; current land use; etc.

Online Audiovisual Materials

An essential part of preserving and revitalizing a language is to sample its sounds. In June 2006 we made audio recordings of George Adams (Syélpx̱en) pronouncing all the place names included in this book. These recordings, along with colour photos of most of the places and of the Nooksack elders who participated in the research, can be accessed through http://hdl.handle.net/2429/34111.

A Few Phonological Comments

As work with Nooksack proceeds, it should be possible to add more phonemic interpretations and corrections and more etymologies to the Nooksack place names. So far, some Halkomelem and Lushootseed influences can be seen, such as Lushootseed /a/ for Nooksack /æ/ in places, and Halkomelem /á/ for Nooksack /ó/ in places. Both sporadically fill in a gap in the Nooksack vowel system left by the historical shift of Proto-Central Salish */á/ to Nooksack /ǽ/.

Other Halkomelem influences are /ə/for unstressed Nooksack /æ/ and /o/ in some cases (see Galloway 1982, 1983a), /θ/ for Nooksack /c/, /θ’/ for Nooksack /c’/, /c ~ č/ for Nooksack /č/, /c’ ~ č’/ for Nooksack/č’/, and loss of /ʔ/ before consonants and after resonants. These shifts are verifiable because of attested variation and correction to the Nooksack versions (either attested in the place name citations or in their etymological roots and affixes where etymologies are certain). In cases where this variation is not verifiable, we have phonemicized with /θ/, /a/, and so on. As more Nooksack vocabulary in modern transcription is brought to bear, /ʔ/ will probably be added adjacent to consonants in a number of words. Lost knowledge of how to pronounce Nooksack place names will sometimes be impossible to recover: one cannot be certain whether some place names may have really dropped the /ʔ/ present in some roots or affixes.

4
Analysis of the Place Names

1. Sq'eláx̲en An area on the southeast bank of the Nooksack River that includes the prairie between Tennant Lake and Barrett Lake. **Map 6**

> <**Sq'eláx̲en**> [sq'əlǽx̣ən] /s-q'əlǽx̣ən/, [sq'əlǽx̣ən] (PFM). ***Fenced off*** or ***go around/over the side (e.g., of a logjam).*** The Nooksack word for *fence* is <q'élex̲in ~ q'élax̲en ~ q'élex̲en> (PF:GS), <asq'eláx̲en> *to be fenced off* (PF:GS, file card box 2, card 552, 7 September 1950). Upriver Halkomelem has cognate <q'eléx̲el> *fence,* probably from root <q'el> *go around, go over* + <-ax̲el> *side (of something constructed);* Squamish /q'iáx̣an/ *fence, stockade, fortification;* there were logjams on the river at or near this location that people had to portage or go around, so this may be the origin of the place name rather than specifically the meaning *fence.*

This name also refers to a group of people occupying this area in the early to mid-19th century. According to Jeffcott (1949, 138), "a small band of Indians had their homes on a small prairie that extended from the east bank of the Nooksack back to near Nu-klus-kum (Barrett Lake) and Deer Creek ... Also it was the natural habitat of the camas and shu-guack or wild carrot." Jeffcott (1949, 138) further states that John Tennant claimed a portion of this prairie, implying that it extended south to Tennant L. (see discussion under place 2). According to Fetzer (1951a, 19), the area immediately east of Ferndale was still occupied by the Sq'eláx̲en in 1850. Sometime before 1820, the Sq'eláx̲en group occupied the mouths of the Nooksack R. and controlled the surrounding salt-water areas, including Lummi Bay and portions of Bellingham Bay (Suttles 1951, 35-41). The name "Sq'eláx̲en" was also used historically to refer to a Lummi fishing site on the lower river (Fitzhugh 1856). An "Indian village" is shown on a Boundary Survey field map (Series 69, unidentified map in folder following Map 76) on the east side of the east branch of the river near the present Slater Road bridge.

1A. T'elt'álaw7 The place where the Nooksack River splits at the head of its delta. **Map 6**

> <**T'elt'álaw7**> GA:Agatha McCloskey (daughter of Julius Charles, the father of Al Charles, all Lummis). From <t'elt'álaw7> /t'əl-tǽlæwʔ/ ***many arms.***

At the head of its delta, the Nooksack R. divided into two main channels in the 19th century. The right branch carried the most water and flowed west to Lummi Bay, while the left branch flowed south to Bellingham Bay. The right branch is called the Lummi R. or Red R. today and is closed off, carrying a minimal flow of water except during high floods. The left branch flowing to Bellingham Bay is the present main channel of the Nooksack R. There were also several smaller channels and sloughs in the 19th century that still carry occasional floodwater today. The location of T'elt'álaw7 is one mile upriver from the Slater Road bridge.

---

2. Solá7atsich Settlement at the north end of Tennant Lake. **Map 6**

> <**Solá7atsich**>, "**Si-lats-its**" (PJ-TL). Vill. at N end of Tennant L., last vill. or camp of the /sq'əlǽx̣ən/ people, abandoned 1850s. Poss. a /sq'əlǽx̣ən/ name, but more likely a Nooksack name, <Solá7atsich> or <Solátsich>, meaning ***largest willow mat on/ in the back***. The root is certainly the Nooksack word [sólɛ́ɛc] (in Fetzer's transcription) or [solǽʔæ¢] <solá7ats> or [solǽ·¢] <solá:ts> in our modern IPA and orthography, which Fetzer glossed as "willow mat (largest size) used for summer roofs and winter wind-breaks–lined walls etc." PF:GS (20 July 1950) (NKF1.1046) (Fetzer's Linguistic Field Notes, file card box 1, card 1046). The suffix is Nooksack <-ich ~ -its> *on the back, in the back*. Thus, the settlement may have been made with the largest willow mats as roof, to line walls, and/or just as windbreaks. This would be very appropriate for a temporary camp while hunting waterfowl on the lake, as mentioned below.

This is possibly the location of a village occupied by remnants of the Sq'eláx̲en people in the early 19th century, based on Jeffcott (1949, 138), who discusses the claim of John Tennant's Indian wife to lands surrounding Tennant L. Sullivan (1978, 59) describes "Sil-ats-its" as a temporary camp used by both the Lummi and Nooksack people while hunting waterfowl. The "Sil-ats-its" site is on the high ground just west of the north end of Tennant L., in an area where prehistoric artifacts have been found and where John Tennant established his homestead in 1858.

2A. The main Nooksack River. **Map 6**

The portion of the Nooksack R. from its mouth to the forks at Nuxw7íyem (place 92) apparently had no distinct name in Lhéchelesem. The Nooksack people probably used the term <stólaw7>, meaning *river,* since this was *the* main river (the largest river in a territory often had no special name; for example, Upriver Halkomelem has no word for the Fraser R. except <stó:lō> *river*). The river is named "Nooksahk" or "Nooksaak River" in the 1857-62 Boundary Survey records, and similar forms are found in other early historical sources. Gardner (1857a) states that above the delta channels and the first jam, "the Indians living on the river are different bands of the Nook-sahk tribe and call it the Nook-sahk river." The Lhéchelesem form, <Nuxwsá7aq Stólaw7> may have been used prior to this, although originally <Nuxwsá7aq> was specific to Anderson Cr. and the area at its mouth (see place 78).

---

3. Tiytásem River crossing at Ferndale. **Map 6**

> <**Tiytásem**> "Ta-tas-um" (PJ), [teytǽsəm] (OW-PJ), prob. /tiyt-ǽs-əm/. PJ says it means ***above us;*** it may in a sense, because the root Nooksack <tiyt> means ***upriver***. Poss. a Lummi name, as this was the furthest they went upriver.

Within six miles above the first jam, which was at the head of the main delta channels, the Boundary Survey team lead by G. Clinton Gardner passed two "Indian villages," the first on the NW bank at Ferndale near Pioneer Park (Series 69, unidentified map in folder following Map 76). It was stated by tribal elders that a Nooksack fishing weir was located at Pioneer Park in Ferndale around 1870 (Richardson 1974, 57).

---

4. Xwx̱ách'tem Location at or near Ferndale on the northwest bank of the Nooksack River, also camp 1½ miles upriver on same bank. **Map 6**

> <Xwx̱ách'tem> ~ <Xwx̱átstem> [xʷx̣ǽctəm] (WS:AJ), /xʷ-x̣ǽct-əm/ or prob. /xʷ-x̣ǽč̓t-əm/. ***Always-fireweed-place to get*** from Nooksack [x̣ǽcət] *fireweed* (WS:AJ); peeled fireweed shoots were eaten in spring. The meaning of Nooksack -əm here is not certain yet, prob. (as in Halkomelem) *get* or (*verbalizer*) and secondarily *place to get.* Prob. /č̓/ rather than /c/ because other Salish cognates of *fireweed* all have glottalized reflexes of č̓; Nooksack speakers influenced by Halkomelem, like AJ here, often have [c̓ ~ č̓] and [c ~ č], as in Halkomelem. Compare PF:GS (27 July 1950) /x̣έ·c̓i·t/ *fern* (prob. sic for *fireweed*). Galloway's *Dictionary of Upriver Halkomelem* (2009) has:
>
> > <**x̱áts'et**>, us //x̣έc̓ət//, EB [*'fireweed'*], [*'Epilobium angustifolium'*], ASM ['peeled shoots are eaten raw in spring before they flower, a good vegetable but somewhat slimy, late summer seed fluff was gathered and mixed sometimes with dog wool and mountain goat wool for blankets'], syntactic analysis: noun, nominal, attested by Elders Group (5/7/75), AC (11/26/71 forgot name), Salish cognate: Squamish /x̣áč̓t/ *fireweed* W73:101, K67:368.

A camp and house used historically by elk hunters and people travelling to Bellingham Bay were located about 1½ miles above Ferndale on the northwest bank of the river, upriver from the mouth of Ten Mile Cr. Joe Louie said: "We had a big smokehouse just above Ferndale" (AR interview with Joe Louie, 31 July 1975). Here people switched from the shovel-nosed river canoes to high-bow saltwater canoes (Richardson 1974, 57). A Boundary Survey field map (Series 69, unidentified map in folder following Map 76) shows an Indian settlement on the SE bank upriver from the mouth of Ten Mile Cr., close to the same position on the river but on the opposite bank. Archaeologists have identified an early historical site on the NW bank of the river ½ to ¾ mile upstream from the prehistoric site 45-WH-34, which is on the upstream side of the I-5 bridge (Grabert 1983, 4, 7, 59). This is very likely the historical Nooksack camp location. Xwx̱ách'tem is often used to refer to this camp location as well as the site of Ferndale. The locations of this place name and others nearby are shown on Map 6.

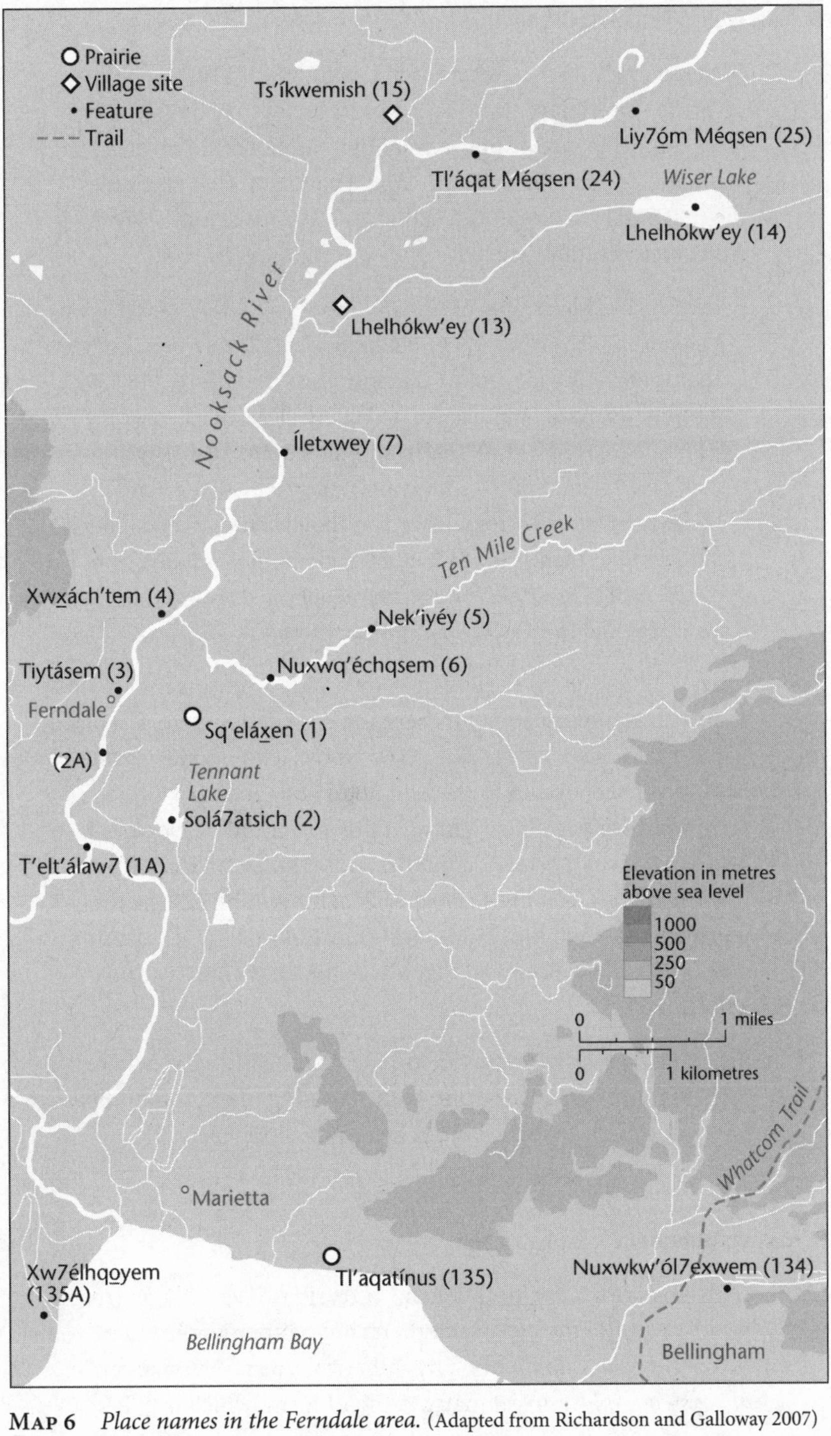

Prairie
Village site
Feature
Trail
Ts'íkwemish (15)
Liy7o̱m Méqsen (25)
Tl'áqat Méqsen (24)
Wiser Lake
Lhelhókw'ey (14)
Nooksack River
Lhelhókw'ey (13)
Íletxwey (7)
Ten Mile Creek
Xwx̱ách'tem (4)
Nek'iyéy (5)
Tiytásem (3)
Nuxwq'échqsem (6)
Ferndale
Sq'eláx̱en (1)
(2A)
Tennant Lake
Solá7atsich (2)
T'elt'álaw7 (1A)
Elevation in metres above sea level
1000
500
250
50
0 1 miles
0 1 kilometres
Whatcom Trail
Marietta
Xw7élhqo̱yem (135A)
Tl'aqatínus (135)
Nuxwkw'ól7exwem (134)
Bellingham Bay
Bellingham

MAP 6 *Place names in the Ferndale area.* (Adapted from Richardson and Galloway 2007)

5. Nek'iyéy Ten Mile Creek. **Map 6**

(<**Nek'iyéy**>? or <Nuxwk'iyéy>? or <Niqiyéy>?) [nıkiyéy] (WS:AJ), [nux^{w}kiáy] (PFM). [ey] or PF's [áy] may be /-iy ~ -əy/ *place* but [k] is rare or non-existent in Nooksack. Upriver Halkomelem has a borrowing from Thompson that resembles the first two syllables if [k']. Galloway's *Dictionary of Upriver Halkomelem* (2009) entry is:

> <**sk'ek'iyáp ~ slek'iyáp**>, df //s=k'ək'iyέp ~ s=lək'iyέp//, [sk'ık'iyǽp ~ slık'iyǽp], EZ [*'coyote'*], [*'Canis latrans lestes'*], borrowed from Thompson /snk'y'ép/ *coyote* (Thompson and Thompson 1980:58), syntactic analysis: nominal, attested by AC, DM, other sources: JH:DM /skəkiyé·p/, also <**snek'iyáp ~ snek'eyáp**>, //snək'iyέp ~ snək'əyέp//, [snık'iyǽp ~ snık'əyǽp], attested by BJ 5/64 and 12/5/64; probably borrowed with the Thompson <s=> and reduplication, rather than as the root in the Thompson word then with UPRIVER HALKOMELEM s= and reduplicated prefix added. The word may end in <=ap> *rump* in Thompson.

(The "=" sign means derivational affix and "-" means inflectional affix in Galloway 2009.) If there is a connection here, the place name could mean *coyote place*. The Nooksack word for coyote has not yet been found in the field notes and tapes. If PF's transcription with [nux^{w}] is right, that portion could be Nooksack <nuxw-> *always; people of,* but the root is still a mystery. The third spelling given in the Nooksack orthography reflects the less likely possible root Nooksack <niq-> *dive,* as in <níq-im> *dive (into water);* however, that leaves the following <iy> unaccounted for.

In most sources, Nek'iyéy is used to refer to Ten Mile Cr., whereas Agnes James states that the name is specific to the crossing of the trail to Bellingham Bay at Ten Mile Prairie (Wayne Suttles field notes). See place 51.

---

6. Nuxwq'échqsem Barrett Lake. **Map 6**

"Nu-klus-kum" (PJ), [nuklə́skəm] (OW-PJ). *Silver salmon (coho)* says PJ because they spawned there, but neither Nooksack /k^{w}óx^{w}əc/ *coho salmon* nor a hypothetical */nux^{w}-k^{w}úx^{w}əc-əm/ *always-coho-place-to get* matches the PJ form, which implies poss. <Nu(xw)tl'ésqem>; with root or stem <tl'esq> not found yet. However, compare Lummi /q'əčqs/ *coho* (which would be <q'echqs> in Nooksack orthography); the consonant cluster would make this hard to hear and transcribe properly, yielding <tl'> for <q'> and <sk> for <chqs> in Jeffcott's version – his transcriptions are among the least accurate in the early transcriptons that we have found. The most likely form is therefore **<Nuxwq'échqsem>** ***always place of coho salmon.***

This place name is used by Jeffcott (1949) to refer to Barrett L., and apparently also Ten Mile Cr. (place 5 Nek'iyéy), which flows through Barrett L. Barrett L. is a swampy expansion of Ten Mile Cr. caused by a beaver dam half a mile above the mouth and extending for 1½ miles. No specifically Nooksack use of the Barrett L. area has been recorded, although this area became part of Nooksack territory following its abandonment by the Sq'eláx̲en (Richardson 1974, 57).

---

7. Íletxwey A location three to five miles above Ferndale, on the southeast bank of the river. **Map 6**

<Íletxwey> [ʔílətx^{w}e] (WS:AJ), /ʔílətx^{w}-iy/. A big bend on the SE bank of Nooksack R. about three miles above /sq'əlǽx̣ən/. ***Plank-place***, from /ʔílətx^{w}/ (WS:AJ) or /s-ʔílæltx^{w}/ (BG:LG) or /s-ʔílætx^{w}/ (PA:GS or SJ 1955) *plank, board;* so called because a projecting plank underwater moved up and down and caused canoe accidents here. PJ calls it "La-plash," Chinook Jargon for *board, plank.*

According to Agnes James, this place is perhaps 3 miles above Sq'eláx̲en, which she placed above Ferndale. R.E. Hawley (1971, 46) discusses "Laplash Bend" about 1½ miles below Bertrand Cr., where a board (or plank) used to stick out from the bank, "laplash" being the Chinook Jargon name for board. This presumably refers to the same location, although the location derived from Agnes James's description is about 3 miles below Bertrand Cr. The location is probably between Mile 9 and Mile 11 of the Nooksack R. (US Geological Survey 1972 7½′ quadrangles), possibly as far downriver as the west end of Lattimore Road or as far upriver as 1½ miles below Bertrand Cr. The map in Jeffcott 1964 shows "La-Plash" a short distance below the mouth of the creek draining Wiser L. (about Mile 10 of the river).

---

8. Ts'xwíl7min7 Lake Terrell. **Map 5**

<Ts'xwíl7min7 or Tsxwílmin> [cxʷílmɪn] (WS:AJ), [c'xʷ ílsmin] (PFM), prob. /c'xʷ-íl?-min?/. The etymology is unclear but might be analyzed with either a prefix Nooksack <ch>, Upriver Halkomelem <ts> *have* + Nooksack root <xwil> or a root like Nooksack <ts'ixw> ***help, pity*** + Nooksack <-íl ~ -íl7> ***come, go, get;*** <ts'ixw> was suggested as a possibility before we found the PFM materials and is further supported by them since his [c'] is <ts'> in the Nooksack orthography; the [s] is uncertain unless there is a suffix <-ils> related to Nooksack <-als> *patterned activity* (an intransitivizer). Nooksack suffix <-min7> ***part*** is probable here. People training for power or to be Indian doctors often bathed or dove into lakes to get help/pity from spirits there.

The area surrounding this lake was good for elk hunting, and it was here that Louis Sacquilty killed the last elk around 1920. Elk hunting by the Nooksacks in this area is also discussed by Jeffcott (1949, 383), with an "elk trail" from the camp above Ferndale (see place 4) to Lake Terrell shown on his "Nooksack Geography" map. Ts'xwíl7min7 is shown in Photo 10.

---

9. Tl'eqx̲ California Creek. **Map 5**

<**Tl'eqx̲**> or <Tl'eq'x̲>? "Kluk'h" (BS). Gibbs's apostrophe usually indicates clusters (not digraphs) and rarely glottalization, however "kl" usually represents [ƛ'] <tl'>. This name could be Semiahmoo. Poss. root and suffix cognate with Upriver Halkomelem <tl'iq> ***soggy*** + <-x> ***spread all around.*** Galloway's Upriver Halkomelem dictionary (2009) states:

> <**tl'íq**>, probable root //ƛ'íq//, meaning related to soggy, as in: <**tl'ítl'eqel**>, rsls //ƛ'í[=C_1ə=]q=əl//, FOOD ['*(go/get/become) soggy*'], DESC, root meaning unknown, probably <**=R1=**> *resultative,* probably <**=el**> *go, come, get, become,* phonology: reduplication, syntactic analysis: adjective/adjectival verb, attested by BHTTC (10/76), Elders Group (3/9/77), for example: <**tl'ítl'eqel seplí:l**>, //ƛ'í[=C_1ə=]q=əl səplí·l//, /'*soggy bread*'/, attested by Elders Group.

Photo 10 *Place 8 Ts'xwíl7min7, Lake Terrell, looking east, with place 114 Kweq' Smánit, Mt. Baker, in the distance. 4 October 1980.* (Photo by B. Galloway)

This creek enters Drayton Harbor two miles south of Blaine, with headwaters in the bogs of the Custer area extending to within two miles of the Nooksack R. Traditional Nooksack use of the California Cr. watershed was probably limited to the harvesting of plants in these extensive bogs. Nooksack people came to this area in the historical period to pick cranberries, blueberries, and swamp tea (LG).

---

10. Kw'ol7óxwem Dakota Creek. Map 5

<Kw'úl7uxwem> or <**Kw'ol7óxwem**> or <Kw'eló̲xwem> "Kwuh-láh-hoom" (BS), poss. /k'ʷólʔoxʷ-əm/ from Nooksack <kw'ól7oxw ~ kw'úl7uxw> (Halkomelem <kw'ó:lexw>) **dog salmon** or Halkomelem-influenced /k'ʷəláxʷ-əm/ ***dog salmon-place to get***.

This large creek enters Drayton Harbor one mile south of Blaine. The upper portions of the Dakota Cr. watershed are close to the Nooksack R. and Bertrand Cr., and were on the edge of the Nooksack area. The trail following Dakota Cr. was referred to as "this Nook'sahk trail" in 1858 (Custer 1858a, 2), which may imply that its primary use was by the Nooksack, or perhaps just that it went to the Nooksack area. The lower areas nearer Drayton Harbor were definitely Semiahmoo territory up to the 1850s. Dakota Cr. and possibly California Cr. were fished for salmon by the Nooksack in the late 19th and early 20th centuries (Richardson 1974, 70). The Indian name for this creek is known only through the 1857-62 Boundary Survey records, although Semiahmoo ethnographic materials have not been studied in any detail.

---

11. T'ex̲t'éx̲em North Fork Dakota Creek. **Map 5**

<**T'ex̲t'éx̲em**> "Tuch-tuch-hum" (BS), prob. /t'əx̣t'ə́x̣əm/ ***many forks (of a creek).*** Compare Nooksack [st'ə́x̣əs] (LT:LG) *fork of tree,* Halkomelem /s-t'ə́x̣/ *fork of creek, fork of tree,* Nooksack $C_1V_1C_2$- *plural (many).*

This place name is known only from the 1857-62 Boundary Survey materials. "Indian Nomenclature" (Gibbs 1857-61) describes "Tuch-tuch-hum" as "first large branch of Kwul-láh-hoom," which is Dakota Cr. (place 10), and on the manuscript and field maps this clearly corresponds to the North Fork Dakota Cr. Where the North Fork joins the main creek near Custer School Road, Dakota Cr. has three forks, which appears to be the basis for the name. The Indian trail followed by Henry Custer in 1858 was indistinct and difficult to follow west of this tributary, whereas to the east, towards the Nooksack area, the trail was "distinct and well trodden" (Custer 1858a, 3). This suggests more use of the area by Nooksack people than by other Indian groups. Custer's Indian guide maintained a "hunting station" where the trail crossed "Tuch-tuch-hum"; unfortunately, his group affiliation is never stated.

---

12. Qel7áw7eliy Upper northeast tributary to Dakota Creek. **Map 5**

<**Qel7áw7eliy**> "Ka-láh-wul-leh" (BS), poss. /qəl(ʔ)ǽwʔ-əl-iy/ ***beaver-come/get-place.*** Poss. from (say LG, EF) *beaver* [sqəlǽ·wʔ] (BG:SJ) ~ [sqəlʔǽwʔ] (BG:LG; LT:SJ and LT:LG).

Based on the Boundary Survey maps, this is a small creek that flows southwest into Dakota Cr., crossing Loomis Trail Road 0.2 mile east of Sunrise Road.

Extensive beaver workings were noted on the main creek near this tributary (Custer 1858a, 3). This creek is about 3 miles west of Bertrand Cr., in an area that was probably used by the Nooksack.

---

13. Lhelhókw’ey Nooksack village site occupied “long ago,” on the southeast bank, possibly at the mouth of the creek draining Wiser Lake. **Map 6**

<Lhelhókw’ey> [ɬəɬák’ʷe] (WS:AJ), [ɬəɬɔ́q’ʷe] (WS:AM), respectively, /ɬəɬák’ʷ-əy/ and prob. /ɬəɬók’ʷ-əy/. ***(Many-)flying-place*** from Nooksack [ɬúk’ʷ] /ɬók’ʷ/ *to fly* (LT:LG) (cf. Halkomelem /ɬá·k’ʷ/ *to fly*, /ɬáɬək’ʷ/ *flying*). [ɔ] is an allophone of /o/ in Nooksack (and an allophone of /a/ in Halkomelem); the [a] version is prob. Halkomelem-influenced here.

A location at the mouth of the creek draining Wiser L. is based on the name’s being a variant of the name for Wiser L. The only ethnographic source for this site is Agnes James, who stated that it was across from Fishtrap Cr., which previously entered the river (with Bertrand Cr.) two miles above the creek draining Wiser L. At present, the best access to the mouth of the creek draining Wiser L. is through the farm on its north bank, west of Northwest Road.

---

14. Lhelhókw’ey Wiser Lake. **Map 6**

<Lhelhókw’ey> [ɬəɬák’ʷay] ([ay] is sometimes heard for /əy/), /ɬə-ɬák’ʷ-əy/. Wiser L., so named because lots of birds land there. *Many-flying-place.* EF, who pronounced this for us on several occasions, gave it with Halkomelem-influenced /a/.

This is a shallow lake with a marshy border good for waterfowl.

---

15. Ts’íkwemish Bertrand Creek and village site at the mouth of Bertrand Creek. **Map 6**

<Ts’íkwemish> or <Ts’íkwema7x> [c’íkʷəmɛʔxʸ] (WS:AJ) ~ [cí·kʷəmɪxʸ] (WS:GS), /c’íkʷə-mǽxʸ/ ~ prob. /c’íkʷə-mixʸ/, [síkʷomaxʸ] (PFM). The root could be from /c’íkʷə/ *left side,* several elders thought (EF, LG) /xʸ/ is prob. from Halkomelem influence, replacing Nooksack /š/ here; the suffix could be /-mixʸ

~ -mix^{w} ~ -miš/ *people* or /-ómiš/ *appearing, -looking.* From *A Stó:lō–Coast Salish Historical Atlas* (Carlson et al. 2001, 136, 146) comes <Seqwoméqwel>, Bertrand Cr., no translation. This seems to be a different name if accurately transcribed, since all the consonants and vowels are different except the <m> and the <e>. It may be either a best guess as to how an early Canadian recording "Sekomekl" was pronounced, or an attestation of a form from an elder that Galloway never heard or recorded while working with the elders. If Halkomelem, it could be compared to Upriver Halkomelem <qwóm> *lump* or <qwò:m ~ qwà:m ~ qwám> *moss* or <síqw'em ~ síkw'em> *peel cedar bark, skin or bark peels off* or related <sekw'emiy> *birch.* The <-eqw> *at the head (of a river), on the head (of a creature)* and <-el> *come, go, get* suffixes probably complete the Halkomelem form. Possible literal meanings may be *get a lump, moss, or peeled bark at the head (of the creek).* If the lump or moss words are the root, the <se> is probably mistranscribed for <s> *stative aspect.*

Before 1900, this was also the mouth of Fishtrap Cr., which joined Bertrand Cr. about ½ mile upstream above a small lake. The 1873 Land Survey map (United States General Land Office 1859-90) shows the creek mouth and main river channel about 200 feet north of their present locations. The village site, which was occupied some time prior to the historical period ("long ago," according to Agnes James), was on the west bank of the creek (based on Fetzer and Jeffcott maps). Jeffcott (1964, 3, map) names this village "Wha-wa-qu-lam," a variant of Xwkw'elám (place 30), Fishtrap Cr. This village was also shown on George Swanaset's map prepared in the 1920s for the Court of Claims case *Duwamish et al. v. United States of America.* At present, access to the mouth of Bertrand Cr. is by a dirt road west of the west end of River Road, which is a side road off Guide Meridian southeast of Lynden.

---

16. Qalqálqx̲w First westerly tributary of Bertrand Creek. **Map 5**

<**Qalqálqx̲w**> or <Qalqálqey> "Kál-kalk-ku" (BS). Prob. from Nooksack /qal-qálq / ***many wild roses*** or /qal-qálq-ey/ *many wild rose bushes.* Also compare possible Nooksack cognates with Upriver Halkomelem <-xw> *round, around,* <x̲w> *lump-like, round,* <qw'> *around in circles,* or <kw' ~ -ekw'> *around in circles.* The final consonant in the Nooksack place name could

> be <kw'> or <qw'> or <xw> or <x̲w>, depending on which cognate exists in Nooksack; there is evidence so far that both <xw> and <x̲w> exist in that language; see Nooksack <span-xw> *camas* (lit. "something-planted-lump like") and <sts'om-x̲w-eláx̲en> *elbow* (lit. "bone-round/around in circles-in the arm"), respectively. In Upriver Halkomelem, <qálq> means *rose hips, rose flower.* The resultant Nooksack literal meaning would be something like ***many round wild rose hips*** or *many wild roses around in circles.*

This name is from the 1857-62 Boundary Survey, and is described in "Indian Nomenclature" (Gibbs 1857-61) as "first creek running to Nooksack." This creek was named in a sequence travelling from Drayton Harbor to the Lynden area, following a trail that is shown on this route on the Boundary Survey manuscript map (Series 68). This map and the field map (Series 69, Map 23) both show the creek flowing directly to the Nooksack R., but the only creek in the area of the trail crossing is a tributary to Bertrand Cr., and it is unlikely that it could have flowed directly to the Nooksack R. in 1858. This creek crosses Birch Bay–Lynden Road ⅛ mile east of Bob Hall Road.

---

17. "Tsáh-nung" Small tributary of Bertrand Creek, entering from the east. **Map 7**

> **"Tsáh-nung"** (BS). Although within Nooksack territory, a Straits name or Straits pronunciation of a Nooksack name (with /ŋ/ for /m/ and /a/ for /o/). Perhaps [¢ánəŋ] or [¢'ánəŋ], or the first vowel may be [ǽ] <á>. Compare, however, Lummi [¢áŋən] ***go up*** with root /¢áŋ-/ and suffix /-ən/, whose final consonants may have been switched; thus perhaps **<Tsó̲ngen>** since the tributary "goes up" from Semiahmoo to Nooksack, and the word is probably in the Northern Straits language (either Semiahmoo or Lummi dialect).

This place name is known from a Boundary Survey field report (Custer 1858a) and "Indian Nomenclature" (Gibbs 1857-61), which describes it as "creek running to Seh-ku-mich" (place 15 Ts'íkwemish, Bertrand Cr.). Based on these sources, "Tsáh-nung" is a small creek shown but not named on the 1857-62 Boundary Survey manuscript map, which now enters Bertrand Cr. from the east, near Birch Bay–Lynden Road.

---

18. Mó̲meqwem Bertrand Prairie and the village located there. **Map 7**

<Mó̲muqwem> [mámukʷəm] (WS:AJ), [mámokəm ~ má·maqʷəm] (PF:GS; PFM), "Máh-moo-koom" (BS), <**Mó̲meqwem**> [máməqʷəm] (WS:AJ), prob. /máməqʷəm/ ***Cranberry marsh***. [á] /á/ replacing [ɔ] /o/ may be by influence of Halkomelem /máqʷəm/ and Lushootseed /báqʷəb/ *cranberry marsh, sphagnum bog;* if so, this influence goes back at least to 1858 (as in BS spelling); /ə/ instead of /o/ in AJ's (and poss. GS's) pronunciation also shows Halkomelem influence. She quotes [máqʷəm] *cranberry marsh* as the root (this form is found in all place names involving this word for marsh, swamp, cranberry marsh); -C_1ə- is a Halkomelem reduplication pattern (-C_1V_1- in Nooksack); unstressed Proto-Central Salish *u > Nooksack u, Halkomelem and Straits ə normally (see Galloway 1982). It seems likely that the Nooksack language, in this root and a few others, had begun to participate in the same sound shift that Halkomelem and Straits did, Proto-Central Salish *u > a, since even the least Halkomelem-influenced speakers, SJ and LG, used /a/ <o̲> in this and a few similar roots.

The prairie was on both sides of Bertrand Cr. extending from ½ to 1½ miles south of the International Boundary and to the northeast to near the Guide Meridian border crossing. The village was located on the east bank of Bertrand Cr. ½ to 1 mile south of the International Boundary, near H Street Road. Based on the memory of Jess Cole and on the 1857-62 Boundary Survey map, the village was about 100 yards *north* of H Street Road. Jeffcott (1949, 39-41) and title records would indicate a location in the first ¼ mile *south* of H Street Road. The village was definitely occupied between 1850 and 1880, receiving new residents from Chmó̲qwem in the 1850s. Residents included Qeléyelh "Savage" and Joe Lox̲él'wó̲nxw, the grandfather and father of Stick Peter, Dick Harry, and Andy Joe. "Indian Nomenclature" (Gibbs 1857-61) includes: "Máh-moo-koom – Prairie at Skul-leh-itl house." Other Boundary Survey records refer to this as "Ske-léh-yo prairie" (Harris 1858, 3), and "a prairie, inhabited by a small tribe of hostile Indians, a detached section of the Nook'sahk tribe" (Custer 1858a, 4). Series 69, Map 23, has "Skaleighes Prairie" for this location. These alternate names for the prairie are all variants of the name of its leading resident, Qeléyelh. The village was abandoned between 1878 and 1882 due to a non-Indian homestead claim, with the residents moving to Méqsen (place 21).

---

19. Sosx̲áy Swampy area at the head of Campbell River. **Map 5**

> "So-sái" (BS) <**Sosx̲áy**> or poss. <Sosáy>, poss. a Semiahmoo name. Compare <Susx̲áy> /sosx̣ǽy/, place 81. If a Nooksack name, the final "ái" could be Nooksack <-ay7> *plant* or Nooksack <-ey ~ -iy> *place,* and the root could be <sos> or <sox> with infixed reduplication <-s->. GA provides a Straits (Lummi or Semiahmoo) form that may be more likely, <Sesx̲ó̲y7iy> *a kind of grass; hay;* compare Lummi [səsx̣ay'iʔǽwʔx̣.] (<sesx̲o̲y7i7áw7x̲> in Nooksack orthography), which means *barn* (lit. "hay building").

This place name, known only from the 1857-62 Boundary Survey materials, is located near 16th Avenue and 240th Street in British Columbia, east of White Rock. This area drains into the Campbell R., which flows to Semiahmoo Bay; even so, it is only ½ mile west of Bertrand Cr. and 2½ miles from the Nooksack village of Mó̲meqwem (place 18). It is likely that Nooksack people were familiar with the area and used it for some purposes.

---

20. "Koh-kwun-nés-tum" Howes Creek. **Map 7**

> **"Koh-kwun-nés-tum"** (BS). Poss. <Kwokwenástem> or <Kw'oqwenístem> or other variants with the BS <ko> and <kw> replaced by other various combinations of <qw>, <qw'>, <kw'>, and <kw>. If the word has reduplication, the first two consonants will be the same. Poss. compare Nooksack root <kw'oqw> *club, hit with sticklike object* or <kwoxw> *knock, rap* and Nooksack suffixes <-enís> *on the teeth* + <-t> *do purposely to someone* + <-em> *passive,* which would indicate *got clubbed/knocked in the teeth. A Stó:lō–Coast Salish Historical Atlas* (Carlson et al. 2001, 136, 146) has Qwóqwélestem, Howes Cr., translation 'talking to a group of people.' This could be an Upriver Halkomelem pronunciation of this name and is a plausible etymology from Upriver Halkomelem <qwóqwel> *talking, speaking,* or <qwṓlqwel> *talking together, all talking together, telling news, warning (birds and other creatures do this)* or more likely <qwélqwelàtstem> *to squeal on someone* (cf. <qwéqweláts> *to gossip*). For the Nooksack form, however, the root that means talk is <níchim> and the root <qwel> is found only in a few longer words, like <shqwélten> *language,* and does

> not have a form with <n>. The BS form with <n> could be related to this root only if it was given by a speaker of the Musqueam subdialect that converted all "l's" to "n's" or by a Nooksack speaker who misconverted the Halkomelem form changing the "l" in this word mistakenly to Nooksack "n" on the theory that since Upriver Halkomelem converts all Nooksack "n" to "l," the reverse must be true.

This name is given to a large easterly tributary of Bertrand Cr. north of the border on the 1857-62 Boundary Survey manuscript map (Series 68). The form "Cocolesta" appears on Series 69, Map 23. Although the drainage patterns do not correspond well to the modern situation, the only likely creek is one now called Howes Cr. This creek crosses 272nd Street, north of 8th Avenue, which is about 1¼ miles north of Méqsen (place 21).

---

21. Méqsen Village known as "Stick Peter's place," Matsqui Indian Reserve No. 4. **Map 7**

> <**Méqsen**> [mə́qsən] /mə́qsən/, [mə́qsɪn] (PFM). ***Nose*** because of a story after the time of /x̣ǽ·ls/, the Transformer, about a man sneezing as a sign of coming disaster (WS:AJ). *A Stó:lō–Coast Salish Historical Atlas* (Carlson et al. 2001, 136, 144) has Méqsel (the Upriver Halkomelem pronunciation or form), "significance, 'large transformer rock in Aldergrove Park, X̱á:ls transformed the nose of a sneezing man as a sign of coming disaster,' translation 'nose.'" The map location is about one mile or a bit less northeast of the village site. It also has Qwóqweléqwem, a settlement, translation 'foggy area,' located on the map at our Méqsen village site. This seems to be an additional Upriver Halkomelem name in the area, but the meaning *foggy area* is not one that we would give to the form Qwóqweléqwem. There are several words in Upriver Halkomelem for kinds of fog, which are similar in form to the place name <Qwóqweléqwem>, i.e., Upriver Halkomelem <qwétxem> *getting foggy,* <qwelxel> *get fog on the water,* and <qwelqwélxel> *fog appearing on the water.* The Halkomelem place name <Qwóqweléqwem> may be a Matsqui dialect form that is a border dialect between Upriver and Downriver Halkomelem and has some different pronunciations and grammar than Upriver Halkomelem. Looking at the form <qwóqweléqwem> as an Upriver Halkomelem form, we

would compare <qwóqwel> *talking,* also *warning,* -eqw *at the head, on the head,* -em *place to get or have or find.* This could very likely be a direct connection with the sneeze, with a literal meaning ***a place to get/have/find warning on the head.*** This etymology would not work as a Nooksack etymology, as Nooksack has a different word for *warn,* perhaps <ay(e)qeláltux̲> or <qelálikwolh> *be warned* or <kw'álex̲stínex̲> *to warn someone* (NKF2.135, NKF2.1235, NKF2.1277 resp.) and a different word for fog (<sqwetshán>).

The village location is ¼ mile north of the International Boundary and ½ mile east of the Aldergrove Customs (Guide Meridian border crossing from the US). Stick Peter's house and farm were located next to a small permanent creek NW of the present Indian home on the west side of 272nd Street. This location is shown in Photo 11. The village was definitely occupied following the abandonment of Mó̲meqwem. Occupation prior to 1878 is not certain, although long traditional occupation is implied by the designation of the Nooksack village as a Matsqui Indian Reserve by the Canadian Indian Reserve Commission in June 1880. The commission agreed to let Stick Peter and family (Nooksacks) remain in exchange for the land's becoming a Canadian Indian Reserve. The Boundary Survey materials do not mention a settlement here, although a "trail from Masqui to Skeleko Prairies" is described as crossing the International Boundary very close to the site of Méqsen (US National Archives, Field Notes, RG 76, E 200).

---

22. Xwq'écheqsem Double Ditch Creek(?). **Map 7**

<**Xwq'écheqsem**> "Hoo-kutch-uk-sun" (BS). This name poss. relates to the story in /mə́qsən/ above, since "uk-sun" here could be the Nooksack /-əqsən/ *nose; point,* and this creek just N of the border flows within ¼ mile. of /mə́qsən/ vill. More likely, <Xwq'écheqsem> with Nooksack <xw-> *always, place to always,* stem poss. <q'echeqsen or q'echeqs> cognate with Lummi <q'echqs> *coho, silver salmon,* and Nooksack <-em> *get.* This last interpretation (**place to always get coho salmon**) is quite likely since silvers or cohos still run up Double Ditch Cr.

This Indian name is applied to a northerly tributary to Fishtrap Cr. on the 1857-62 Boundary Survey manuscript map, in both formal script and rough handwriting. This map shows a single stream flowing south from the Méqsen

Photo 11 *Place 21 Méqsen* (nose), *village known as "Stick Peter's place," Matsqui Indian Reserve No. 4, showing Nooksack elder George Cline and local resident at village site. 9 July 1981.* (Photo by B. Galloway)

area to Fishtrap Cr., although at least two streams draining the extensive wet area north of Lynden are more likely. The name "Hoo-kutch-uk-sun" does not appear in the Boundary Survey field reports or the field map of this area (Series 69, Map 23), but is found on a sketch map in E 223 with the "Indian Nomenclature" (Gibbs 1857-61), where it designates a creek and lake near "See-ko-mich" village (see place15). In his notebook "No. II Journals & Notes N.W.B.S., 1855-1858," Gibbs (1853-58) wrote: "The See-ko-mich ... Their river runs into the Nooksahk, & heads in a small lake called Hoo-kutch-uk-sen." There may well have been open water fitting a description as a lake in the wet area just south of the International Boundary that was a major source of water for the Bertrand Cr.–Fishtrap Cr. system. The mouth of Double Ditch Cr. is located 1 mile west of place 28 Chmó̱qwem village, and although fishing here is not documented, Indian elders state that silver salmon still run in this creek (Ernie Paul). This creek flows as a natural creek north of the border, where it is called

Pepin Cr. (see place 40 “Tse-tséh-ne-wun”), but is diverted into two ditches when it enters the US. Just north of the border, Pepin Cr. flows within ¼ mile of place 21 Méqsen.

---

23. Noxwqwo7ópey Tributary of Fishtrap Creek west of Guide Meridian(?). **Map 7**

> Prob. <**Nuxwqwó7opey**> or <**Nuxwqwo7ópey**> or <**Noxwqwó7opey**> “Noo-kópe” (BS). Prob. /nox^w-/ [nux^w- ~ nox^w-] prefix, ***always***, <qwó7op ~ qwú7up ~ qwo7óp> ***crab-apple***, and either <-ay> ***plant/tree*** or /-iy ~ -əy/ ***place***, thus prob. lit. *always crabapple trees* or *always crabapples place.*

This place name is known only from the Boundary Survey materials and it is difficult to determine what it referred to. “Indian Nomenclature” (Gibbs 1857-61) describes “Noo-kópe” as a “larger fork of Séh-ku-mich” (following “Tsáh-nung”), and then describes “Kwool-laām” (place 30 Xwkw’elám, Fishtrap Creek) as a fork of “Noo-kópe.” From this evidence, “Noo-kópe” might be considered a name for the lowermost portion of Fishtrap Cr. above its former mouth into Bertrand Cr. The Boundary Survey manuscript map has “Noo-kópe” pencilled in as another name for “Hoo-kutch-uk-sun” (see place 22), possibly Double Ditch Cr. When the trail route used in the Boundary Survey is considered, and Custer’s report (1858a) is read carefully, it is most likely that “Noo-kópe” refers to the tributary of Fishtrap Cr. located west of the present Guide Meridan near Tromp Road. This was probably a significant drainage for the extensive wet area north of Lynden.

23A. “Pook” Tributary of Fishtrap Creek. **Map 7**

> **“Pook”** (BS), “Poowk” (BS-Custer). Perhaps compare Upriver Halkomelem <péqw> [pʊ́q^w] *split off, break off (often used of riverbanks), split in two,* which may have a cognate in Nooksack, or Upriver Halkomelem <pekw’ ~ peqw’> *puff out (dust, plant fluff, smoke).* The orthography could reflect either <p> or <p’> and <o> or <u> or <e>, and either <kw>, <kw’>, <q>, <q>, <qw>, or <qw’>.

This name is known only from the Boundary Survey field materials. In Henry Custer’s Topographical Notes, E 201, “Poowk” names a creek meeting Cullam at a small bluff. On the field map (Series 69, Map 23), “Pook” appears to name the same creek, referred to as “Noo-kópe” in the field report (Custer 1858a) (see place 23).

---

24. Tl’áqat Méqsen Ox-bow in Nooksack River above Bertrand Creek. **Map 6**

<Tl’áqat Méqsen> **“Yo-kit Mux-in”** (PJ), [yókɨkt mə́ksən] (OW-PJ). The form quoted by Jeffcott is partly Chinook Jargon: “yo-kit,” spelled “youtl-kut” and “youtlkut” in Shaw (1909, 30), means *long* in Chinook Jargon; “Mux-in” is Nooksack /mə́qsən/ *nose,* but the whole expression is “broken” Nooksack since /mə́qsən/ does not mean point of land; place names use a root plus /-əqsən ~ -ələqs/ *nose; point of land* (see place 26 and Galloway 1977, 177, 182, 537, 632). If, however, the Chinook Jargon word for long is replaced by Nooksack /ƛ̓æqat/ <tl’áqat> *long,* the name is <Tl’áqat Méqsen>, prob. **long point (of land)**.

This name was applied to a great ox-bow bend in the Nooksack R., a short distance above Bertrand Cr. (PJ), difficult to navigate due to its swift water. The location was “just above the Little Jam” (Jeffcott 1964, 3).

---

25. Liy7ó̱m Méqsen “Devil’s Bend” in Nooksack River. **Map 6**

<Liy7ó̱m Méqsen> “Le-om Mux-in” (PJ), [liyʔá·m mə́ksən] (OW-PJ). Again “broken” Nooksack; /liy(ʔ)ám/ *devil* is borrowed from Chinook Jargon. Lit. ***devil nose/devil point.***

Devil’s Bend is a bend in Nooksack R. formerly with rapids and many snags causing many canoe and riverboat accidents, located “a short distance below the site of the present Guide Meridian bridge” (Jeffcott 1964, 3-4). This is probably the same meander referred to in place 26, Schúkweleqs.

---

26. Schúkweleqs A point at the end of a long narrow meander loop of the Nooksack River ¼ mile west of Guide Meridian. **Map 7**

<Schúkweleqs> [sčúkʷələqs] (WS:AJ), /s-čókʷ-ələqs/. ***(Nominal)-distant, far-point*** from root /čókʷ/ *far, distant.*

The point was originally on the south bank of the river, but the loop has been cut across, placing the loop and the point to the north of the present river

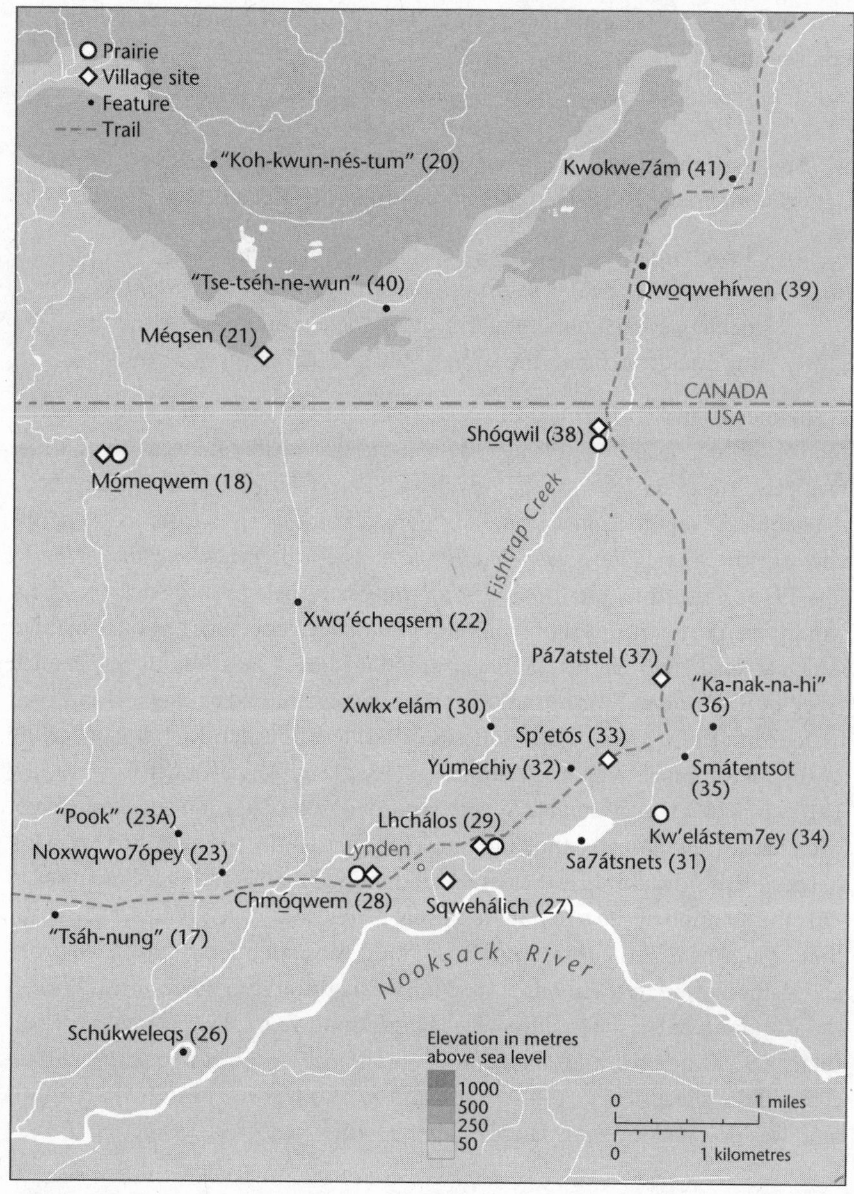

Map 7 *Place names in the Lynden-Northwood area.* (Adapted from Richardson and Galloway 2007)

channel. The location is north of River Road ¼ mile west of the north end of the Guide Meridian bridge, northwest of Bode's Redi-Mix and Gravel. This place and others near present-day Lynden and the Northwood area to the northeast are located on Map 7. The villages shown on this map associated closely together, and formed a somewhat separate group within the broader Nooksack community.

---

27. Sqwehálich Village on the south bank of the Nooksack River across from Lynden on Stickney Island; Lynden Jim's place. **Map 7**

> <**Sqwehálich**> [sqʷəhǽlıč ~ sqʷəhǽlič] /s-qʷəhǽ-lič/, [skʷəhǽlič] (PFM). ***(Nominal)-go through an opening-at back?*** since it was by an opening through a logjam on the bend that is now Stickney Island: the suffix could be /-ič/ *on the back.*

Stickney Island was formed between 1895 and 1906 when a broad meander loop (½ mile long and ¼ mile across the neck) was deliberately cut off by white farmers. The exact location of Sqwehálich on Stickney Island has not been determined. George Swanaset stated: "opposite side of river from Lynden, just above bridge – on place now called "Stickney Isle" (interview by Paul Fetzer, 14 July 1950). Unfortunately, there are two bridges: the bridge onto Stickney Island would seem to be the most obvious, but the main river bridge opposite Lynden (since at least 1895) is the Hannegan Road bridge. A location for Sqwehálich (specifically Lynden Jim's house) near the Hannegan Road bridge was specified by Jeffcott (1949, 32) and by Ella Reid (interview by Allan Richardson, 1 July 1975), and implied by Sindick Jimmy (interview by Allan Richardson, 10 July 1975). In 1857, the Boundary Survey recorded two houses on the west side of what became Stickney Island, and one house across the river on the NW bank bordering the lower prairie (Series 69,unidentified map in folder following Map 76). The location of the two houses closely matches George Swanaset's description, assuming that the Hannegan Road bridge was intended. Sqwehálich probably gained more residents after 1860 following the arrival of white settlers and the abandonment of the traditional villages Chmó̲qwem (place 28) and Lhchálos (place 29). Lynden Jim (Selhámetan) was the "headman" at Sqwehálich, and claimed the site and over 150 acres of land as a homestead in 1874. Part of this land was donated for the Stickney Home mission school in 1890.

---

28. Chmó̲qwem Main village at Lynden. **Map 7**

> <**Chmó̲qwem**> [čmáqʷəm] (WS:AJ; BG), [čəmɔ́·kʷəm ~ čəmá·kʷəm] (WS:GS), [čəmá·qʷəm] (PF:LG; PFM), /č-máqʷəm/ (poss. /č-móqʷəm/ for GS variant with [ɔ́·]). ***Have-marsh/ cranberry bog*** because semi-cultivated plant foods grew here

in the marsh: camas, chocolate lily, and [c'ə́θələ] (a plant with white flowers and white roots like big buttons). Nooksack <ch- ~ che-> *have* could be a prefix in this name.

This was a major village in the early 19th century, with many residents and three longhouses totalling 300 feet in length. The village location is in the western part of the downtown business district of Lynden, near Front Street. This was on a hill overlooking the river, with a natural prairie (an important source of plant foods) located between the base of the hill and the river and extending one mile or more west from the downstream side of the Stickney Island meander loop. The Boundary Survey materials call this the "lower Nook'sahk prairie" and state that it was two miles long and 400 yards wide, with a considerable number of Indians of the Nook-sahk tribe in the area (Custer 1858a, 5-6). The Boundary Survey manuscript map has "Kweh-sa-litch Pr." (see place 27). The unidentified field map of 1857 shows a building at the Chmó̲qwem location. The village was abandoned following the "Indian Wars" of the late 1850s and the claiming of the site by Colonel Patterson around 1860.

---

29. Lhchálos Village at the east edge of the old part of Lynden. **Map 7**

<Lhchálos> [ɬčǽ·los] (PF; BG; PFM), [ɬčɛ́losəm ~ ɬəčɛ́losəm] (WS:AJ), /ɬčǽlos/. Etymology unknown so far (although Nooksack /-ǽlos/ <-álos> may be *eye, in appearance, colour,* or it could be a suffix cognate with Upriver Halkomelem /-ǽ:ləws/ <=**á:lews**> *leaf, leaves.* It is not clear whether the root is related to the one in Nooksack, <lhch-il> *arrive* (<-il> *come, go, get, become*), or is cognate with one in Halkomelem, <lhet> *tremble* or <lhéch> *feel like singing a spirit song, be in a trance, making sighs and crying sounds before singing a spirit song.* The name is the source of the language name Lhéchelesem /ɬə́čələsəm/ (from */ɬə́čælosəm/). The language name (in Halkomelem) /hɛlq'əmɛ́yləm/ *Halkomelem language; to speak Halkomelem* has a similar etymology, from /hɛ-ləq'ɛ́məl-íl-əm/ *(continuative)-Nicomen Island-go/come to-(verbal suffix).*

This village was closely connected with Chmó̲qwem. It was considered part of the same settlement by Agnes James, and locations were reversed in some sources. According to AJ, the ordinary class of people lived here, whereas the high-born people lived in Chmó̲qwem. Lhchálos was located about one mile northeast of Chmó̲qwem, near Front Street east of Nooksack Avenue. This is

Photo 12 *Place 29 Lhchálos, village at the east edge of the old part of Lynden, source of the language name Lhéchelesem. Photo taken from Stickney Island, near the location of place 27 Sqwehálich. 18 September 1980.* (Photo by B. Galloway)

in the area northeast of Stickney Island on the hillside overlooking the river, shown in Photo 12, and near another prairie area that extends over a broad area to the northeast. The Boundary Survey materials (Custer 1858a, 7) refer to this as the "upper prairie" and state that it is much larger than the lower one (see place 28). The Boundary Survey manuscript map names the upper prairie "Kwo-las-ta-meh Pr." (see place 34). The portion of the prairie near Lhchálos was important for root digging, and was also claimed by a white settler around 1860 (Hawley 1971, 35), which probably caused the village to be abandoned.

---

30. Xwkw'elám Fishtrap Creek, and a fishtrap location with a drying house on Fishtrap Creek. **Map 7**

<**Xwkw'elám**> or <Xwqw'elám> ~ <Xwixwkw'elám> or <Xwixwqw'elám> [xʷkʷəlɛ́·m] (WS:AJ), [xʷuxʸk’ʷəlɛ́m] (WS:GS),

prob. /xʷkʼʷəlǽ-m/ ~ /xʷi-xʷkʼʷəlǽ-m/, [kukʼʷəlǽm] (PFM). ***Scouring rush-place to get*** and ***little-scouring rush-place to get;*** AJ says the first form means *rushes;* GS says [xʷuxʸkʼʷə́lə] is *scouring rush;* /kʼʷ/ in both may be /qʼʷ/ instead, as in Halkomelem /xʷəqʼʷə́lɛ/ <xweqw'éla> *scouring rush. A Stó:lō–Coast Salish Historical Atlas* (Carlson et al. 2001, 139, 145) has Qólem, Fishtrap Creek, translation 'dipping in (soup or water).' This is clearly a different name from the Nooksack name and is based on the Upriver Halkomelem word <qó:lem> //qá·=əl=əm//, *to scoop, to dip, dip water, to scoop (e.g., oolachens, eulachons)* (but the -ing translation is incorrect for Upriver Halkomelem since *dipping, scooping* is <qóqelem>).

The fishtrap location is 400 yards upstream from Lynden City Park. Numerous pit houses have been identified on the north bank of the creek west of the park and near the fishtrap location (Jeffcott 1949, 11; Emmons 1952, 52), implying a large prehistoric population. These pit houses were designated as archeological sites 45WH7 and 45WH8 (Emmons 1952, 52). The area is now predominantly residential housing, but two possible pit houses were observed in 1980 on school property west of the park and north of the creek. The early historic villages of Chm̱ó̱qwen (place 28) and Lhchálos (place 29) were located ¾ mile to the southwest and ½ mile to the southeast, respectively, from the fishtrap location. The fishtrap was maintained and used by Lynden Jim and others until the end of the 19th century.

---

31. Sa7átsnets A shallow lake in the low area east of Lhchálos (place 29) and west of Kw'elástem7ey (place 34). **Map 7**

<Sa7átsnets> [sɛʔɛ́cnəc] (WS:AJ). If the final [c] were Halkomelemized by AJ to [c ~ č] from [č], /-nəč/ ***(on the) bottom*** could be involved; [ɛ́] may be [ǽ] in line with normal Nooksack allophony. Perhaps the Nooksack root is cognate with Lummi <sa7át> ***raise, lift,*** i.e., **raised/lifted bottom** due to the shallowness of the lake.

The lake was habitat for beaver, geese, and swans, and formerly extended for about ½ mile to ¾ mile west of Northwood Road. It is now bisected by a railroad grade and is dry except in winter. The lake area is drained by a creek that enters the Nooksack R. at the upper end of the Stickney Island meander loop.

---

32. Yúmechiy A creek northeast of Lynden, entering place 31 Sa7átsnets lake from the north. **Map 7**

> <**Yúmechiy**> [yúməči] /yóməč-iy/. ***Spring salmon-place*** as spring salmon ran in this creek; the first of three such place names from Nooksack <yúmech> *spring salmon* + <-iy> *place.*

Spring salmon ran in this creek, which flows next to the pit house site of Sp’etós (place 33). The creek flows southeast from the corner of Line Road and Kamm Road.

---

33. Sp’etós Village longhouse and pit house site in the prairie area northeast of Lynden. **Map 7**

> <**Sp’etós**> [sp’ətó·s] (WS:GS; PF; PFM), /s-p’ətós/. EF and LG compare Nooksack [pətó·s] ***suddenly broke through (brush, anything requiring struggle to get through)*** and Skagit [p’ət’ósəb] *brush hair back away from one’s face.*

Most of the prairies in the Nooksack area are low wet places, some of which were bogs that would have been naturally treeless. The hillside prairie from Lynden northeast to Northwood Road is not likely to have formed naturally unless by fire and, as with many of the lower and wetter prairies, was almost certainly artificially maintained by burning. The Sp’etós pit houses were located on the hillside just west of Yúmechiy (place 32). This location is northeast of the corner of Line Road and Bradley Road, and was designated as archeological site 45WH6 (Emmons 1952, 52). These pit houses were last occupied some time before the 1850s; unfortunately, the site was bulldozed for ease of farming in the 1950s.

The Sp’etós plank longhouse was located at the base of the hill just southwest of the corner of Kamm Road and Northwood Road, almost half a mile east-northeast of the pit house site. These locations and the surrounding area are shown in detail in Map 8. Both Sp’etós locations were within the homestead claim of McClanahan, a white man married to Lynden Jim’s sister (LG). This property later became the Bradley farm, with the Bradley farmhouse adjacent to the pit house location (Jeffcott 1949, 34). The plank longhouse was probably occupied until the Land Survey of 1872 (United States General Land Office 1859-90), which determined that it was within McClanahan’s claim rather than in one of the adjoining Indian homestead claims. The longhouse was torn down around 1900 and consisted of “just boards” in 1914 (Richardson 1974, 59). The

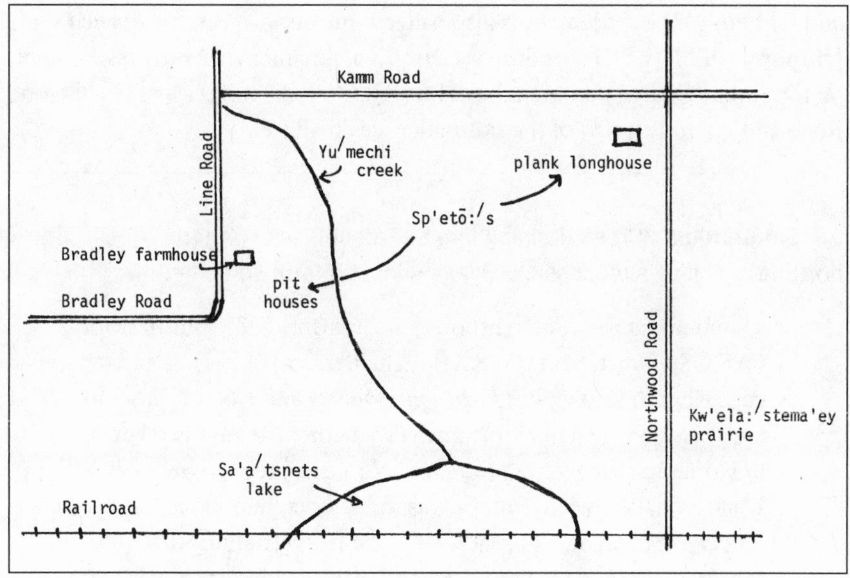

Map 8 *Locations of places 31 Sa7átsnets, 32 Yúmechiy, 33 Sp'etós, and 34 Kw'elástem7ey. Sketch made following a field visit with the Nooksack elders, with the place names transcribed according to the convention being used at the time.* (A. Richardson field notes, 18 September 1980)

name Sp'etós is also applied to the farm settlement established about 200 yards north of the longhouse site, on the homestead of Joe Sx̱éyem.

---

34. Kw'elástem7ey Prairie east of Sa7átsnets lake, possible village site, and farm settlement. **Map 7**

<**Kw'elástem7ey**> [kʼʷəlɛ́·stəmɛʔᵉ] (WS:AJ), /kʼʷəlǽstəmʔ-əy/ or poss. /kʼʷolǽstəmʔ-əy/. ***Saskatoon berry, service berry-place*** because they gathered the [kʼʷəlǽ·stəm] *saskatoon or service berry* (BG:LG) there and *camas* [spǽnənxʷ] (BG:SJ); LG first remembered the Skagit cognate [kʼʷolá·stəb] (BG:LG) [qʼʷəᵒlástəb] (LT:LG) *service berry.*

This is the easternmost portion of the prairie area that extended west to Lhchálos. Kw'elástem7ey was important for berry picking and root digging. There is no firm evidence of a traditional village here; the "village" often mentioned always seems to refer to the house (farm settlement) of Sumas George and Old Polly. The settlement is also called Chítmixw (/čítmixʷ/ ***horned owl***), [čítmox̣ʷ] (PFM), which was Sumas George's nickname. The house (settlement) on the Sumas George homestead was located about 0.3 mile east of Northwood Road and 0.2 mile north of the railroad, on a small hill.

---

35. Smátentsot Creek draining into Sa7átsnets lake from the northeast, fishing site, possible village site, and farm settlements. **Map 7**

> **<Smátentsot>** ~ <Smátenthot> [smɛ́·tɛnΘot] (PF), [smɛ́·tənΘot] (WS:GS), [smɛ́təncut] (WS:AJ), [smǽtænΘot] (PFM), /s-mǽtən-cot/. Root unknown but /s-/ *(nominalizer)* and /-cot/ *(reflexive)* are affixes in the name. It is unclear whether the root is related to Nooksack <máts'en> *proud* or a Nooksack root cognate with Upriver Halkomelem <met'->, as in Halkomelem <met'mét'> *limber, supple.* The Nooksack <o> is in free variation with <u> in the language, and we have used either the predominant variant or the only variant in each case used by the recorded speakers who pronounced the names or words.

This creek was historically known as Worthen Cr. and is now called Kamm Slough, or Kamm Ditch, reflecting the extent to which its course has been altered for drainage. The creek was fished for silver salmon into the 20th century. A traditional village location on this creek is uncertain. The name "Smátentsot" is used most frequently to refer to the farm settlements on the homesteads of Jobe (Chúm) /čóm/ and Tenas George (shown in Photo 13). Jobe's house was located near the cemetery on his homestead on the east side of Northwood Road. Tenas George's house was located by Smátentsot creek ½ mile east of Northwood Road, northeast of the right angle turn in Kamm Road. Also on the Tenas George place was a longhouse built in the historical period and used in the early 20th century for ceremonial gatherings.

---

36. "Ka-nak-na-hi" Longhouse on Worthen Creek. **Map 7**

> **"Ka-nak-na-hi"** or "Knak-ni-hi" (both PJ), [kənǽkənəhay] (OW-PJ). Prob. has /-əy ~ -iy/ ***place*** and perhaps before that <-(e)x̲> *all around.* Poss. <Qanáx̲enex̲éy> or <Q'anáx̲enehéy> or <Qanáx̲en7éy> (no "k" in Nooksack), which could mean that the root may be related to Nooksack root <qan> *steal* as in <qánqan> *thief* or another Nooksack root that could begin with

Photo 13 *Tenas George, also known as George James, whose trust homestead was located east of Lynden, by place 35 Smátentsot, Worthen Creek or Kamm Slough. (Nooksack Indian Tribe 1974)*

<q> or <q'> or <x̲> and end with <n>; the name may have the Nooksack suffix <-áx̲en> *arm, side of house (angular/ perpendicular extension),* as in Nooksack and Halkomelem <sq'eláx̲en> *fence* and cognate with Upriver Halkomelem <-áx̲el ~ -ex̲el> /-ɛ́x̣əl ~ -əx̣əl/ *end or side of a house (inside/outside), angular or perpendicular extension.* This suffix is likely involved in the place name since it refers to a smokehouse site and the suffix is in the same domain as buildings and houses. Plank houses were sometimes erected or moved by making a new frame and taking (thus, steal) the planks from an old house or smokehouse that was no longer used. If the etymology was

<Qan-áx̲en-ex̲-éy>, this would mean *place to steal (house) sides all around.*

This place name is said to refer to "the old smokehouse on Worthen Creek" (Jeffcott 1949, 57). Worthen Cr. is place 35 Smátentsot, yet the nearest certain "old smokehouse" was the plank longhouse of place 33 Sp'etós located ¼ mile northwest of the creek. Jeffcott also states (1949, 34) that Lynden Jim held a large potlatch in the "old smokehouse" in the 1880's. At that time, the Sp'etós longhouse was probably the only one standing in the area, and it was in ruins soon after. After 1900, a new ceremonial "smokehouse" was built more directly on Worthen Cr. on the Tenas George place (see place 35), and it is possible that Jeffcott mistakenly considered this to be the "old smokehouse." Since "Ka-nak-na-hi" is not known from any other sources, its location remains uncertain.

---

37. Pá7atstel Village site and prairie area near Northwood Road north of the Jobe Cemetery. **Map 7**

<**Pá7atstel**> [pɛ́ʔɛctəl] (PF:LG), [pɛ́·^Θtəl] (WS:AJ), [pǽ(ʔ) æc'təl] (PFM), [pǽʔæΘtəl] (BG:EF) /pǽʔæc-təl/. AJ notes the name is from /spɛ́·Θ/ *black bear,* using the Halkomelem form for Nooksack /spǽʔæc/ ***black bear;*** /-təl/ resembles Halkomelem /-təl/ *device, thing for,* and resembles Halkomelem [pǽ˙Θtəl] ***bear trap*** (lit. "device to get bear"), but Nooksack has /-tən/ as in /ɬǽč'-tən/ *knife.*

This village was last occupied around 1820 (based on genealogical data); its exact location is uncertain. The most likely area is the northwest corner of the Jobe (Chúm) homestead north of the cemetery, east of Northwood Road and south of the Northwood Store on East Badger Road. The house that previously belonged to Frank George still stands here. Frank George and Louis George [LG of PF's notes] are both grandsons of Jobe.

---

38. Shó̲qwil Trail crossing, fishing site with drying houses, and small prairie area on Fishtrap Creek just south of the International Boundary near Northwood Road. **Map 7**

<**Shó̲qwil**> or <**Sháqwil**> [šá·qʷil ~ šá·kʷɪl ~ šxʸá·kʷɪl] (PF), [šxʸá·kʷel] (PFM), [šxʸá·kʷɪl] (WS:GS), [šyákʷɪl] (WS:AJ; BG:EF), [šáqʷil] (BG:SJ), /šáqʷ-il/ or prob. /šǽqʷ-il/. ***Crossing (of water)*** or ***cross (water)-go, come, get*** from Nooksack [šǽqʷiˇl] *go across*

(LT:LG), cf. also [šxʷšǽ·ˇqʷil] *bridge, something one goes across on* (LT:LG); Skagit has /šáqʷil/ *cross a river or lake* and Halkomelem /xʸ/ corresponds to Nooksack /š/ here; the Nooksack forms appear to be influenced by both Halkomelem and Skagit.

The trail from the Nooksack villages in the Lynden area to Matsqui crossed Fishtrap Cr. at Shó̲qwil. This was ¼ to ½ mile south of the border based on the 1857-62 Boundary Survey manuscript map, Series 68, or about 0.2 mile south of the border based on the 1875 Land Survey map (United States General Land Office 1859-90). The primary traditional use of Shó̲qwil was for catching and drying silver salmon in the fall, with some plant gathering in the surrounding prairie. There was probably also a permanent village settlement here at some time in the past. The Boundary Survey report of Henry Custer (1858a, 8) includes the following: "Having crossed the Creek about 10-15 ft. wide we found ourselves before a large Indian house of most solid structure. The Indians informed us that this was a hunting & fishing station of the Ska-leih-hes Indians. A short distance from here a trail was leading off to their prairie (Máh-moo-koom) in an almost due westerly direction." The Shó̲qwil site was claimed as an Indian homestead by Dick Harry (Hawley), with an adjacent 160 acres east of Northwood Road claimed by Louis Sacquilty (shown in Photo 14). Dick Harry's house and orchard were located on the small hill about 100 feet north of Fishtrap Cr. and 100 feet west of Northwood Road (EF), which would be on the trail shown on the 1875 Land Survey map (United States General Land Office 1859-90).

---

39. Qwo̲qwehíwen Peardonville, British Columbia, located on the west bank of Fishtrap Creek one mile north of the border. **Map 7**

<**Qwo̲qwehíwen**> [kʷakʷəhéwən] (WS:AJ). ***Cut ravine.*** Halkomelem has cognate [qʷɔqʷəhíwəl] /qʷaqʷəh-íwəl/ also *cut ravine,* prob. from /qʷəhɛ́/ *go through an opening* (as in Nooksack also, see place 27) and /-íwəl/ *on the inside;* this suggests Nooksack /qʷaqʷəh-íwən/ or, if [a] is really [ɔ], then /qʷoqʷəh-íwən/.

This was on the trail to Matsqui about 1½ miles upstream from Shó̲qwil (place 38). A sketch map in the Boundary Survey materials (RG 76, E 201, Topographical Notes) shows a "trail to Skaleigh Prairie" meeting the trail from the main Nooksack prairies at about this location. The present location is just north of the corner of Huntingdon Road and Peardonville Road.

Photo 14 *Louis Sacquilty, whose trust homestead was located on Northwood Road adjacent to place 38 Shó̲qwil.* (Nooksack Indian Tribe 1974)

40. "Tse-tséh-ne-wun" Pepin Creek. **Map 7**

"Set-séh-no-wa" ~ "Seet-seh-no-wa" (BS) ~ **"Tse-tséh-ne-wun"** (Harris 1858). Poss. <Tsetsíniwen> or <Ts'ets'íniwen> or <Tsitsíniwen> with root something like <tsin> or <ts'in> + prefixed reduplication + suffix, perhaps <-iwen> *on the inside;* or the root could be something like <tsits>, <sits'>, or alternatives with either or both <ts> being <ts'> or plain + <-ín> + <-iwen>. Of these possibilities, Upriver Halkomelem has a variant root <ts'i> (from <ts'a:> *on top*) used with suffix <-t> *do to s-th/s-o purposely,* yielding <ts'it> *greet s-o, thank s-o* (s-o =

> someone; s-th = something) (some speakers pronounce this <th'it>). Nooksack has both -t and -n transitivizers with similar meaning but <-n> adds a completive element (*do on purpose completely to s-o or s-th*); other possible cognates to the root here are Upriver Halkomelem <sits> *proud* and the root in <si:ts'-elhp> *vine maple*. Nooksack also has a suffix <-áy(7)> *tree, plant, wood* and if this combined into <sits'-áy-n-iwen> it could mean something like *vine maple wood/tree on the inside* (although BG:SJ has Nooksack <síč'ɛɬp> *vine maple*). The versions ending in <owa> are less likely since no Nooksack suffix <-owa> or <-owe> has been found, even after analysis so far has shown about 170 lexical affixes (mostly suffixes). *A Stó:lō–Coast Salish Historical Atlas* (Carlson et al. 2001, 136, 142) has Leqlétsel, Pepin Cr., translation 'a stretch of the foothills.' This is an Upriver Halkomelem name that is different from the Nooksack name. Its literal translation cannot be verified from Galloway's Upriver Halkomelem dictionary (2009) since the six words for types of hills do not have a root remotely resembling that in Leqlétsel. One could compare <lhéq'qel> *end of a falling section of land, end of a level stretch of land (head of a creek or island* or <léq'> *level, flat* or <q'ál> *go over or around (hill, rock, river, etc.)* + <-étsel> *on the back, at the back* with prefix le (xw) = *always* (the le- allomorph is very rare, and is only in old place names), but the Upriver Halkomelem root <léq> means *dive*. The etymology of this Upriver Halkomelem name remains unclear.

The Nooksack place name is known only from the Boundary Survey materials. The large manuscript map shows "Seet-seh-no-wa" as the first of the upper tributaries of Fishtrap Cr. above Peardonville. Study of other Boundary Survey materials indicates that the location of "Seet-séh-no-wa" on the manuscript map was probably an error. Custer's field report (1858a) and field map (Series 69, Map 23) show that the trail from the Nooksack prairie to Matsqui did not cross this creek; rather, it (the creek) was encountered on the return trip to the west of Kwokwe7ám (place 41) and is clearly Pepin Cr. Harris (1858, 3) reports that the "Tse-tséh-ne-wun" crosses the boundary line two miles east of Bertrand Cr., which is the exact location of Pepin Cr. Pepin Cr. was the main stream entering an extensive wet area with outflow south to Fishtrap Cr. (see place 22 Xwq'écheqsem and 23 Noxwqwo7ópey), or possibly southwest to Bertrand Cr. (Harris 1858, 3).

41. Kwokwe7ám A branch of Fishtrap Creek above Peardonville. **Map 7**

<Kwokwe7ám> "Ko-kwa-ahm" (BS), [kʷakʷəʔɛ́m ~ kʷəkʷəʔɛ́m] (WS:AJ), [kʷukʼʷəlɛ́·m] (PF:LG), prob. /kʷokʷəʔǽm/. Perhaps compare Nooksack <skwá7am> *fish trap basket* with Upriver Halkomelem <skwá:m> *storage basket (for oil, fruit, clothes), burial basket for twins, round basket (any size, smaller at top), clay jug (to store oil or fruit)* from root <kwá:m> *round;* the first syllable in the place name could be prefixed *diminutive* reduplication, here <kwe->. Another possible root is Nooksack <kwe7á>, as in <kwe7át> *leave it alone,* with <-m> *middle or passive voice* replacing the <-t> *transitive* (cf. Upriver Halkomelem <kwikwe'át> *leave s-o alone, stop pestering s-o). A Stó:lō–Coast Salish Historical Atlas* (Carlson et al. 2001, 139, 147) has Si:tel, Waechter Creek, significance "possibly 'cedar-gathering place.'" It has Kwókwechíwel for a site in the headwaters of this creek, significance "a viewpoint from which to watch for raiders," translation 'lookout' (Carlson et al. 2001, 139, 142). Kwókwechíwel is a place name shown in the Upriver Halkomelem dictionary as Kw'okw'echíwel, a correction that should be made in *A Stó:lō–Coast Salish Historical Atlas,* since the name and derivation and meaning (*lookout*) are identical to the one in the dictionary. Kw'okw'echíwel is also used for a different lookout place name, *Wahleach Bluff, a lookout mountain with rock sticking out over a bluff, also the lookout point on Agassiz Mountain.*

There was a house here for drying fish, and perhaps a fishtrap, according to Agnes James (Wayne Suttles's interview). Also according to James, this name refers to "a branch of Fishtrap Creek that runs east from Peardonville." Since there are no side creeks to the east, this may refer to the main creek, which makes a sharp turn to the east going upstream above the first northwesterly tributary. The Boundary Survey field materials all have "Ko-kwa-ahm" as the first northwesterly tributary north of the boundary. This is probably the stream that crosses Peardonville Road one mile northeast of Echo Road, although a 1914 map (BC Department of Lands) has a rather different drainage pattern for this area just west of the Abbotsford International Airport. The form "O'kwa'am" appears in Henry Custer's "Topographical Notes" field book (RG 76, E 201).

---

42. "Pehp-she" Second main tributary of Fishtrap Creek above Peardonville. **Map 5**

> **"Pehp-she"** (BS), "Pipehi" (BS-Custer),<Pípshiy> or <P'íp'shiy?>, prob. /pípš-iy/ or /p'íp'š-iy/. Root <piš> or <p'iš>, poss. compare Nooksack <pipíš> *kitten* (<píšpiš> cat) + <-ey> *place.*

The 1857-62 Boundary Survey field materials show "Pehp-she" as the second northwesterly branch of Fishtrap Cr. crossed by the trail to Matsqui north of the border. The form "Pipehi" is used in Henry Custer's field notebook (RG 76, E 201, Topographical Notes). "Pehp-she" is most likely the creek that now crosses Mt. Lehman Road 0.2 mile north of Marshall Road. The Nooksack had a fish-drying house at nearby place 41 Kwokwe7ám, and travelled through this area going to Matsqui (see place 43 Yilhíxwich).

---

43. Yilhíxwich The last branching of Fishtrap Creek near the old Trans-Canada Highway (Old Yale Road). **Map 5**

> <**Syilhíxwich ~ Yilhíxwich**> "Seet-le-wheetsh" (BS), [yɪɬéx^{w}ɪč] (WS:AJ), prob. /yəɬíx^{w}-ič/ or /yiɬíx^{w}-ič/, poss. /yi-ɬíx^{w}-ič ~ s(y)i-ɬíx^{w}-ič/. ***Creek-in back*** from Nooksack [yɛɬíx^{w}] (LT:LG) (/yəɬíx^{w}/ or /yiɬíx^{w}/ *creek* (cf. Skagit /jɬíx^{w}/ *creek*); possible alternative is ***three creeks-in back***, suggested by a similar Halkomelem place name /sí-ɬíx^{w}/ *Mahood Cr.*, which has three branches from Deer L., near Harrison L. The BS version shows that an <s-> *nominizer prefix* is sometimes present. *A Stó:lō–Coast Salish Historical Atlas* (Carlson 2001, 139, 146) has Selxwí:chel, translation 'centre of something,' 'the middle of three.' This is an Upriver Halkomelem name for the same place, derived from <**alxwítsel**>, //ʔɛlx^{w}=íc(=)əl//, *middle (in age or spatial position), between,* possibly with <**=íts(el)**> *in back.* So the meaning is not literally 'the middle of three' but merely *middle,* so it can be a different or same item between two or more other items. Thus, *middle (of three)* is quite poss. a literal meaning here, since the Nooksack name also refers to three creeks.

This is described by Agnes James as "the last place going up Fishtrap Creek on the way to Matsqui" (WS:AJ). The 1857-62 Boundary Survey maps and reports have "Seet-le-wheetsh" for the uppermost northerly tributary of Fishtrap

Cr. The upper section of Fishtrap Cr. trends northeast going upstream, with a tributary entering from the north just south of the present Trans-Canada Highway. This tributary splits into two branches ⅓ mile upstream, south of Old Yale Road near Townline Road, west of Clearbrook, BC.

---

44. Sq'éq'ayex̲ Village site and fishing location on the south bank of the Nooksack River, between the south ends of Northwood Road and Notter Road (Timon School site), both on the north bank. **Map 9**

> <**Sq'éq'ayex̲**> [sk'ákayəq] (WS:AJ), [skə́qayəq] (WS:GS), prob. /s-q'ə́-q'æyəx̣/. ***Whirlpool*** (WS:AJ), so called because the fast narrow stretch of water with whirlpools and eddies was and still is a good fishing spot (inherited). Cf. Halkomelem /q'ɛ́yə́x̣-əm ~ q'ə́yə́x̣-əm/ and Squamish /s-q'yax̣-atq^{w}úʔm/, both *whirlpool.*

This is a fast, narrow stretch of the river with whirlpools that was Louis Sacquilty's main fishing place early in the 20th century (Richardson 1974, 59). It was also fished in the late 19th century (Hawley 1971, 59) and is still being fished today. The location on the south bank was a former village site, according to Agnes James. A viewpoint on the north bank can be reached by a dirt road south from Timon Road ⅛ mile east of Northwood Road. A Boundary Survey map from a trip taken in late August 1857 (Series 69, unidentified map in folder following Map 76) shows three houses 1 mile below here next to a weir or small logjam. Related written records (RG 76, E 201, Topographical Notes) state that these houses were in the mouth of a "dry channel of River." Thus, this was probably a seasonal fishing site.

---

45. Ey7í7shil7 Location near the mouth of Timon Creek. **Map 9**

> <Ey7í7shil7>; [ʔé·yʔx^{y}ɪl] (BG) is a Matsqui Halkomelem version of this Nooksack name. The Halkomelem means *bring(ing) a load of food (by canoe) for trade;* Upriver Halkomelem also has /ʔí·x^{y}əl/ *paddling a canoe;* Nooksack has [ʔíšilʔ] /ʔíšilʔ/ *paddle a canoe* and /ʔəy ʔíšilʔ/ ***paddling a canoe*** (BG:SJ).

This is the name for a trading place near the mouth of Timon Cr. where the Lummi and Nooksack would bring loads of food by canoe for trading (EF). This place was also said to be near Kilcup's house. Timon Cr. has been ditched and disrupted so that the former mouth is hard to find. Its drainage can be traced downstream as far as an old crossing of Timon Road 0.1 mile west of Notter Road (based on the 1908 Sumas 15′ quadrangle map, US Geological Survey). Daniel Kilcup's homestead was located north of Timon Road near here, while another Kilcup lived more recently south of Timon Road and east of Notter Road. Most of this area is also within Timon Prairie (place 46 Kwets'kwets'éy).

---

46. Kwets'kwets'éy Timon Prairie. **Map 9**

> <Kwets'kwets'ó̲y> or better <**Kwets'kwets'éy**> [kʷɔckʷʊc'á·y] (PF:LG; PFM), [kʷəθ'kʷəθ'áy] (WS:GS), [kʷaθ'kʷəθ'áy] (WS:AJ), poss. /kʷəc'kʷəc'-áy ~ kʷac'kʷac'-áy/. *Willow (ruffed) grouse* /kʷə́c'kʷəc'/ (Halkomelem /skʷə́θ'kʷəθ' ~ skʷə́θ'/, both /kʷ/ ~ /qʷ/). ***Willow grouse-place*** from the Nooksack word for *willow grouse* + Nooksack <-éy ~ -iy> *place,* which seems to have a stressed variant, <-ó̲y>, here.

According to Agnes James: "This was open ground with vegetables growing, a good deer hunting ground, and good for willow grouse" (interview by Wayne Suttles, 13 August 1952). A location 100 yards south of the corner of Slotemaker Road and Timon Road was specified by Louis George (interview by Paul Fetzer, 18 October 1950), although a broader surrounding area historically known as Timon Prairie was presumably also covered by the name. Also see place 45 Ey7í7shil7.

---

47. Mách'aney Location about four miles east of Lynden. **Map 9**

> <**Mách'aney**> "Mat-cha-ni" (PJ), [mə́tčənə] (OW-PJ), prob. /mǽč'æn-əy/. ***Black hawthorn berry-place,*** cf. Halkomelem /mɛ́c'əl/ *black hawthorn berry.*

This place name is known only from the following statement: "MAT-CHA-NI – black haw berries; a locality about four miles east of Lynden where those berries were plentiful" (Jeffcott 1949, 57). This location would be near the corner of Hampton Road and Trapline Road. The 1908 US Geological Survey map shows a swampy area here extending northeast to Johnson Cr., which is the appropriate habitat for the black hawthorn.

---

48. Sp'ó̲p'qwos Location on the south bank of the Nooksack River below Po̲pehómey (place 52). Map 9

<**S(h)p'ó̲p'qwos**> [šp'áp'qʷos] (WS:AJ), poss. /š(xʷ)-p'áp'qʷ-os/ or more likely /s-p'áp'qʷ-os/. ***Clear bank*** (WS:AJ) with /-os/ being *face; face of bank or cliff.* Louisa George also compares Nooksack [p'ap'qʷós] ***brush hair back away from face.*** Musqueam, but not Nooksack, has /š-/.

This is a place name given only by Agnes James, and without specific uses or an exact location. This place is about 1 to 2½ miles below Everson on the river in the vicinity of Mile 22 of the Nooksack R. (US Geological Survey 1972 7½′ quadrangles). Due to shifts in the river, most of the 19th-century south bank in this area is located north of the present river channel. The best present access to this area is via a gravel road south from Stickney Island Road ½ mile west of Trapline Road. This area has been fished with set eddy nets as recently as the 1950s (George Cline).

---

49. Kw'íshilwalh Fountain Lake. Map 9

<**Kw'íshilwalh**> ~ <**Qw'íshilwalháy**> [k'ʷéixʸɪlwɛɬ] (WS:GS), [q'ʷí·xʸɪlwɛɬá·y] (PF:GS, NKF2.2308) (Fetzer's Linguistic Field Notes, file card box 2, card 2308). So far, it is unclear how to phonemicize and segment, poss. /k'ʷíyš-ilwæɬ/, /k'ʷíš-il-wæɬ/, /q'ʷíyš-ilwæɬ-ǽy/, /q'ʷíš -il-wæɬ-ǽy/, etc. Various Nooksack morphemes might be compared: /k'ʷiš ~ k'ʷəš/ (Upriver Halkomelem /k'ʷəxʸ/) *count,* /-álʔwəɬ ~ -ílwəɬ/ *side,* /-wəɬ ~ -wiɬ/ *canoe,* and /-ǽy/ *tree, plant.* These suffixes are all feasible for this place name since one way to harvest wapatos/Indian potatoes was by hanging over the *side* of the *canoe* and uprooting them with one's toes and letting them float to the surface. [xʸ] is Halkomelem-influenced for /š/. Nooksack has a root <kw'iš ~ kw'eš> *count,* as in Nooksack <ch'exwkw'ésh> *twenty* (LG) and <ch-kw'exʸ-álh> (PF:GS) *twenty* and Upriver Halkomelem has a root <kw'íy> *climb* that has not yet been found in Nooksack. *Climb over the side plant* might be a good literal meaning and name for what is done to gather wapatos, but this is so far just a possibility, not a certainty. It may be the reason both PF and GS recorded the place name and the note about gathering Indian

potatoes on the same card. No root of shape <qw'ish> in Nooksack or <qw'ix> in Upriver Halkomelem has been found yet.

This is a small lake with a marshy border. Wild cranberries and Labrador (swamp) tea used to grow in a bog off the east side of the lake. Indian potatoes were also gathered in the lake, according to PF:GS (6 September 1950, NKF2.2308). The only access to this lake at present is through the Hardy farm north of Pole Road, one mile east of Hannegan Road.

---

50. Sqeláw7 Green Lake. **Map 9**

<**Sqel(7)áw7**> [sqəlǽwʔ] (BG:EF), /sqəl(ʔ)ǽwʔ/. ***Beaver*** from [sqəlʔǽwʔ] (LT:LG, LT:SJ, BG:LG), [sqəlǽwʔ] (BG:SJ, BG:EF) *beaver;* Upriver Halkomelem has cognate /sqəlɛ́·w/ *beaver.*

This lake is located ¼ mile south of Pole Road and 1 mile west of Noon Road, with access through private property at the end of Lunde Road. Green L. drains into Ten Mile Cr. It is small and shallow, with beaver workings visible in the swampy border of the lake. No specific Nooksack use of this lake is recorded, although hunting of beaver and waterfowl and gathering of useful plants would have been possible.

---

51. Nek'iyéy Ten Mile Prairie. **Map 9**

<**Nek'iyéy**>? or <Niqiyéy>? [nɪkiyéy] (WS:AJ). The form "Lequiei" is given for the creek at this location in Henry Custer's field notes (RG 76, E 202).

This place name also applies to Ten Mile Cr. (see place 5). Ten Mile Prairie was located where the trail to Bellingham Bay crossed Ten Mile Cr. In reference to the prairie location, Agnes James states that "Joe Pete testified to a village on Ten Mile Creek" (Wayne Suttles field notes), and R.E. Hawley (1971, 80) states that "the Hudson Bay Company had established a Trading Post at Ten Mile Creek." The trail from Kwánech (place 54) (at Everson) to X̲wó̲tqwem (place 133) on Bellingham Bay became known as the Whatcom Trail and later as the Telegraph Road. The Telegraph Road crossing of Ten Mile Cr. is located on a long driveway leading to a group of older houses north of Hemmi Road, ¼ mile east of Hannegan Road (see Jeffcott 1949, 196). The location of the prairie is indicated today by the low wet area crossed by Hemmi Road from ½ to ¾ mile east of Hannegan Road. Upper portions of Ten Mile Cr. were fished for silver salmon, according to Sindick Jimmy (Richardson 1974, 63).

51A. “Spelcoke” Deer Creek. **Map 9**

> “**Spelcoke**” (BS-Custer). Possibly <Sp’ólqw’eqw> *foam at the head* or <Sp’álq’eqw’> *glitter around in circles,* from Nooksack <sp’olqw’-em> *foam* + <-eqw> *on top of the head/hair,*or compare Upriver Halkomelem <p’álq’-em> *glitter, flash, sparkle* + -(e)qw’ *around in circles;* or a number of other pronunciations are possible, as is the Nooksack suffix <-ey> *place* at the end of the first two possible etymologies.

This name is known only from the field notes of Henry Custer’s reconnaissances (RG 76, E 202). His party left Ten Mile Cr. on the trail to Whatcom at 11:43 and at 12:20 they “crosse a little stream, Spelcoke.” They would have crossed one of the two upper branches of Deer Cr., which joins Ten Mile Cr. at Barrett L.

---

52. Po̲pehómey Location on the south bank of the river at Nooksack Crossing. **Map 9**

> <**Po̲pehómey**> “Pop-a-ho-my” (PJ), [papəhomiy] (OW-PJ), [pap^{a}hó·may] (WS:AJ), [papəhomay] (BG:EF), /papəhóm-ay/. ***Frog, toad-place*** from Nooksack /pipəhómʔ/ (LT:LG, LT:SJ) + <-ey ~ -iy ~ -ó̲y> *place.*

Nooksack Crossing was the location of the first ferry crossing and first store in the upper Nooksack valley, and was a focus of non-Indian activity from the 1850s until the coming of the railroad around 1890, which caused the abandonment of Nooksack Crossing and the founding of Everson. Nooksack Crossing was located near the present Everson Rodeo grounds on the Pete Harkness homestead just west of Trapline Road and south of Stickney Island Road. Po̲pehómey was the name for a location on the south bank opposite Nooksack Crossing, which places it between 0.2 and 0.4 mile below and west of the present highway bridge at Everson. At present, the best access to view this location from the north bank is to reach the river through Everson City Park and then walk downriver on gravel bars. Po̲pehómey and other named places near Everson

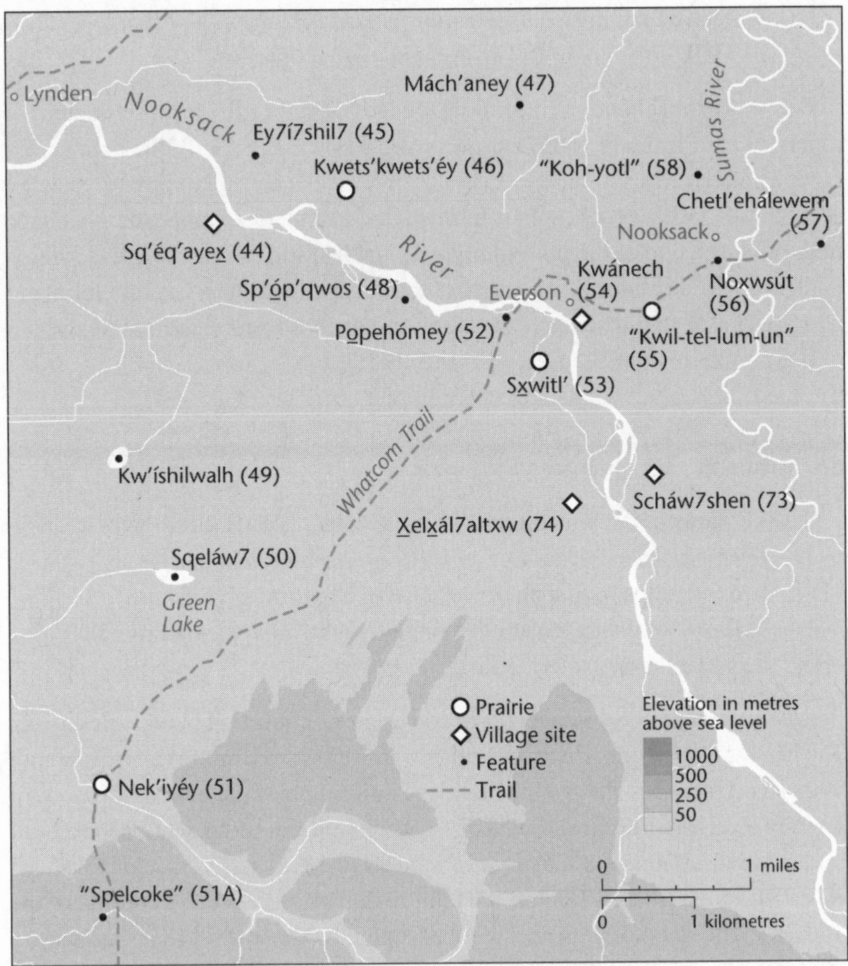

MAP 9 *Place names in the Everson area.* (Adapted from Richardson and Galloway 2007)

are located on Map 9. The villages shown on this map formed a community with its centre at Kwánech (place 54).

---

53. Sx̲witl' Captain John's place and prairie, across the river from Kwánech. **Map 9**

<**Sx̲witl'**> [sx̣ʷéyƛ̃'] or [sx̣ʷé·ƛ'], /sx̣ʷíƛ'/, [swé·ƛ'] (PFM). Apparently named after Captain John's nickname, /sx̣ʷíƛ'/,

which in turn means ***bush robin (varied thrush)*** in Nooksack; cf. Halkomelem /sx̣ʷíkʼ/ *bush robin, varied thrush.*

This was probably not a traditional village but rather the farm settlement of a man named Captain John, who was also known as Sx̱wítlʼ. The area across from Kwánech was a natural prairie and historically an Indian potato-growing area (Smith 1950, 332). Captain John settled immediately opposite Kwánech, near the south end of the present highway bridge, and another Nooksack man, Old Alec, settled about ¼ mile further south (upriver). Both Captain John and Old Alec failed to file homestead claims and were driven off their land and out of their homes by a white setter around 1882.

---

54. Kwánech Village located at Everson. **Map 9**

<**Kwánech**> [kʷǽ·nəč], /kʷǽnəč/, [kʷə·nɛč] (PFM). EF derives it from Nooksack /kʷǽ/ ***lots*** and /-nəč/ ***at the bottom*** because of two fish traps at /papəhómay/; LG (in LT) thinks it refers to a shallow-water stretch at Everson, over which people had to pull their canoes instead of poling.

This was a major traditional village and home of important Nooksack leaders. The last "chief" of this "district" (village cluster) was George Welósius, whose homestead included the Kwánech village and much of the area of the present town of Everson. The first Methodist church and boarding school were built under the direction of Welósius at Kwánech in 1876. The village of Kwánech was abandoned around 1888 in the land rush that preceded the coming of the railroad. The site of Kwánech is now occupied by the former Kale Cannery to the east of the highway bridge on the northeast bank of the river.

---

55. "Kwil-tel-lum-un" Prairie between the Nooksack and Sumas Rivers east of Everson. **Map 9**

"Kwil-tel-lum-un" (BS). Poss. <Kwiltelemen or Kw'iltelemen>, or first consonant could be <Qw> or <Qw'> and/or either or both of the last two vowels could be <e>; the stress is on either the first or third vowel. Poss. <-tel> *each other, reciprocal,* poss. <-ámen ~ -ámin> *in the mind, thinking about* (if vowel 1 is stressed, the <á> could become <e> in a Halkomelem-accented Nooksack). Poss. compare Nooksack cognates, as in <as-kwálil>

hidden and <temqw'ílos> *spring (time things sprout up)* with the following Upriver Halkomelem roots: <kwil-> *hide* (Lummi <kwil-> *hide*), <qw'il> *uncover,* as in <qw'il-t> *uncover it,* and <qw' íles> *sprout up (lit. uncover the face),* or Lushootseed roots <kwil> *pick berries* (Hess, 1976) or <kwil(i)-> *peek, peer, look from behind s-th, peer around s-th.*

This Indian name is known only from the 1857-62 Boundary Survey materials. It is listed in "Indian Nomenclature" (Gibbs 1857-61) with places on the Sumas R., and is described as a "prairie near Nooksaak." On the manuscript map (Series 68), it is placed between the two rivers crossing the trail from Whatcom east of the present town of Everson, the centre of the prairie being about ½ mile east of the city centre. In contrast, a Boundary Survey field report (Gardner 1857a) states that the trail to Sumas Prairie leaves the Nooksack R. just above a large Indian village, and goes through dense timber to reach the Sumas R. There is no clear record of this prairie in either ethnographic or later historical sources. Fitzhugh (1858, 328) mentions first "a large prairie" and then prairies (in the plural) for the Everson area, either of which could refer to this prairie in addition to the prairie on the southwest side of the river (see place 53 Sxwitl'). The portion of "Kwil-tel-lum-un" south of Main Street was part of the George Welósius homestead.

---

56. Noxwsút Charley Lewiston's place, at the east edge of the town of Nooksack, on the Sumas River near the mouth of Breckenridge Creek. **Map 9**

<Noxwsút> [nuxʷsú·t] (PF), [noxʷsú·t] (PFM), prob. /noxʷ-sót/. Prob. <nuxw- ~ noxw-> ***always; people,*** perhaps <sut> is related to Upriver Halkomelem **<sát>**, bound root //sɛ́t// *reach, pass on, pass along,* as in **<sóstem>**, //sɛ[=AáC_1ə=]t=əm//, ABDF [*'lost (deceased)'*] (from Galloway 2009). Or, just as plausibly, one could compare Nooksack <sot'onas> *take it in* (NKF 2.1455) and cognate Lushootseed root /sut'u-/ *draw in* or the Nooksack root in <sótič> *northeast wind, cold north(east) wind* (PA:GS, story of the North Wind People in LT:LG, card 46.12). This last is plausible if the transcribers of the place name missed the last syllable. It is also plausible since the area is more exposed to the northeast wind than many locations in this set of Nooksack sites.

This was the homestead of Charley [læwíčtən] /læwíčtən/ (anglicized to Charley Lewiston), not a traditional village, but probably named before homesteading. In 1874, Charley Lewiston, also known as Charlie Swim and as Seqó7e, filed a homestead claim of 160 acres, including this site. Lewiston is an anglicized form of his father's name, Lawéchten. Charley Lewiston's house, the place named Noxwsút, was located near an old orchard west of the Sumas R., about ¼ mile south of Breckenridge Road, according to George Cline, although other sources imply a location east of the Sumas R. The Boundary Survey reported "an unoccupied Indian hut" in this area (Gardner 1857a), with a field map (Series 69, Map 31) showing a house on the east side of the Sumas R. upstream (south) from Breckenridge Cr. Charley Lewiston may have built a new house across the small Sumas R. from an older structure.

---

57. Chetl'ehálewem Breckenridge Creek. **Map 9**

> <**Chetl'ehálewem**> [čəƛ'əhǽləwəm], prob. /čəƛ'ə-hæləw-əm/ or /čəƛ'əhǽ-ləw-əm/. ***Rocky bottom creek*** from root [čƛ'ǽ] (BG:LG) ~ [č'íƛ'æ] (LT:LG) *rock* (cf. Northern Lushootseed /č'ƛ'áʔ/, Southern Lushootseed /č'ə́ƛ'əʔ/ *rock*).

This creek was fished traditionally for silver salmon, and there were fish-drying houses at some location on the creek. Chetl'ehálewem is also referred to as the creek by Antone's old house, which specifies the location of most activity following homesteading in the 1870s. Antone's old house, shown in Photo 15, was on his trust homestead on the north bank of Breckenridge Cr. about 50 yards east of Goodwin Road. Salmon and trout were fished here early in the 20th century (AH).

---

58. "Koh-yotl" Creek tributary to the Sumas River in the town of Nooksack. **Map 9**

> **"Koh-yotl"** (BS), poss. <Kweyúlh ~ Kweyólh> [kʷəyúɬ] (BG:LG). Poss. compare Nooksack <-olh> *in past, former, deceased.* If the first consonant is glottalized, the root may be cognate with Upriver Halkomelem <kw'iy ~ kw'ey> *climb, ascend,* or more likely <q'oy> *die* (Nooksack <q'oy> /q'oy/ *die*), thus <Q'oyólh> *(where they) died in the past.* A similar set of roots is found as possibilities in place 101.

Photo 15 *Antone's place, on the trust homestead at place 57 Chetl'ehálewem, Breckenridge Creek. On the left is Agnes Antone (Agnes James), and on the right is Belinda Antone (Belinda Cline, Alice Hunt's mother), ca. 1900.* (Nooksack Indian Tribe 1974)

This creek is shown on the Boundary Survey manuscript map (Series 68, Folder 1, Map1) and described in "Indian Nomenclature" (Gibbs 1857-61) as a "creek running through it" in a listing following "Kwil-tel-lum-un" prairie. Although part of the prairie is drained by Johnson Cr., this creek is shown as a tributary to the Sumas R. near the present town of Nooksack. The one possible creek is presently unnamed, and appears to have shifted to different remnant channels of the Sumas R. through time. The present mouth of "Koh-yotl" is near Gillies Road ½ mile north of Breckenridge Road; the mouth on the 1874 Land Survey map (United States General Land Office 1859-90) is about ½ mile upstream, and in 1858 the mouth apparently was more than 1 mile upstream at a location above the mouth of Breckenridge Cr. near Noxwsút (see place 56). In the town of Nooksack, the present "Koh-yotl" crosses Nooksack Avenue

(Highway 9) north of Lincoln Street. A creek was located in this same channel in 1874, but may have been in another channel ⅓ mile to the south in 1858. These various channels all originate in an area north of Main Street east of Everson, which is within the area of place 55 "Kwil-tel-lum-un" prairie.

---

59. Xwmó̲lsemelhp Marshes on the west side of the Sumas River two miles south of Sumas, Washington. **Map 10**

> <**Xwmó̲lsemelhp**> ~ <**Mó̲lsemelhp**> "Hoo-mal-so-melp" (BS), [má·lsəmət] (PF:LG), [má·lsəməɬp] (PF:LG), prob. /xʷ-málsəm-əɬp ~ málsəm-əɬp/. ***Always-tall marsh blueberry-bush*** from Nooksack <noxw- ~ xw-> *always* + <mó̲lsem> *tall marsh blueberry* + <-elhp> *tree, bush.*

Native tall marsh blueberries and cranberries grew here, and people also got témelh /tə́məɬ/ *ochre clay* here along the river to burn and dry for red face paint (Paul Fetzer interview with Louis George, 18 October 1950). A village of Mó̲lsemelhp was mentioned by Josie George (interview by Paul Fetzer, 17 October 1950) but not included in any other sources. The marshes are shown as "Hoo-mal-so-melp Prairie" on the 1857-62 Boundary Survey manuscript map, and the same area is called Fern Prairie on the 1875 Land Survey map (United States General Land Office 1859-90). Today this location is near the corner of Telegraph Road and North Pass Road. This and other places near Sumas, Washington, can be located on Map 10. Villages in this area were part of the bilingual Nooksack-Halkomelem community discussed in Chapter 1.

---

60. "Yuch-wun-neh-ukw" Prairie east of Sumas River one mile southeast of Sumas, Washington. **Map 10**

> **"Yuch-wun-neh-ukw"** (BS). Poss. <Yux̲wuníqw> or <Yex̲weníqw> /yox̣ʷ(-)on-íqʷ/ or /yəx̣ʷ(-)ən-íqʷ/ but /qʷ/ could be /q'ʷ/ or /x̣ʷ/ instead. Perhaps compare Nooksack <yóx̲won7> *arrow* + <-iqw> *in the hair, on top of head;* or possible root cognate with Upriver Halkomelem <yéx̲w> *broke down, came (un)loose, came apart, (got) untied, loose, unravelled.*

This prairie was ½ to ¾ mile wide and extended 1 to 1½ miles along the Sumas R. opposite and upstream from the mouth of Johnson Cr. and the village of Temíxwten (place 61). This prairie is shown on the 1875 Land Survey map (United States General Land Office 1859-90), and shown and named on the

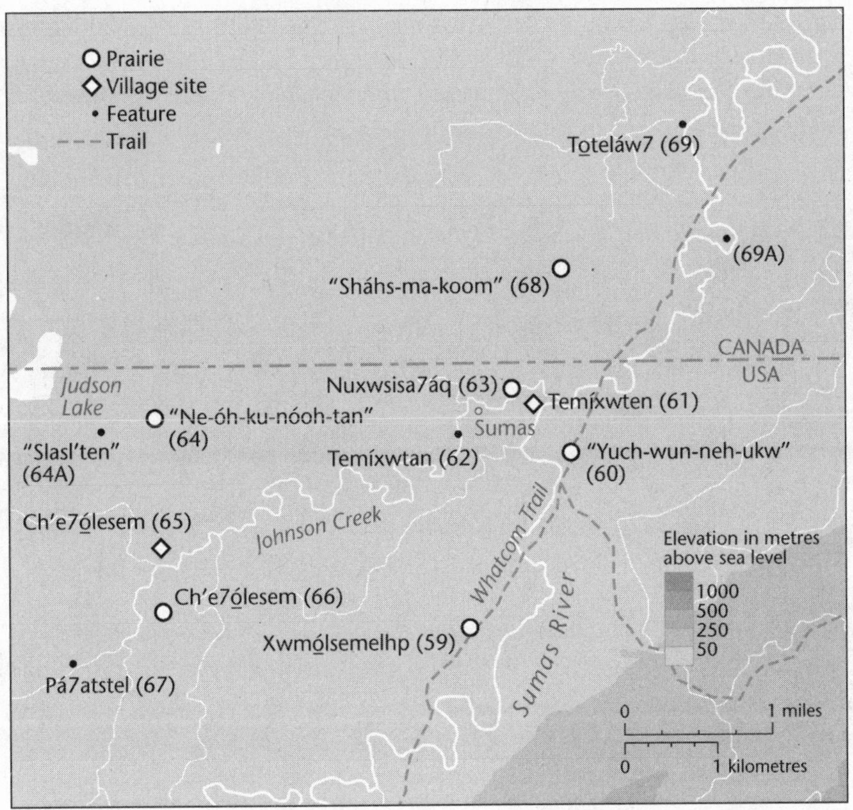

Map 10 *Place names in the Sumas, Washington, area.* (Adapted from Richardson and Galloway 2007)

1857-62 Boundary Survey manuscript map. Series 69, Map 31 shows a house in this prairie at the junction of a trail from the North Fork Nooksack R. at Kendall Cr. (see place 100) with the trail from Whatcom to Sumas L. In "Indian Nomenclature" (Gibbs 1857-61), "Yuch-wuh-néh-ukw" is described as the "1st small prairie on Tah-ta-láo" (place 69), the upper Sumas R. The centre of this prairie is near the corner of Rock Road and Sumas Road.

---

61. Temíxwten Nooksack village at Sumas, Washington. **Map 10**

<**Temíxwten**> [təmí·x^{w}tən] (PF; WS:AJ; WS:GS; BG:LG), /təmíx^{w}-tən/. ***Earth-device***, probably also *pit house,* though not the usual word for pit house in Nooksack, which is <sqemín> /sqəmín/ (Halkomelem /sqə́məl/).

Photo 16 *Place 61 Temíxwten* (earth-device), *a major Nooksack village with pit houses at Sumas, Washington, near the junction of Johnson Creek and the Sumas River. 8 March 1980.* (Photo by B. Galloway)

This was a major village with pit houses. Lottie Tom stated (Paul Fetzer interview, 23 October 1950) that when her great-grandfather was a young adult (around 1825), the people moved out of their pit houses because of a flood and built longhouses. Not too many years later, the village was entirely abandoned, with people moving to the location of Sumas Indian Reserve No. 7 (place 69A Upper Sumas Village) and to the Goshen area. The village of Ye<u>x</u>sáy (place 84, in the Goshen area) was apparently founded at this time (Paul Fetzer interview with George Swanaset, 14 September 1951). A descendant of the Temíxwten village married a white man named Johnson, who homesteaded the village site. The 1875 Land Survey map (United States General Land Office 1859-90) shows the building and fields of Robert Johnson south of the mouth of Johnson Cr. on the west bank of the Sumas R. This area, shown in Photo 16, is also the location of an archeological site, 45WH5 (Emmons 1952, 51-52). The location of the prehistoric site, the Johnson homestead, and Temíxwten is at the north end of Victoria Street at the east edge of the town of Sumas, northeast of the Sumas Elementary School. Also see place 62 Temíxwtan creek and place 63 Nuxwsisa7áq prairie.

---

62. Temíxwtan Johnson Creek. **Map 10**

> **<Temíxwtan>** "Tum-mehw-tan" (BS), certainly /təmíx^{w}-tæn/.
> ***Earth-device.***

This name from the 1857-62 Boundary Survey materials is presumably equivalent to Temíxwten (place 61). "Indian Nomenclature" describes "Tum-méhw-tan" as "Creek entering Tahtaláo below pre. [prairie]," yet three prairies have just been listed. Johnson Cr. is located below the first, place 60 "Yuch-wun-neh-ukw," but the Boundary Survey manuscript map places "Tum-méhw-tan" on Breckenridge Cr., which enters the Sumas R. below place 55 "Kwil-tel-lum-un." This placement is almost certainly incorrect since three more prairies are listed for "Tum-méhw-tan"; there are no prairies on Breckenridge Cr. but three known prairies on Johnson Cr. Further indication of a map error comes from the additional factor that a creek and the village at its mouth usually have the same name, and the village of Temíxwten is located at the mouth of Johnson Cr.

---

63. Nuxwsisa7áq Prairie at Sumas, Washington. **Map 10**

> **<Nu(xw)sisa7áq>** "Ne-see-sa-áhk" (BS). Prob. <Nu(xw)sisa7áq>
> /no(x^{w})-si-sæʔǽq/ ***always-little-bracken fern root.***

"Indian Nomenclature" (Gibbs 1857-61) describes this as "small pre. at mouth of Tum-mehw," which corresponds with a small unnamed prairie just above the mouth of Johnson Cr. on the Boundary Survey manuscript map. This prairie was immediately west of place 61 Temíxwten village. The location today, shown in Photo 17, is an area near the corner of Mitchell Street and Gough Street in Sumas, extending towards the mouth of Johnson Cr. to the northeast.

---

64. "Ne-óh-ku-nóoh-tan" Prairie west of Sumas, Washington. **Map 10**

> **"Ne-óh-ku-nóoh-tan"** (BS). Poss. <Noxwnúqwtan> or
> <Noxwnúx̲wtan??> or <Noqwnexwtan??>, or more likely
> **<nuqwnúqwtan>** from Nooksack root and prefixed *plural*
> reduplication in (PF:GS, NKF 2.648) <ay nuqwnúqwum>

Photo 17 *Place 62 Temíxwtan, Johnson Creek, facing east, downstream, near Sumas City Park. The area of place 63 Nuxwsisa7áq is in the distance to the left. 22 November 1980.* (Photo by B. Galloway)

> ***waving many times (like grass in the wind)*** + **<-tan>** ***something, thing for/to.*** The same root seems to be found in <núqum> *shake* and <ay nuqnúqum te temíxw> *many earthquakes* (PF:GS) (lit. *the earth shakes many times*). The first two (less likely) etymologies begin with <noxw- ~ nuxw> *always, place that always* + either <nuqw> *shake, wave (like grass in wind)* or a so far unattested root <nuxw> or <nu<u>x</u>w> + *thing for/to, device;* the third (less likely) etymology begins with root <nuqw ~ noqw> *shake, wave* + <-nexw> *happen/manage to do to s-th* (s-th = something) + <-tan>, as above.

"Indian Nomenclature" (Gibbs 1857-61) describes this as the second prairie of Tum-méhw-tan (see place 62). This is perhaps the low wet area about one mile in diameter, located between the International Boundary and Johnson Cr., mostly north of Halverstick Road and northwest of the former Milwaukee Road Railroad. This area is shown as a swamp on the 1908 US Geological Survey Sumas 15′ quadrangle map, which might be considered a prairie, and the 1857-62 Boundary Survey manuscript map places "Ne-óh-ku-nóoh-tan Pr." roughly in this area. Custer's report (1858a) describes an impassable swamp along the boundary west of the Sumas R. His party travelled for three hours on "the trail to Nooksahk prairie" following the north bank of Johnson Cr., then after reaching the end of the swamp, they turned northwest through dense timber and underbrush for an hour before reaching the Ne-óh-ku-nóoh-tan prairie. Custer also states that this prairie was of "small extent." A location on higher ground three miles west of Sumas, Washington, is most likely.

64A. "Slasl'ten" Prairie west of Sumas, Washington. **Map 10**

> **"Slasl'ten"** (BS). Poss. compare (PF:GS, card 2.778) <sél7sel7tan> ~ <sélseltan> *hand spinner device* (lit. "something for spinning by hand many times") and (PF:GS, card 2.312) <ay sélsel> *to spin by hand.*

This name, known only from the Boundary Survey (Series 69, Map 23), may be an alternate name for "Ne-óh-ku-nóoh-tan" prairie, which is not on this map. The map shows a large prairie extending from the location described in the report for "Ne-óh-ku-nóoh-tan" and expanding west to the area between Judson and Pangborn Lakes. "Slasl'ten" might be more narrowly applied to this area to the west.

---

65. Ch'e7ó̲lesem Village, fishing site, and prairie on Johnson Creek at Clearbrook, Washington, three miles southwest of Sumas, Washington. **Map 10**

> **<Ch'e7ó̲lesem>** [c'əʔá·ləsəm] (PF:LG), [cc'á˙ləsəm] (PFM), [c'əʔáləsəm] (WS:GS), Nooksack [č'əʔáləsəm] (WS:AJ) versus Halkomelem [c'əʔáləsəm] (WS:AJ), /č'əʔáləs-əm/. ***Resting place*** (WS:GS), cf. Halkomelem /c'á·lə́s-əm/ ***turn around***, with /c'/ corresponding to Nooksack /č'/; further support for /č'/ in place 66.

Ch'e7ó̲lesem was consistently included as a village by Nooksack elders of the 1950s and 1970s, although there is no basis through genealogy or otherwise of determining when or whether it was occupied in the historical period.

Occupation of Ch'e7ólesem in the year 1800 or later is likely based on its recognition as a traditional village. Ch'e7ólesem was also important as a camping ground for groups in transit, and was a good place for roots and berries in summer. There were one or two Indian houses here, and a vegetable patch where chocolate lily, camas, and /c'ə́Θələ/ were raised (WS:AJ). Historical records show a prairie extending a mile or more south of Clearbrook, primarily southeast of Johnson Cr. (see place 66 Ch'e7ólesem prairie). Historically, a fishtrap was located at the Ch'e7ólesem site (Richardson 1974, 60). Clearbrook is located on Clearbrook Road, at the crossing of the former Milwaukee Road railroad. This is on a hill on the northwest bank of Johnson Cr., just below the mouth of the creek draining Pangborn L. (see place 67).

---

66. Ch'e7ólesem Prairie at the head of Johnson Creek near Clearbrook, Washington. **Map 10**

> **<Ch'e7ólesem>** "Cháh-á-la-sun" ("corrected" to "Cháh-la-sum") (BS), [c'əʔá·ləsəm] (PFM), prob. <Ch'e7ólesem> /č'əʔáləs-əm/. Prob. ***Resting place*** or ***turn around place***, as in place 65.

This name from the 1857-62 Boundary Survey materials is presumably equivalent to Ch'e7ólesem (place 65). "Indian Nomenclature" (Gibbs 1857-61) describes it as a prairie on the head of "Tum-méhw-tan." Although the manuscript map places "Cháh-la-sum" at the head of Breckenridge Cr., it almost certainly belongs on Johnson Cr., where Ch'e7ólesem is located. The error made for "Tum-méhw-tan" was extended to "Cháh-la-sum."

---

67. Pá7atstel Squaw Creek, or possibly the creek draining Pangborn Lake. **Map 10**

> **<Pá7atstel>** [pɛ́ʔɛctəl] (WS:LG), [pɛ́ʔɛctəl] (PFM), /pə́ʔæc-təl/. Probably a Halkomelem-influenced term for ***bear trap***, with Nooksack <pá7ats> *get bear* + <-tan> (Upriver Halkomelem <-tel>) *device.*

The best information on this place name is Paul Fetzer's interview with Louis George (18 October 1950), which includes "Páatstel Creek, goes to Pangborn Lake." The creek draining Pangborn L. (unnamed on recent US Geological Survey maps) enters Johnson Cr. at Clearbrook, Washington, although it is not certain that this creek was being referred to since it is a considerable distance from place 37 Pá7atstel village. Squaw Cr. enters Johnson Cr. from the west ¾ mile south (upstream) from Clearbrook and is closer to Pá7atstel village, draining an area between the village and Pangborn L. Paul Fetzer's map uses [pɛ́ʔɛctəl] to name Johnson Cr. and [c'ʔá·ləsəm] to name Squaw Cr. Since the first of these is certainly wrong, it could be that Louis George gave Páatstel as the name for Squaw Cr. The creek draining Pangborn L. enters Johnson Cr. at place 65 Ch'e7ó̲lesem, and is more likely to share this name. (Note: Louis George is a man, and different from Louisa George, whom we worked with. He is from an earlier generation, and these two Nooksack elders are not related.)

---

68. "Sháhs-ma-koom" Large marshlike prairie area north of Huntingdon, BC. **Map 10**

> **"Sháhs-ma-koom"** (BS). "Sháhs-" is unclear unless Nooksack <sh-> *nominalizer* + <7as-> *stative, have, be* (thus ***"something that has swamp tea"***) or, less likely, Halkomelem /šxʷ-/ (*nominalizer*), but "ma-koom" is both Nooksack and Upriver Halkomelem /máqʷəm/ ***cranberry marsh, sphagnum bog; Labrador tea;*** this is the kind of bog that grows Labrador tea, cranberries, and tall marsh blueberries; blueberries are still grown in the area commercially. Poss. <Sh7asmo̲qwem> or <Shxwmó̲qwem>; it could be a Nooksack name or a variant of the Halkomelem name, respectively. *A Stó:lō–Coast Salish Historical Atlas* (Carlson et al. 2001, 139, 142) has Lexwmo:qwem, translation 'always swamp tea.' This should be Lexwmó:qwem and the literal meaning given is quite correct for the Upriver Halkomelem name.

This name is given on the 1857-62 Boundary Survey manuscript map for a large swampy area extending from the border near the present Huntingdon north to Lonzo Cr. near the present Trans-Canada Highway, a distance of 2 miles. The southeast edge of "Sháhs-ma-koom" is within ½ mile of the Nooksack village of Temíxwten (place 61), and the east edge is within ½ mile of the part-Nooksack village at Upper Sumas (place 69A). The former location of this swampy area is now indicated by rich black soil and deep drainage ditches with pink spiraea and cattails.

---

69. To̲teláw7 The upper Sumas River above Sumas Lake. **Map 10**

> <**To̲teláw7**> "Tah-ta-lá-o" (BS), poss. /tatəlɛ́·w/ (Halkomelem), poss. /totəlǽw7/ (Nooksack). This name resembles Halkomelem /s-tátəlo(w)/ ***creek*** as found in *A Stó:lō–Coast Salish Historical Atlas* (Carlson et al. 2001) and may be a Sumas dialect Halkomelem name; Upper Sumas Village (place 69A), otherwise unnamed, might be expected to have this name, being so close to the mouth of upper Sumas R. Contrast Nooksack <stólaw7> *(big) river* (GA) and Nooksack /stótələw/ *little creek. A Stó:lō–Coast Salish Historical Atlas* (Carlson et al. 2001, 139, 149) has Stótelō, Sumas River, translation 'little creek.' The place probably had both names, depending on which language the speakers were using.

This name was recorded as "Tah-ta-lá-o" by the 1857-62 Boundary Survey, presumably in the Halkomelem-speaking area near Sumas L. Although the upper Sumas R. is an important part of Nooksack geography, a definite Nooksack name has not been recorded. The Sumas R. above Temíxwten (place 61) was fished with fishtraps in the late 19th century (Richardson 1974, 61).

69A. Upper Sumas Village. **Map 10**

This settlement was located on the upper Sumas R. within the boundaries of Sumas Indian Reserve No. 7, south of Vye Road near the present Upper Sumas Elementary School. On the east and crossing the southeast part of the reserve is Whatcom Road, a remnant of the Whatcom Trail, later Telegraph Road, which follows the Sumas R. southwest 1½ miles to the border and extended originally to the town of Whatcom on Bellingham Bay. The Whatcom Road station of the BC Electric Railroad was formerly located at the northeast corner of the reserve. Nooksack Indians and their Sumas Indian relatives definitely lived here in a village that seems to have had a dual or intermediate identity. This location is about 2 miles from the Nooksack village Temíxwten (place 61) and about 3 miles from the Sumas village at Kilgard. Lottie Tom stated (Paul Fetzer interview, 23 October 1950) that when the village of Temíxwten was abandoned (between 1825 and 1850), families with closer Sumas ties moved to "'Whatcom,' just past the Sumas Customs," presumably a reference to the Whatcom Road station. The place name "Təmí˙xʷtən (in Canada)" in Paul Fetzer's field notes probably refers to this same location. Lottie Tom also stated that the Səmɛ́˙Θ Nooksack families later moved to Kilgard (PF transcriptions have been modernized slightly throughout by writing stress over the vowel instead of after, and by writing ə for ɑ). Further information on this village might be included in archival records of the Sumas Indian reserves and in other historical and ethnographic sources related to the Sumas Indians.

---

70. "Klaalum" Saar Creek. **Map 5**

> "**Klaalum**" (BS). Probably Nooksack <**Lhálem**> ***land oneself (in a canoe);*** see entry found in Carlson et al. 2001 below. Compare Nooksack /ɬǽl-il/ *land a canoe* and <lhal> *come ashore* + <-em> *middle voice (do it oneself). A Stó:lō–Coast Salish Historical Atlas* (Carlson et al. 2001, 136, 144) has "Q'élem, Saar Creek, significance 'Nooksack translation is "land a canoe"', Stalo translation 'camp'; 'rest.'" The word <**q'élém**> means to *camp, rest* in Upriver Halkomelem (note high tone on both vowels, a correction), while Nooksack has <q'el7mín> *to make camp, to camp, a camp* and <lhálil> *land a canoe,* not <q'élem>. So this creek has both a Nooksack name <**Lhálem**> and a Halkomelem name <**Q'élém**>, both referring to people landing and camping there.

This place name from the 1857-62 Boundary Survey materials is clearly applied to Saar Cr. This creek drains an area east of Sumas, Washington, flowing roughly parallel to the Sumas R., and formerly entered Sumas L. on the southwest shore about two miles from Kilgard. The Halkomelem name was probably given by Halkomelem speakers near Sumas L., while the Nooksack name was probably given by Nooksack people more familiar with the upper part of Saar Cr., nearer the Nooksack villages. The Boundary Survey field map (Series 69, Map 51) shows the "Indian trail to the Nooksahk" heading south from Sumas L. east of Saar Cr. to a gap in Vedder Mountain. This trail reached the North Fork Nooksack R. at the mouth of Kendall Cr. (see place 100).

---

71. "Kwul-stánn" Creek entering Sumas Lake on the south shore. **Map 5**

> "**Kwul-stánn**" (BS). Prob. a Nooksack name due to probable final /-ǽn/ ***place*** (as in Kwelshán *Mt. Baker* or /-tǽn/ ***device*** (Downriver Halkomelem has /-tən/, Upriver Halkomelem has /-təl/). <**Qwel7stán**> or <**Qw'elstán**> (the first of these would mean either *something to boil with* or *place to boil things;* the

second would mean *something to cook with* or *place to cook things*). So far, we have found Nooksack <qwél7s-nóxw> *manage to boil s-th, succeed in boiling it* (PAC860) (Pamela Amoss file cards, card 860); (<-noxw> can be replaced by <-t> *do it on purpose to s-th*),<ta sqwél7es> *something boiled* (PAC854), <qw'ílam> (*to bake on a stick*), <sqw'élem> *bake or roast over open fire, barbecue.* Compare several entries from Upriver Halkomelem from Galloway's dictionary (2009): "<**qwéls**>, FOOD /*'to boil, make boil'*/, *see* qwó:ls /*'boiling, making boil (cooking in boiling liquid)'*/" and "<**qwélst**>, FOOD [*'boil s-th'*]"; and "<s-qw'éls> *something cooked,*" and "<qw'él-ém> *roast, bake, boil, cook.*" *A Stó:lō–Coast Salish Historical Atlas* (Carlson 2001, 139, 145) has Qwélstém, significance "the creek that formerly ran SW-NW along Vedder Mountain and drained into Sumas Lake, probably a Nooksack name," translation 'transdivider' or 'device'; 'cooking or meeting place.' This last name, <Qwélstém>, appears to be a Halkomelem name, whereas the first name (<**Qwel7stán**> or <**Qw'elstán**>) appears to be a Nooksack name. The Nooksack name does in fact mean ***place to cook/boil things***. The Halkomelem name means *something boiled.* This name might be appropriate especially if there were a hot spring in the area, but it may have just been a good cooking place.

This place name from the Boundary Survey is difficult to locate today due to the draining of Sumas L. and the ditching and relocating of creeks. On the Boundary Survey manuscript map (Series 68) and field map (Series 69, Map 32), "Kwul-stann" is close to the base of Vedder Mountain. It may be the creek that crosses Wells Line Road ⅛ mile east of Dixon Road, or possibly a second creek about ½ mile to the west. Arnold Slough, which drains an area south of the border, entered Sumas L. on the south shore in 1914 (BC Department of Lands map), and is another possibility for "Kwul-stánn." Nooksack familiarity with "Kwul-stánn" would probably have been associated with use of the south shore of Sumas L. (see place 72).

---

72. Semáts X̲ácho7 Sumas Lake. Map 5

<**Semáts X̲ácho7**> [səmǽc x̣ǽčoʔ] /səmǽc x̣ǽčoʔ/ ([səm'ǽc] [LT:LG] may point towards a variant /səmʔǽc x̣ǽčoʔ/), Halkomelem [səmǽ·θ x̣á·cɛ] /səmɛ́θ x̣á·cɛ/. ***Level place lake*** (Wells 1966; the same source gives the literal meaning of

> [mǽθəx^{w}i] /mέθəx^{w}i/ *Matsqui* as *a rising ground*). Since no dialect of Halkomelem has /c/ consistently corresponding to Upriver /θ/ but Nooksack has, it seems /səmǽc/ or /səmʔǽc/, as given by Nooksack elders, is a true Nooksack version of this name; even so, the lake name was prob. Halkomelem in origin. *A Stó:lō–Coast Salish Historical Atlas* (Carlson et al. 2011, 139, 146) has Semá:th, significance "has to do with the thick grass and reeds that used to grow in the shallow parts of this lake," translation 'level place lake.'

This large shallow lake filled the lower Sumas valley in British Columbia, bounded by Sumas Mountain on the NW and Vedder Mountain on the SE, until it was drained in 1920-23. Although this is outside the Nooksack area, many Nooksacks went here in early spring to fish for steelhead and sturgeon, to hunt ducks, and to dig wapatos (arrowleaf tubers) (Richardson 1974, 61). The most likely areas for Nooksack use of Sumas L. would be the southern shore or near the mouth of the upper Sumas R. on the western shore, which would be near relatives' homes at Kilgard. The former southern shoreline can be reached on Dixon Road ⅓ mile north of Wells Line Road. This location is on a rise that is probably the remnant of an early historical dike built to control extensive seasonal flooding caused by high water in the Fraser R.

---

73. Scháw7shen Village on the east bank of the Nooksack River about two miles upriver from Everson. **Map 9**

> **<Scháw7shen>** [sčá^{w}x^{w}x^{y}ɪn ~ cčá·^{w}wɪšx^{y}ɪn] (PFM), [čáuʔx^{y}ɪn ~ cčáuʔx^{y}ɪn] (WS:GS), [ščáuʔišεn] (WS:AJ), prob. /s-čǽwʔ-šən/ or /s-čǽwʔ-šin/, poss. /č-čǽwʔ-šən/. ***Trail coming to river/beach*** from /s-/ (*nominalizer*), /čǽwʔ/ *down to/on the beach,* /-šən/ or /-šin/ *on the foot or leg;* if [cč] is genuine, it is prob. a Halkomelemization of Nooksack [čč] (preconsonantal /c/ → [¢] in Halkomelem), and Nooksack /č-/ is attested elsewhere, e.g., place 28.

A trail, probably from the Sumas R., came out to the Nooksack R. at this village; when no one was home, travellers shouted across the river to <XelxáI7altxw> /xəlxǽlʔæltx^{w}/ to be taken across. Historically, this village became known as Jim Kelly's place, and 160 acres, including the village site, was a trust homestead. Jim Kelly is also known as Jim Unchochanon or Leqwelqéynem <Leqwelqínem> /ləq^{w}əlqínəm/. The village site is located about ½ mile west of Highway 9 and

Photo 18 *Place 73 Scháw7shen (*trail coming to river/beach*), village on the east bank of the Nooksack River about two miles upriver from Everson, known as Jim Kelly's place; view upriver. 14 August 1980.* (Photo by B. Galloway)

⅔ mile south of Massey Road. Present access to the east bank of the river in this area is by way of a gravel road south from Massey Road (½ mile west of Highway 9), which reaches the northwest corner of the Jim Kelly homestead. From here, a dirt road reaches the present riverbank about 200 yards due west of the Scháw7shen site and directly across the river from place 74 X̱elx̱ál7altxw. This place where the modern "trail" comes to the river is shown in Photo 18.

---

74. X̱elx̱ál7altxw Village on the west bank of the Nooksack River opposite Scháw7shen. **Map 9**

> <**X̱elx̱ál7altxw**> [x̣əlx̣ɛ́lɛltxʷ] (WS:GS, WS:AJ), [x̣əlx̣ɛ́lɛ́ltxʷ] (WS:GS), [x̣əlx̣əlɛ́ltxʷ] (PFM), /x̣əl-x̣ǽlʔ-æltxʷ ~ x̣əl-x̣æʔ-ǽltxʷ/. Village with a big longhouse painted with stripes of /tə́məɬ/ *red ochre* to ward off disease. ***Painted up house***, lit. *many times-paint/mark/write-house.* Cf. Nooksack /x̣ə́lʔ-ənʔ/ *write or mark something.*

The traditional longhouse here was occupied until at least 1885. Around 1890, this site, shown in Photo 19, became the location of a Methodist church and two houses, and by 1910 a barn had been built directly on the longhouse site. This is on the John Suchanon (Long Johnny /səq'qínəm/) homestead, better known as the Johnnie place. Access today is from Mission Road via a dirt road on the DeJaeger farm along the southern boundary of the homestead. The longhouse site was in the northeast part of a field directly on the riverbank in 1980, as shown on Map 11. This is also a known fishtrap site (Richardson 1974, 62). On this part of the river in 1868, although not necessarily at this location, Edmund Coleman observed the construction of salmon traps for use in a fish weir at a spot adjacent to a village (Coleman 1869, 799).

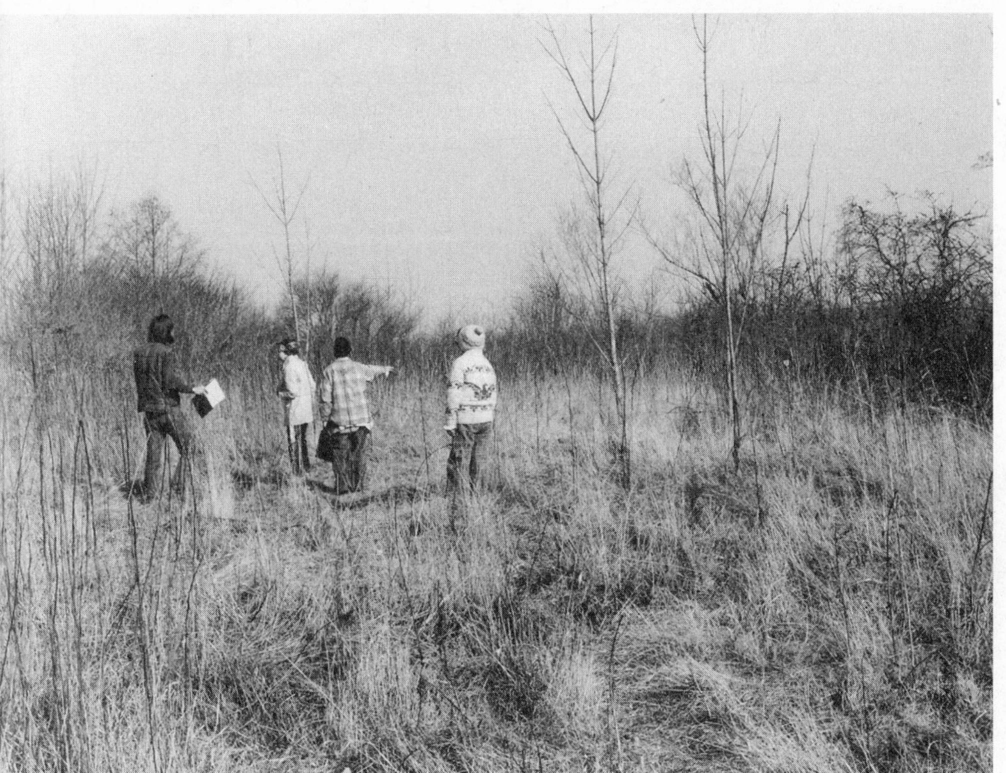

PHOTO 19 *Place 74 X̲elx̲ál7altxw* (painted up house*), village on the west bank of the Nooksack River opposite place 73 Scháw7shen, on the homestead of John Suchanon (Long Johnny). Left to right: Allan Richardson, Alice Hunt, Esther Fidele, and Lucy Fidele, standing in the area of historical houses, with the longhouse site to the right. 8 March 1980.* (Photo by B. Galloway)

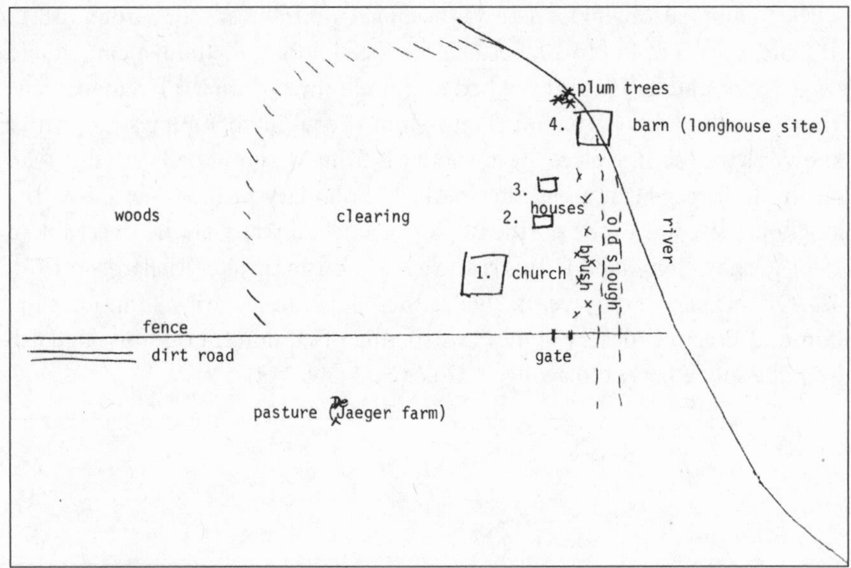

Map 11 *Locations of historical buildings at place 74 X̲elx̲ál7altxw. Sketch made following a field visit with the Nooksack elders.* (A. Richardson field notes, 8 March 1980)

75. Xwch'álsus Fazon Lake. **Map 12**

> <**Xwch'álsus**> [xʷc'ɛ́lsus] (WS:GS), prob. /xʷ-c'ǽl-cot/ or /xʷ-c'ǽlsos/. Fazon L. is said to have acquired its Indian name because it is bottomless, with a hole going out to sea (BG:EF, BG:LG); LG compares Nooksack /č'ǽl-cot/ *whirlwind-like water or hole that people sink through;* cf. also Hess 1976 Lushootseed /ʔu-c'ál-cut/ *hide oneself* with root /c'ál-/ *obstruct the view;* or the final <-us> may be the Nooksack suffix /-os/ [-us ~ -os] *face.*

Wayne Suttles's field notes include this name for a "lake back of <X̲elx̲ál7altxw> /x̣əlx̣ǽlʔæltxʷ/." Fazon L. is located 2¼ miles southwest of X̲elx̲ál7altxw and is the closest lake to this village. It is said to be "bottomless" and used to be called Silver L. (EF). Public access to Fazon L. today is on the south shore, at the end of a road off Hemmi Road.

---

76. Ts'úts'um7als Source of filing rock on the Coffee Johnson place. **Map 12**

> <**Ts'úts'um7als**> [c'úc'umɛ́ls] (WS:AJ), [c'úc'umʔɛls] (BG:EF, BG:LG), /c'óc'omʔ-æls/. ***Little file*** or ***many files*** because

> sandstone slabs from here were used to file things; cf. Nooksack /c̓ó̆mals/ <ts'ómals> *file,* Halkomelem /θ'áməls/ *to file* (with Nooksack /-æls/ and Halkomelem /-əls/, both meaning *do as a structured activity*). Either prefixed or infixed reduplication, *diminutive* or *plural.*

This is a sandstone outcrop west of the railroad tracks (since removed) west of Roberts Road, ½ mile north of Martin Road on the Coffee Johnson trust homestead. The overhanging rock here drips water and ices up in winter, and is the source of sandstone slabs used as filing rock. This place and others in the Goshen area, and the Lawrence area across the river, can be located on Map 12. The villages included on this map formed another of the village clusters within the larger Nooksack community. Families from all Nooksack villages owned root-digging plots at place 78, Nuxwsá7aq, which is also the source of the name "Nooksack."

---

77. Temíxwten A place near or on Coffee Johnson's homestead. **Map 12**

> **<Temíxwten>** [təmíxʷtən] /təmíxʷ-tən/. ***Earth, dirt-device, thing for; pithouse.***

A place near <Ts'úts'um7als> /c̓óc̓omʔæls/, where some Nooksacks got /tə́məɬ/ *red ochre clay.*

---

78. Nuxwsá7aq Anderson Creek and the area at the mouth of Anderson Creek. **Map 12**

> **<Nuxwsá7aq>** ~ <Xwsá7aq> [nəxʷsǽ·q ~ xʷsǽ·q ~ xʷsɛ́ʔɛq] (WS:GS), [xʷsɛ́ʔɛq'] (PF), [nʊxʷsǽʔæq ~ nʊxʷsǽ·q] (BG, various elders), [nuxʷsǽʔæq ~ nuxʷsǽ·q] (BG:SJ), /noxʷ-sǽʔæq ~ xʷ-sǽʔæq/. ***Always-bracken fern roots;*** cf. Nooksack [nʊxʷ] /nəxʷ-/ ~ /xʷ-/ *always* and /sǽʔæq/ and Upriver Halkomelem [sǽ·q] /sɛ́·q/ *bracken fern root;* this place name is the source of the name for the people, Nooksack; the creek mouth formerly had many bracken ferns growing by it whose roots could be harvested for food.

The name Nuxwsá7aq is consistently applied to Anderson Cr., which was an important fishing stream for silver salmon, steelhead, and trout. The name is applied to the prairie (Goshen Prairie) west of the creek mouth in some sources,

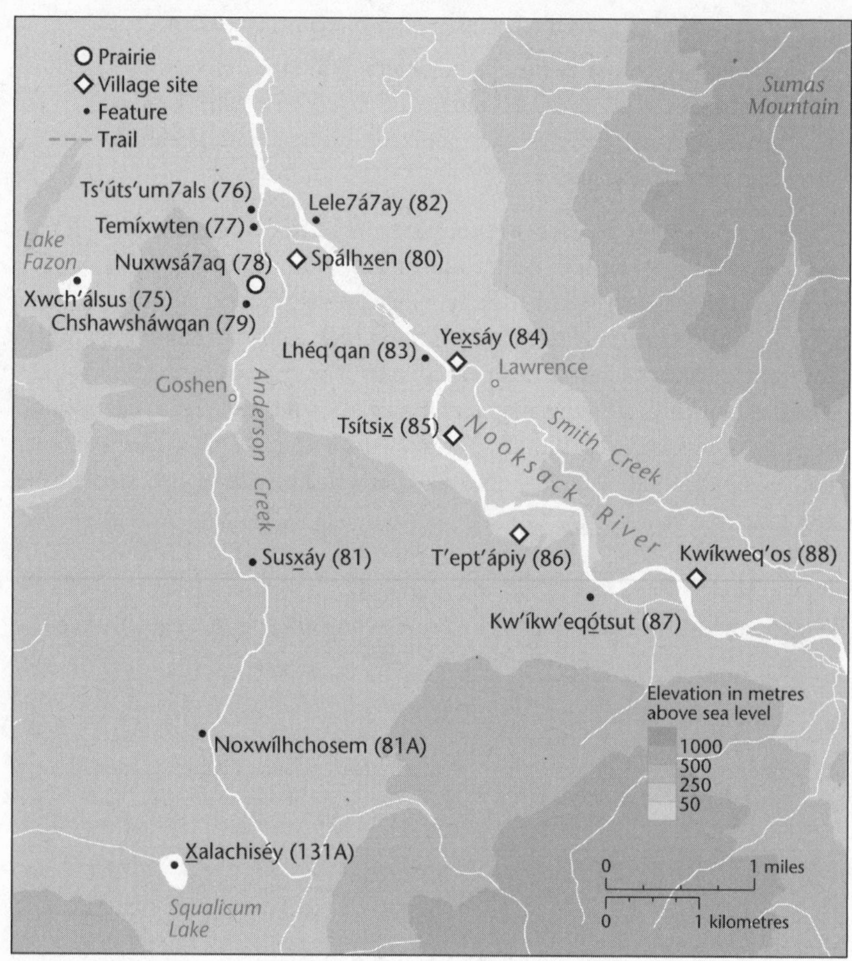

Map 12 *Place names in the Goshen-Lawrence area.* (Adapted from Richardson and Galloway 2007)

whereas other sources call this prairie Spálhx̱en. In a few sources, Nuxwsá7aq is also considered to be the name of a village, perhaps the same as Spálhx̱en (place 80) or a separate settlement located more directly on Anderson Cr. George Swanaset stated (Paul Fetzer interview, 17 July 1950) that there had been longhouses on both sides of the river here, but that both were part of the Spálhx̱en village.

The prairie west of the 19th-century mouth of Anderson Cr., shown in Photo 20, was important for the digging of bracken fern roots and "wild carrots." In this prairie, there were carefully marked family-owned plots for the harvest of the "wild carrots" (Smith 1950, 335-36; Amoss 1972: 12-13). This is the only known Nooksack case of private ownership of resources. "The importance of the wild carrot root crop can be judged from the fact that carrot plots were owned by families. The limits of each plot were marked off with large rocks. When they dug the carrots, the women were very careful to replant the tops" (Amoss 1972, 12-13). The "wild carrots," or <sháweq>, were probably the roots of *Perideridia gairdneri,* also known as wild caraway and yampah. The prairie is in the river floodplain extending from the base of the hill east of Roberts Road to Anderson Cr. and from near the location of Martin Road north for about 0.2 mile. The northern part of the prairie borders the 19th-century main river channel below the mouth of Anderson Cr. and is directly across this river channel from the Spálhx̲en village. Tommy Tuchanon's homestead cabin was located at the north end of the prairie and present cleared area, near a group of evergreen trees. Robert Sulkanum's first cabin was located west of Anderson Cr., on what is now Martin Road.

A Boundary Survey field map shows two buildings located in the prairie on the south bank of the river below the creek mouth (Series 69, unidentified map in folder following Map 76). At this time, the prairie measured "perhaps ½ mile long and 300-400 y wide & covered with an immense growth of ferns" (Custer 1858b). Also on this date, 20 June 1858, "numerous Indians were here occupied to cultivate their potato fields" (Custer 1858b).

---

79. Chshawsháwqan "Wild carrot" plots near Anderson Creek. Map 12

<Chshawsháwqan> "St-yhaw-yhau-yhan" (Jeffcott 1964). Prob. <Tsxawxáwqan ~ Chshawsháwqan> /c-x^{y}æw-x^{y}ǽwq-æn/ or /č-šæw-šǽwq-æn/ ***has-many-wild carrots-place,*** /č-/ *have* (<ts-> is the Halkomelem accent version), /x^{y}/ Halkomelem-influenced for /š/, Nooksack /šǽwəq/ *wild carrot* (prob. wild caraway, *Perideridia gairdneri*), and C$_1$V$_1$C$_2$- *plural (many);* <-an> *place,* as in <Kwelshán> Mt. Baker. PJ uses "St-" for preconsonantal /č-/ elsewhere, i.e., "St-sew-hal" for place 73 (<Schāw7shen>), presumably to show the alternate [cčǽwʔx^{y}ɪl] (Halkomelemized) for /č-čǽwʔ-šən/.

This is an alternate name for place 78 Nuxwsá7aq prairie, or perhaps a name for just the portion of the prairie where the "wild carrot" plots were located.

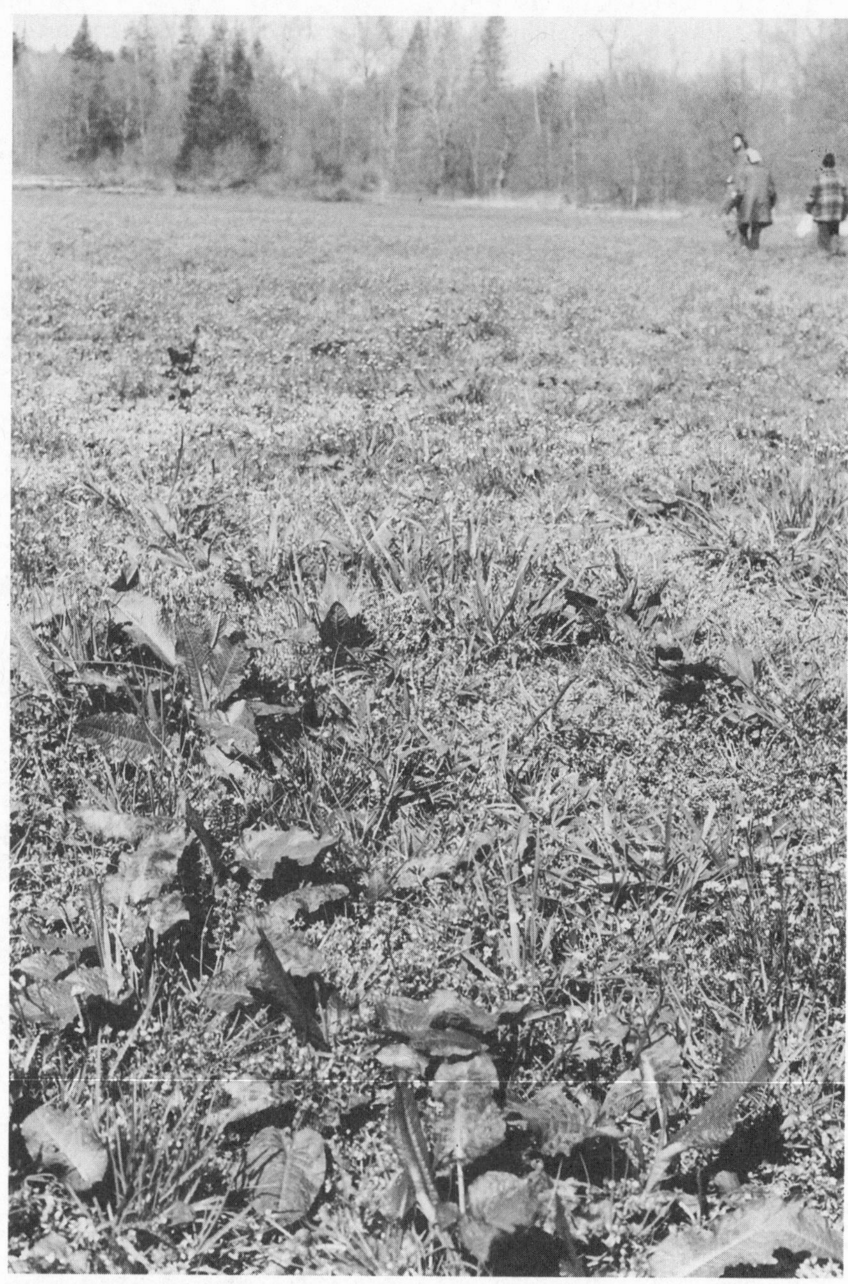

Photo 20 *Place 78 Nuxwsá7aq* (always-bracken fern roots), *Anderson Creek and the prairie at its mouth, important as a place for digging bracken fern roots and "wild carrots," <sháweq>; source of the word "Nooksack"; view north from Martin Road. 30 March 1980.* (Photo by B. Galloway)

Photo 21 *Cedar plank longhouse at place 80 Spálhx̱en, Johnson Island, ca. 1940. People identified as R.E. Hawley and David Johnson.* (P.R. Jeffcott Collection, no. 1361)

80. Spálhx̱en Village on Johnson Island opposite the mouth of Anderson Creek. **Map 12**

> <**Spálhx̱en**> [spǽ·ɬx̣ən] /spǽɬx̣ən/, ([spǽɬx̣æn] (PFM)). ***Prairie, meadow, open land*** (which is what is meant by "prairie" throughout this book).

This was a major traditional village and the location of the last traditional longhouse to stand on its original site. In the 19th century, the river formed an island 1¼ miles long and ¼ to ½ mile wide opposite the mouth of Anderson Cr. The main river channel was the westerly one, which flowed between the prairie (see place 78 Nuxwsá7aq) and the village site. Now the river is located over 1 mile to the northeast, and Anderson Cr. flows in the old main channel below its former mouth. The last longhouse at Spálhx̱en was built by <K'ilíwuselh>, who used the English name Johnson. The longhouse, shown in Photo 21, was dismantled and moved to the Toss Weaxta homestead above Deming in the

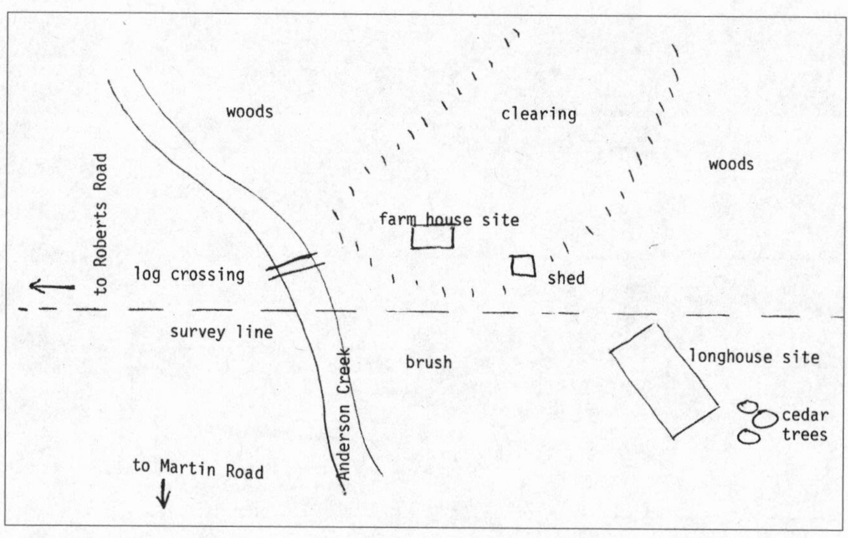

Map 13 *Locations of historical buildings and the last traditional longhouse at place 80 Spálhx̲en. Sketch made following a field visit with the Nooksack elders.* (A. Richardson field notes, 30 March 1980)

1940s (Jeffcott 1949, 12). The Spálhx̲en longhouse site is located between the remnants of later buildings (in an old orchard) and a group of large cedar trees, as shown on Map 13. This is almost exactly ¼ mile north of Martin Road and just under ¼ mile east of Roberts Road on the east side of Anderson Cr.

---

81. Susx̲áy Location near Anderson Creek, about 2½ miles above its mouth. **Map 12**

> <Susx̲áy> [susx̣ǽ·y], poss. /sosx̣ -ǽy/ or /sosx̣-ə́y/. The name is similar or identical to "So-sái" (BS) (place 19) (<Sosx̲áy> or possibly <Sosáy>), which is the swampy head of Campbell R.; this name attested only from a non-speaker of Nooksack, Susan Jimmy, but the wife of SJ. Possibly <-ey ~ -áy> *place* or more likely <-áy7> *tree* with reduplication infixed, and root <sux̲ ~ sox̲> /sox̣/ may be same as in <sox̲áthot ~ sox̲átsot> *sun* (which seems to itself have <-thot ~ -tsot> *reflexive* or *inceptive*); words to compare in sister languages may include: Upriver Halkomelem <stháthqey> *sweet berry shoots* or <sásexem> *bitter*, Lummi /sax̣əŋ/ *taste bitter*, and Lushootseed /sáx̣əb/ *bitter*.

This place name was given by Susan Jimmy, apparently for an area near Anderson Cr. (but not the creek) about 2½ miles above its mouth, near the corner of Sand Road and Smith Road. This name is similar to place 19 Sosx̱áy, which refers to a swampy area. The 1884 Land Survey map (United States General Land Office 1859-90) shows a swamp east of Anderson Cr. extending ½ mile north from the present corner of Sand Road and Smith Road. This may be one of the bogs where cranberries were picked, and is definitely within an area hunted for deer and bear (Richardson 1974, 64).

81A. Noxwílhchosem Small prairie on Anderson Creek, on the trail to Lake Whatcom. **Map 12**

"Nochuilchosem" (BS-Custer). "Nochuilchosem" almost certainly has the Nooksack prefix <noxw-> *always.* For the root, one possibility is to compare the Upriver Halkomelem place name <Swiylhcha> *Sweltzer Cr.,* an outlet of Cultus L. It has Halkomelem prefix <s-> *nominalizer,* root <wiy- ~ way-> *warn,* and suffix <-elhcha> *dirty water,* from a tradition about supernatural creatures that were like swirling dust in the lake water and made people get sick or die if they saw it; thus, the name Cultus (Chinook Jargon for *bad*) Lake. Nooksack (and the Halkomelem name for Sweltzer Cr. also) may instead have a root <wilhch> that lacks the *warn* meaning and is cognate with Northern Straits dialects Lummi <swilch> *lake* and Samish <swilcha> *lake.* The Nooksack place name may be <Noxwwiylhchosem>, with either the same root and suffix as the Halkomelem or Northern Straits terms, or merely <**Noxwílhchosem**>, with a placeholder root <i>, sometimes used to make lexical suffixes into roots as in Halkomelem. In either case, it seems likely that the Nooksack word has suffix <-élhcho7> ***dirty/unclear water*** (as is also found in Nooksack words <tl'lhélhchu7 ~ tl'álhchu7> *sea, salt water* (LT:LG and BG:LG) [tl'(a)lh- *salt*] and <ts'kwálhcho [PA:GS] ~ th'ekwélhcho [PF:GS, NKF 2.913]> *pond,* and then has Nooksack <-os> ***in the face, round thing*** plus Nooksack <-em> ***(place to) get/have*** or ***middle voice (one's).*** This would give a literal meaning ***always dirty water in the face (place to) get/have*** or ***always get dirty water in one's face.***

Another reference, found recently in Paul Fetzer's ethnographic field notes (vol. 4, p. 8 of Roland Holterman's typescript of the notes), may be a more recent recording of the same place name as [xʷiyé·lq'ʷosəm] *(place) back of Goshen where lots of [spέ·ɬxʷ] grows.* It is mentioned in context with three well-known place names as one of four where large quantities of this plant grow. The plant is identified elsewhere by Fetzer as *black onions* (compare Upriver Halkomelem /spǽ·lxʷ/ *camas; any underground root vegetable*). This place name is for a prairie that is "back of Goshen" and, if it is the same name better recorded, it would be spelled in the Nooksack orthography as <Xw(i) yílqw'osem> or <Xwyélqw'osem>. The initial <xw> may be the same prefix <noxw- ~ xw-> ***always,*** and the suffixes are also the same as identified for the first proposed etymology, Nooksack <-os> ***in the face, round thing*** plus Nooksack <-em> ***(place to) get/have*** or ***middle voice (one's).*** The root has not yet been found in Nooksack. One might compare Upriver Halkomelem forms <yó:lqw'> *mess up, make a mess,* <yélqw't> *mess s-th up, upset a bed,* <yó:lqw'es> *make a real mess,* <xwiyó:leqw> *(become/get) upside down,* <xwiyó:leqwt> *turn something upside down.* The root of these stems is <yó:l- ~ yél-> *turn;* the first set has suffix <-qw'> *around in circles, circular,* while the second seems to have suffix <-qw> *on top of the head* in Upriver Halkomelem. The *upside down* stem seems to have prefix <xwe-> *become, get,* which can become <xwi-> before <y>. <yó:lqw'es> *make a real mess* may have <-es ~ -os> *on the face, circular object,* as the Nooksack place name has. The literal meanings suggested, if these are cognates with the Nooksack place name, range from *always place to get one's face messed up* to *place to get one's face upside down,* but none of these can be confirmed by physical characteristics or stories about the place name, unless one turns one's face upside down or gets it messed up while gathering black onions or other vegetable roots such as camas. The *messed up* etymology allows a match between Fetzer's glottalized <qw'> and the <qw'> of Upriver Halkomelem.

This place name is located mainly from a brief entry in the field notes of Henry Custer for 1858, in his "Reconnaissances Fort Langley trail, Trip to Sumass Whatcomb Lake & Whatcom trail 1859 [sic]" (RG 76, E 202). Custer's party was travelling on the "Nucksack Trail" from L. Whatcom to the Nooksack R.

following the "Sack stream"(place 78). They departed from Squalicum L. at 10:05 AM and at 11:45 they reached "a little prairie Nochuilchosem." Continuing to follow the "Sack stream," they reached the Nooksack R. at 4:00 PM. By estimating distances based on these times and referring to the field map (Series 69, unidentified map in folder following Map 76), one would place the location of this prairie near or south of the Kelly Road crossing of Anderson Cr. If the Fetzer notes apply to the same place, they do not add much more detail except that the prairie would be a place where black onions grow in abundance.

---

82. Lele7á7ay Place of Old Bill Ts'ós on the northeast bank of the Nooksack River. **Map 12**

> <**Lele7á7ay**> [lələʔáʔay] (WS:AJ), [lələʔáʔiy] (BG:EF), prob. /lələʔáʔay/ or better /lələʔǽʔæy/. ***Douglas-fir trees*** from [ləʔǽyʔæy ~ ləʔǽyʔey] (BG:SJ), [lɛʔɛ́y'ɛy'] (LT:LG), [slǽyʔæyʔ] (BG:LG) *Douglas-fir tree* (itself with /-(ʔ)æy/ *tree* or *bark*) plus /-lə-/ infix *plural.*

This location was settled by Old Bill Ts'ós /c'ós/, Bill Soce, at the time of homesteading; there is no record of any earlier village. The original Lele7áy7ay location has been washed away by the river, and the site of a later house, built around 1900, is on the present riverbank. The site of this later house is about 0.2 mile west of Roy George's house at the west end of George Road (on Indian trust land), beyond the last cabin, where the dirt road reaches the river at an open field with fruit trees. The house was near the present eroding riverbank by the seedling plum trees, and the barn was to the north by the cherry trees. The river used to be much further to the southwest, ¼ to ½ mile based on the 1884 Land Survey map (United States General Land Office 1859-90), which shows the house of "Indian Bill" located on the river almost exactly ½ mile directly south of the later house.

---

83. Lhéq'qan Place on the Nooksack River just below where Smith Creek now enters. **Map 12**

> <**Lhéq'qan**> [ɬə́q'qɛn] (BG:SJ), prob. /ɬə́q'-qan/. Cognate with Halkomelem <lhéq'qel> ***end of a falling section of land, end of a level stretch of land.***

Photo 22 *Place 84 Yex̲sáy* (place given as a gift), *a village on the east bank of the river, at the mouth of Smith Creek. The original village site has been washed away. The photo was taken from a remnant of the Sampson Santla (Sátl'e) homestead, view to the south, upriver. 14 August 1980.* (Photo by B. Galloway)

84. Yex̲sáy Smith Creek and village at the mouth of Smith Creek. **Map 12**

<**Yex̲sáy**> [yəx̣sá·y] (PF; WS:GS), [yəx̣sǽ·y] (WS:GS; BG:SJ, BG:LG), ([yəx̣sáy] (PFM)), /yəx̣sáy ~ yəx̣sǽy/. Prob. <-ey ~ -áy> *place* or possibly <-áy7> *tree;* compare Upriver Halkomelem <yex̲ts- ~ yex̲ch-> *give as a gift* as in <yéx̲chet> *give someone s-th as a gift;* this place was settled by people from Temíxwten around the 1830s, so ***place given as a gift*** might well be appropriate; other, less likely but possible comparisons may be Upriver Halkomelem <ye-> *travelling by* + root <x̲es> as in Upriver Halkomelem <x̲ésxel> *deadfall, trap* or Lushootseed /jax(a)-/ *move, shake.*

The village was on the east bank of the river north of the mouth of Smith Cr. in the area shown in Photo 22. The mouth of Smith Cr. was an important fishing site for silver salmon and steelhead. A manuscript map by Paul Fetzer locates a

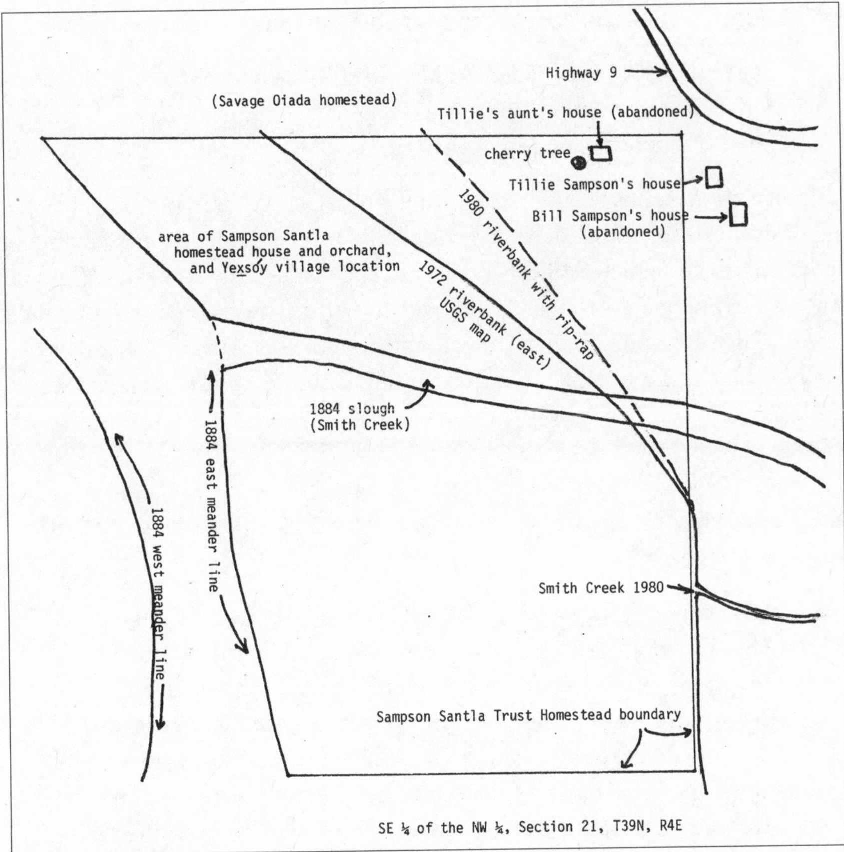

Map 14 *Locations of historical and recent houses, property boundaries, and the river at place 84 Ye<u>x</u>sáy. Sketch made following a field visit with the Nooksack elders, with the place name transcribed according to the convention being used at the time.* (A. Richardson field notes, 14 August 1980)

fishtrap in Smith Cr. at Ye<u>x</u>sáy. Ye<u>x</u>sáy is one of the traditional villages occupied in the historical period, although it was probably first settled around the 1830s, when Temíxwten was abandoned (see place 61). The site of Ye<u>x</u>sáy village was homesteaded by Sampson Santla, Sátl'e /sǽƛ'ə/, with the homestead of his brother, Savage Oiada, adjoining on the north. The village and homestead house site have been washed away by the river, and are now on the west bank. The village site is about 0.2 mile west of the present home, occupied in 1980 by Matilda Sampson (Sampson Santla's granddaughter) and rented by George Adams in 2005. This house is on Highway 9, ¼ mile west of Lawrence. These various locations at Ye<u>x</u>sáy on or near the Sampson Santla homestead are shown on Map 14.

85. Tsítsix̲ Village site east of the river above Yex̲sáy. **Map 12**

> **<Tsítsix̲>** [θí·θix̣] (PF:GS; PFM), [θí·θɪx̣ - cíciəx̣] (WS:GS), /cí-cix̣/. ***Little-spring*** from Nooksack <tsix̲> *spring* + <tsí-> (C_1í- reduplication) *diminutive, little.*

Information on this village has come only from George Swanaset, and includes no basis for determining dates of occupation or an exact location. Statements about the location include "just above Lawrence" and "above the river" (Wayne Suttles field notes), as well as ¼ mile up river from Yex̲sáy (Paul Fetzer field notes). Tsítsix̲ was possibly located in the area southwest of the Lind Road bridge over Smith Cr. and northwest of the end of Back Acre Road ("Back Acre" sign and gate).

---

86. T'ept'ápiy Village site at or near Nugent's Bridge (Mt. Baker Highway bridge). **Map 12**

> **<T'ept'ápiy>** "Dep-dap-y" (PJ), [t’əp’t’ɛ́·p’e] (PF), [t’əpt’ǽpiy] (BG:EF), /t’əp-t’ǽp-iy/, poss. /t’æp-t’ǽp-iy/. ***Many dead trees,*** lit. *plural (many)-die (of tree or plant)-tree* (cf. Halkomelem /t’ɛ́p-iy-θət/ *to die (of tree, plant),* /s-t’ɛ́p-iy/ *dead (of tree, plant);* so named because /x̣ǽls/ the Transformer turned some trees to stone there; EF had some of the stones and they were petrified wood; PJ says it was so named because a forest fire had killed many trees there.

Among the few sources that include this village, there are differences of opinion as to its location. According to George Swanaset (Paul Fetzer interview, 7 September 1951), T'ept'ápiy was on the east side of the river at Nugent's Bridge. Jeffcott locates this place name at Nugent's Ferry (the same location as the present Mt. Baker Highway bridge, based on an 1895 map), and states: "The name was also applied to a large smokehouse that stood there before the whites came" (1949, 54-55). He does not state which side of the river this was on, although "Dep-dap-y" is placed on the southwest bank in his 1964 map. Esther Fidele's statements imply that the T'ept'ápiy was about ¾ mile upriver from the Mt. Baker Highway bridge, and probably on the southwest bank. The date at which this village was last occupied cannot be determined based on information available, although a date prior to 1820 is likely.

---

87. Kw’íkw’eqó̱tsut Rock in the Nooksack River above Nugent’s Bridge, shaped like a person lying on his back. **Map 12**

> **<Kw’íkw’eqó̱tsut>** [k’ʷik’ʷəqácut] (BG:LG), /k’ʷi-k’ʷəq-ácut/ (a Skagit name but prob. very close to the Nooksack also). ***Diminutive-fall or lie on one’s back-(reflexive),*** cf. Hess 1976, Lushootseed /k’ʷə́q/ *fall or lie on one’s back,* Upriver Halkomelem /k’ʷə́q/ *fall or lie on one’s back.*

This is the name of a big rock in the river on the southwest side below Kwíkweq’os (place 88) and above Nugent’s Bridge (see place 86 T’ept’ápiy). Nothing grows on this rock, which looks like a person lying on his back rocking back and forth (LG). The exact location of the rock has not been determined.

---

88. Kwíkweq’os Village, plant gathering site, and fishing site on the north bank opposite the blue clay “white face” slide about 2½ miles upriver from Nugent’s Bridge. **Map 12**

> **<Kwíkweq’os>**, [kʷí·kʷixʸos] (PF, PFM), [qʷéqʷeᵊx̣os] (WS:GS), [q’ʷəq’ʷx̣ʷós ~ q’ʷəq’ʷqʷós ~ qʷq’ʷós] (BG:LG) (all forms with initial qʷ or q’ʷ here are probably Skagit-influenced), prob. Nooksack <Qwíqwix̱wos> ~ <Kwíkweq’os> /qʷíqʷix̣ʷ-us/ ~ /kʷíkʷəq’-os/ ~ Skagit /qʷəqʷq’ʷ-ús ~ qʷq’ʷ-ús/. ***Little-white-face*** from Nooksack /kʷə́q’/ *white,* Skagit /qʷəq’ʷ-/ *white,* Skagit /(xʷ-)qʷq’ʷús/ *bluff of clay or sand (not of rock)* (Skagit from Hess 1976), (*diminutive*) reduplication; the etymology of /qʷíqʷix̣ʷ-os/ is similar, but the root /qʷíx̣ ʷ/ is so far uncertain; PJ says the name means *the place for digging roots.*

Based on the knowledge of present-day elders and consistent statements in other sources, this village was probably occupied early in the 19th century and was located south of Williams Road, near Mrs. Gus Compton’s house at the curve where Williams Road turns north, coming west from Deming. This location was part of the Eck Williams non-Indian homestead. Jeffcott (1949, 55) states that this was a place for digging the roots of a plant similar to the sand rush – probably horsetail, which has *white* wartlike knobs on its roots that are eaten like hazelnuts. This place name and location are also given for a fishing site fished by Ella Reid’s father early in the 20th century.

---

89. Leme7ólh Fishing rocks on the east bank of the Nooksack River ½ mile upriver from Deming. **Map 15**

> <**Leme7ólh**> "Le-ma-oth" (PJ), [ləməó·Θ] (PF:GS), /ləmaʔóɬ/ (BG:LG), poss. <Leme7óts> or <Leme7ólh> /ləməʔ-óc/ or /ləməʔóɬ/. PJ says it means *taking the salt water away,* from a legend about when salt water extended inland to this point; LG and EF say it may be related to Nooksack /ləməʔ-óɬ/ *kicking* (BG:EF) or perhaps better ***kicked (away) long ago***; also cf. Nooksack [ləməʔ-ǽ·n] *kick something;* poss. /-óc ~ -óʔc/ *edge; (perhaps) mouth,* although *mouth* is usually /-ócin/, so more likely /-óɬ/ (*past tense*).

Located directly west of the north edge of Mud L. in the northwest corner of the Skookum George (George Whaholich <Xwó̱xwelech> /xʷáxʷələč/) homestead. This group of rocks, shown in Photo 23, was used traditionally for catching salmon with dip nets and set eddy nets in the downstream eddies. As of 2005, one could still see marks and wear in the rocks from this activity. The area between the two rocks was used for fishing and was deep water with eddies in 1974, but filled with a gravel bar in 1980, then a backwater pool in 2005. At present, access is via the old highway and a trail across the railroad tracks. The locations of Leme7ólh and other places above Deming, where the Nooksack R. branches into its three forks, are shown on Map 15. The villages in this upriver area formed a loose cluster, although only Nuxw7íyem (place 92) was occupied in the mid-19th century and later.

---

90. Kw'élhqwàl7 Fishing rock on the east bank of the Nooksack River ¼ mile downriver from the mouth of the South Fork. **Map 15**

> <Kw'élhqewàl7> or <**Kw'élhqwàl7**>, "Kisk-a-wel" (PJ), [kískəwɛ́l] (OW-PJ), [kʷí·ɬqawɛ·lʔ] (PF:GS), [q'ɛ́ƛkowɛ·l] (PF:AM), [kɛɬkəwɛ́l] (WS:AM). EF says the word means ***under-water eddy that leads out underground to somewhere else***; prob. Nooksack /k'ʷə́ɬ/ *flow, spill* (BG:LG) + <-qw> *around in circles* + <-ál7> meaning unknown. Less likely <Kw'ilhqewál7> or <Q'átl'qwál7>.

This is an important salmon-fishing site for dip nets and set eddy nets that has been fished continuously up to the present. Kw'élhqwàl7 is a very deep spot with an eddy and an undertow. The underwater eddy is said to lead out

PHOTO 23 *Place 89 Leme7ólh, fishing rocks on the east bank of the Nooksack River ½ mile upriver from Deming. Marks and wear in rocks can be seen. View looking south, upriver. 17 July 1980.* (Photo by B. Galloway)

underground to somewhere else, possibly Mud L. across Mt. Baker Highway, L. Whatcom, or salt water. At present, access to Kw'élhqwàl7 is through Vincent Almonjero's driveway and a trail across the railroad tracks. This is located on the Skookum George (George Whaholich), <Xwó̱xwelech>, homestead. According to his daughter-in-law, Louisa George, Skookum George's house was in the area of the present raspberry patch north of Vincent Almonjero's house; the 1885 Land Survey map (United States General Land Office 1859-90) shows Skookum George's house (perhaps an earlier house) to the south, about where Maggie Johnson had a house early in the 20th century in a flat area below Clara Williams's present home. Skookum George's house is sometimes considered one of the houses of the Nuxw7íyem village (Paul Fetzer field notes), or a separate village of Xwó̱xwelech (Richardson 1974, 65).

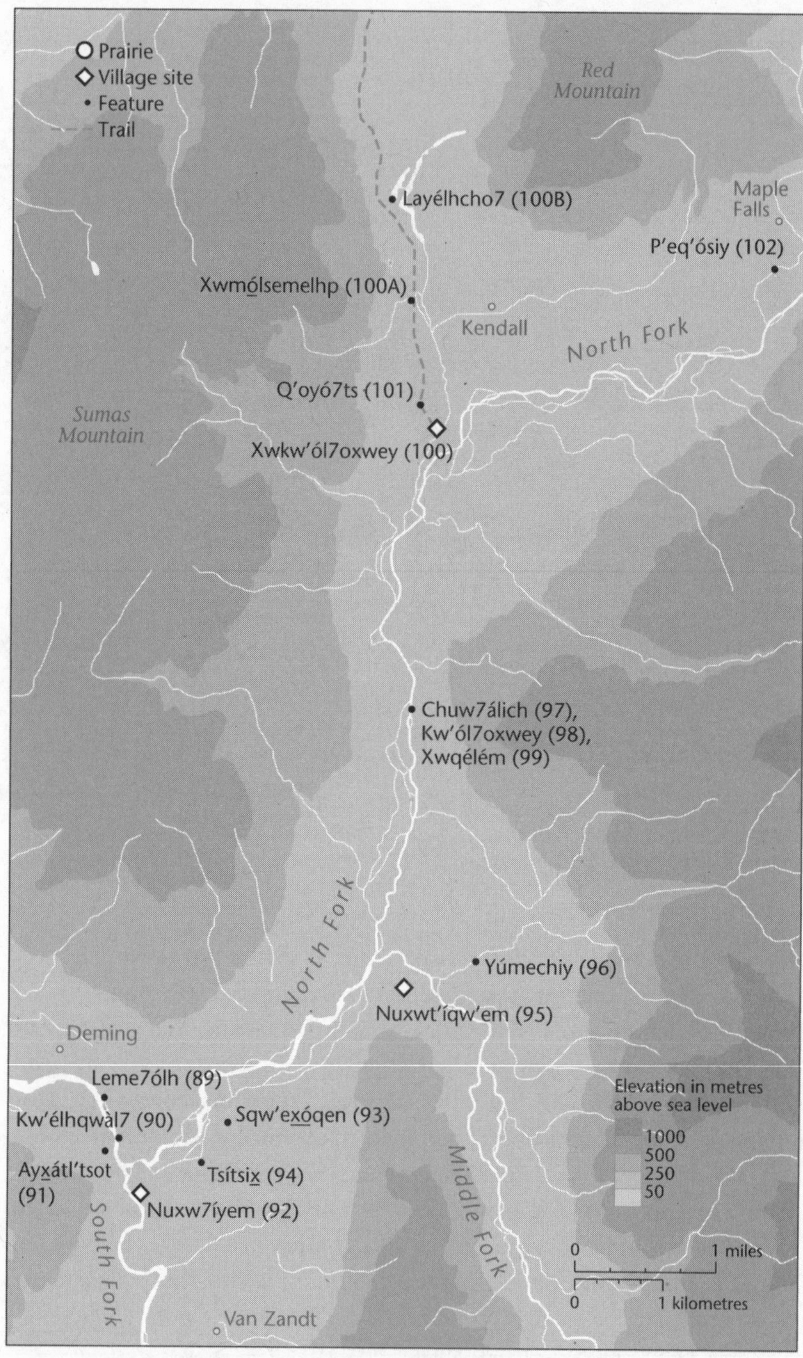

Map 15 *Place names in the Deming-Forks area.* (Adapted from Richardson and Galloway 2007)

91. Ayx̲átl’tsot Rock on the west bank of the Nooksack River immediately downstream from the mouth of the South Fork, also known as “Cooper’s Rock.” **Map 15**

> **<Ayx̲átl’tsot>**, “Ag-a-thot” (PJ), [ʔǽygəθat] (OW-PJ). PJ says that it is the stretch of rapids here and means *swift waters.* Jeffcott’s pronunciation sheds some light on the possible form of this name: the word may begin (as OW-PJ has it) with ʔæy- (*continuative*); there is no [g] in Nooksack but GS has [x̣áƛ’θot] (PF:GS, PA:GS), /x̣áƛ’-cot/ *get rough-flowing (of wind, water),* and LG has [x̣ǽƛ’] *blowing hard (of wind);* so the name may be <Ayx̲átl’tsot> /ʔæy-x̣ǽƛ’-cot/ ***getting turbulent.***

This is on the John Whichtalum /xʷičt’íləm/ place inherited in the Cooper family. The rock is a rocky cliff 200 yards or more in length, where a mountain comes down to the river. Living elders were unable to recall the Lhéchelesem name of this rock, remembering only “Cooper’s Rock.” Jeffcott gives the forms “Ag-a-thot” (1949, 55) and “Aga-thot” (1964 map).

---

92. Nuxw7íyem South Fork Nooksack River and village at mouth of South Fork. **Map 15**

> **<Nuxw7íy(7)em>** ~ <Xw7íy(7)em> [noʔxʷí·əm ~ ʔxʷí·əm] (PF:GS, PF:AM; PFM), [nəxʷʔéəm ~ xʷʔéəm ~ nəxʷʔím] (WS:GS), [xʷʔeʔy’əm] (LT:LG), [nʊxʷʔéyəm ~ nʊxʷʔíyəm ~ xʷʔíyəm] (BG:LG, BG:EF, others), [šxʷʔə́yʔ-ɪm] (BG:SJ), /noxʷ-ʔíy(ʔ)-əm ~ xʷ-ʔíy(ʔ)-əm/). ***Always clear water*** because the water is non-glacial and clear much of the year, in contrast to the other forks.

The village was a large and important traditional village with longhouses on both sides of the mouth of the South Fork, the view shown in Photo 24. This was the major settlement of the upriver area, and the home of <X̲emtl’ílem> /x̣əmƛ’íləm/, an important 19th-century Nooksack leader. The best-known longhouse site is on the Charley Adass place, ¼ mile south of the Highway 9 bridge west of the railroad tracks. Adjacent to the longhouse site (shown in Photo 25) is a log house built before 1900 for Charley Adass by his son-in-law Antone. This house is also shown in Photo 26 (taken around 1940), and was still occupied in 2009. The longhouse was located within 100 feet of the former channel of the South Fork. The probable location of a second longhouse across

Counterclockwise, from top left:

Photo 24 *Place 92 Nuxw7íyem (*always clear water*), South Fork Nooksack River at its mouth, with place 91 Ayx̲átl'tsot on the left. Waters of the North and Middle Forks enter from the right. View to the north, down the main river. 17 July 1980.* (Photo by B. Galloway)

Photo 25 *Place 92 Nuxw7íyem, village location showing log house of Charley Adass. The house is also shown in a historical photo (Photo 26). The site of the traditional longhouse is to the left. 17 July 1980.* (Photo by B. Galloway)

Photo 26 *Log house with dovetail corners at place 92 Nuxw7íyem village site, ca. 1940. The house is also shown in a 1980 photo (Photo 25) and was still occupied in 2009.* (P.R. Jeffcott Collection, no. 1363)

the South Fork on the John Whichtalum place has been washed away. A third longhouse was located ¼ mile to the south along the South Fork on the Tom Hyladdis place, and was the last old traditional house in the area (LG; Paul Fetzer interview with George Swanaset, 25 August 1950). The mouth of the South Fork was an important traditional weir location for catching spring and silver salmon, and has continued to be fished up to the present.

93. Sqw'ex̲óqen Billy Williams's place. **Map 15**

<**Sqw'ex̲óqen**> [sq'ʷəx̣áqən] /s-q'ʷəx̣áqən/, (Skagit [q'x̣ʷáx̣ad] ***upstream side*** [BG:LG]). The Skagit etymology is most likely since it is given by LG, in spite of Nooksack's switching of the labialization of the <q> and <x̲> and changing of the next to last consonant from <x̲> to <q>; her suggestion seems to be based on the Nooksack form's being cognate with the Skagit form. The Nooksack <s-> is *nominalizer, noun forming,* and cognate to the Skagit suffix /-áx̣ad/ *side* (which would be <-óx̲od> in the Nooksack orthography) is Upriver Halkomelem /-ǽx̣əl/ <-áx̲el> *side (geographical)* and perhaps the <áx̲en> in Nooksack <-eláx̲en> *on the arm, side extension;* the Skagit root is /q'ixʷ/ *located upstream.* The suffix on the Nooksack term, however, seems more like <-eqen> *voice, language* or <-qin> *head,* so there are differences between all three consonants in the root and suffix of the Skagit form and the Nooksack form here.

This is the location of three houses built by Billy Williams [wɪlʔíməltxʷ] (later known as [wílləmat] Willemot, then Williams) on his trust homestead between around 1875 and 1900. These houses, and thus Sqw'ex̲óqen, were located between Tsítsix̲ (place 94) and the main channel of the North Fork within ¼ mile to the west and northwest of the tribal fish dam on Tsítsix̲. The original homestead house and first barn, which were about 0.2 mile west of the fish dam, were washed away by the river long ago (GC). Billy Williams's second house was located further north and was also washed out by the river; the 1885 Land Survey map (United States General Land Office 1859-90) shows a house and the name "Indian Billy" at about this location. His second barn and third house were just northwest of the fish dam. This area is river floodplain, with cottonwood trees predominating.

---

94. Tsítsix̲ Tom Williams's Creek, also called Rutsatz Slough. **Map 15**

<**Tsítsix̲**> [cícix̣] /cí-cix̣/$_2$. ***Little-spring*** from Nooksack <tsix̲> *spring* + <tsí-> (C_1í- reduplication) *diminutive, little,* from the many small springs along it even today.

This is a small creek that flows along the south edge of the river floodplain parallel to Rutsatz Road for about one mile, primarily within the Billy Williams trust homestead, and enters the North Fork just above the Highway 9 bridge. The creek is fed by springs, hence its name, and at times by overflow from the main channel of the river. Tsítsix was fished in earlier times for dog salmon, and is now the site of a tribal spawning enhancement project and fish-rearing pond. Also see place 93 Sqw'exóqen, Billy Williams's place.

---

95. Nuxwṭ'íqw'em Middle Fork Nooksack River and the village located at its mouth. **Map 15**

> **<Nuxwt'íqw'em>** ~ <Xwt'íqw'em> [nux^{w}téq'um ~ x^{w}tíq'^{w}əm] (WS:GS), [x^{w}tíʔk'^{w}əm] (PFM, a very inaccurate transcription here), [nʊx^{w}t'íq^{w}əm ~ nʊx^{w}t'íq'^{w}əm] (BG:LG), [x^{w}t'í·q'^{w}əm] (LT:LG), prob. /nox^{w}-t'íq'^{w}əm ~ x^{w}-t'íq'^{w}əm/. ***Always-murky water*** due to its turbulent glacial water. The root is prob. Nooksack /t'íq'^{w}əm/ *muddy or murky water* (BG:LG), the variability in glottalization prob. being due to influence of Skagit /ʔt'íq'^{w}əb/ *murky,* although Halkomelem /t'ə́k^{w}t'ək^{w}/ *muddy,* /t'ə́k^{w}/ *mired,* but cf. also Squamish /tíq^{w}/ *muddy* and /t'ə́k^{w}t'ək^{w}/ *very muddy.*

The Middle Fork had a strong run of steelhead, but smaller runs of other salmon because of its turbulent, cloudy water. The Middle Fork was important as a route to hunting and berry-picking areas on the slopes of Mt. Baker (Wayne Suttles interview with George Swanaset, 26 April 1950). This route to Mt. Baker was also chosen by the Nooksack Indian guides on Edmund Coleman's 1868 climbing expedition, which clearly documents Nooksack familiarity with the area (Coleman 1869). According to George Swanaset (same interview) the village of Nuxwt'íqw'em was located on the flat at the south side of the mouth of the Middle Fork. Little else is known of the village; its date of last occupation was probably prior to 1820. In recent years, the Middle Fork watershed has become the focus of traditional religious activities because it is less disturbed by modern developments than other parts of the Nooksack area. The Nooksack Tribe has gone to court to block hydroelectric projects on tributaries of the Middle Fork, and has requested that the Middle Fork watershed be formally recognized as a traditional cultural property through the National Register of Historic Places (Richardson 1995; Nooksack Tribe 2000). The Middle Fork valley, with place 97 Chuw7álich in the foreground, is shown in Photo 27.

PHOTO 27 *Place 97 Chuw7álich, North Fork Nooksack River, view downriver with place 95 Nuxwt'íqw'em, the Middle Fork, entering from left. The Middle Fork valley is in the centre background, with place 129 Kwetl'kwítl' Smánit, Twin Sisters Mountain, in the distance. 31 July 1980.* (Photo by B. Galloway)

96. Yúmechiy Canyon Creek on the Middle Fork. **Map 15**

<**Yúmechiy**> [yúməči] /yóməč-iy/$_2$. ***Spring salmon-place***. Same etymology as in place 32.

This creek was possibly named Yúmechiy, which refers to spring salmon. Tom Williams (Richardson 1974, 68) and George Swanaset (Paul Fetzer field notes) both stated that this was a good stream for steelhead, and do not mention any other species. Recent consultants stated that the stream was good for steelhead, silver, chum, and sockeye (because of the lake, Canyon L.). The apparent lack of spring salmon in Canyon Cr. could mean that the name Yúmechiy is misapplied, although it may refer to a different creek in this area.

97. Chuw7álich North Fork Nooksack River. **Map 15**

<**Chuw7álich**> [čuɛlɪc ~ čuʔɛ́lɪc] (WS:GS), [čuwʔǽlič] (BG:LG), [xʷčəwʔǽ·lʔič] (LT:LG), /čowʔǽ-lič/. LG compares Skagit [čgʷáʔlič] *the next point* and Halkomelem [čəwǽ] /cəwɛ́/ *neighbouring;* Nooksack <chuwá> [čuwǽ] *next* is the root, with a variant pronunciation [čuwʔǽ] not yet attested elsewhere or with a glottal stop to separate the final vowel from a vowel-initial suffix [-ǽlič]. The Nooksack place name is a word cognate with the Skagit word [čgʷáʔlič] ***the next point.*** There is a Nooksack suffix found in Pamela Amoss's card files of Nooksack, [-ǽlič], apparently meaning *bundle* in one example, [θiy-ʔǽlič-əm] *tie up in a bundle,* with root [ciy] <tsiy> *make, fix* (GS has Halkomelem accented <thiy> instead of <tsiy>, which SJ and other speakers had in this root); it is unclear so far whether this suffix is the same as the one in the place name.

This is the largest and longest of the three forks of the Nooksack R. The North Fork was the route of access to important mountain goat-hunting areas on the slopes of Mt. Baker, Mt. Shuksan, and other peaks. Lower elevations or less rocky areas were also used for hunting other species and gathering berries. The upper North Fork drainage above Maple Falls was to some extent shared with the Chilliwack people, especially the area north of the river that the Chilliwack considered to be part of their territory (Duff 1952, 20-21). The Thompson Indians apparently also hunted in the upper North Fork drainage, considering the extensive knowledge of this area held by Teosaluk, who served as guide and hunter for the US Northwest Boundary Survey. James Teit shows this area as part of Thompson territory (Teit 1900, 1910-13), although clearly the Nooksack and Chilliwack people were not excluded. The North Fork had important runs of steelhead, pink salmon, silver salmon, and especially dog salmon. In some sources, the North Fork is named after the dog salmon (see place 98 Kw'ól7oxwey). The North Fork was fished from Nuxw7íyem to Nooksack Falls, primarily in jams and eddies, or at the mouths of side creeks. See also place 99 Xwqélém.

---

98. Kw'ól7oxwey North Fork Nooksack River. **Map 15**

<**Kw'úlexwey ~ Kw'ól7oxwey**> "Koo-la-wheh" ~ "Ko-la-wheh" (BS), [xʷq'ʷóləxʷé(y)] (PFM), [k'ʷúləxʷey ~ k'ʷúlʔʊxʷey] (BG:SJ),

/k’ʷóləxʷ-iy ~ k’ʷólʔuxʷ-iy/, /k’ʷ/ poss. ~ /q’ʷ/. Alternate name for North Fork. ***Dog salmon-place*** from /k’ʷóləxʷ ~ k’ʷólʔoxʷ/ ~ sometimes /q’ʷólʔoxʷ/ *dog salmon* + /-iy ~ -əy/ *place.* The PFM quotation appears to belong here but has prefix <xw-> [xʷ-] *always,* which is found in place name 100. The Upriver Halkomelem cognate for *dog salmon* is <kw’ó:lexw>.

This is an alternate name for Chuw7álich (place 97) used by some of the present-day elders. A similar form was recorded by Jeffcott (1949, 54), and the form "Koo-la-wheh" is used in the 1857-62 Boundary Survey materials. All of these forms refer to the dog salmon, which had important runs in the North Fork. The most important run entered Kendall Cr., which is known by a variant of the same name, Xwkw’ól7oxey (place 100).

---

99. Xwqélém [Halkomelem] North Fork Nooksack River. **Map 15**

Upriver Halkomelem **<Xwqélém>** [xʷqə́lə́m] /xʷ-qəl-ə́m/. ***Always-dirty water*** from root /qə́l/ *bad, dirty* because of its water from snowmelt and glaciers.

This Halkomelem name for the North Fork has been used by some Nooksack elders (Richardson 1974, 68). Meaning *always dirty water,* it is appropriate because of the snowmelt and glacial water that the North Fork carries through the summer.

---

100. Xwkw’ól7oxwey Kendall Creek and village at the mouth of Kendall Creek. **Map 15**

<Xwkw’ól7exwam ~ Xwkw’ól7oxwey> [xʷk’ólʔəxʷɛm] (WS:GS), [k’óloxʷɪɬ] (PFM), [xʷk’ʷóləxʷi] (BG:SJ), [k’ʷólʔuxʷʔay] (BG:LG), [k’ʷáləxʷi] (BG:EF), prob. /xʷ-k’ʷólʔəxʷ-æm/ ~ /(xʷ-)k’ʷólʔoxʷ-iy/. ***Always-dog salmon-place*** (with /-æm/) and ***always-dog salmon-place*** (with /-iy/).

The creek was a major spawning ground for dog salmon, with truly massive runs (Richardson 1974, 68). Many people came here each fall to catch and dry dog salmon. It has been described as the "biggest camping ground in the valley," and as having "huge smoke houses," possibly as many as four or five (Paul Fetzer field notes). There were permanent residents here early in the 19th century, but after a smallpox epidemic in the 1830s or 1840s, the site was abandoned except

Photo 28 *Place 100 Xwkw'ól7oxwey (*always-dog salmon-place*), Kendall Creek and village. The location of the village is near older buildings of the Washington State Salmon Hatchery in the centre of the photo. 31 July 1980.* (Photo by B. Galloway)

for seasonal use. Early residents of this village included Philomena (Harry) Solomon's great-grandfather, <Yusán>, and his father, <Wíweqs>. Yusán's son (name unknown) had son, Matsqui Harry, the father of Philomena. Philomena was a member of the Halkomelem Workshop along with the other elders who worked with Brent Galloway on that language from 1974 to 1980. George Adams is a grandson of Philomena.

A village is shown on the west bank of the creek mouth on the 1857-62 Boundary Survey manuscript map, although such a village would not have to have been permanently occupied. One of the Boundary Survey field maps (Series 69, Map 31) shows five buildings at the east side of the creek mouth. Series 69, Maps 31 and 51, and the large manuscript map, show Indian trails from the upper Sumas R. valley and Sumas L. to here. The site of Xwkw'ól7oxwey village is now occupied by the Washington State Salmon Hatchery, which has greatly modified the creek mouth area, as can be seen in Photo 28. The last Indian

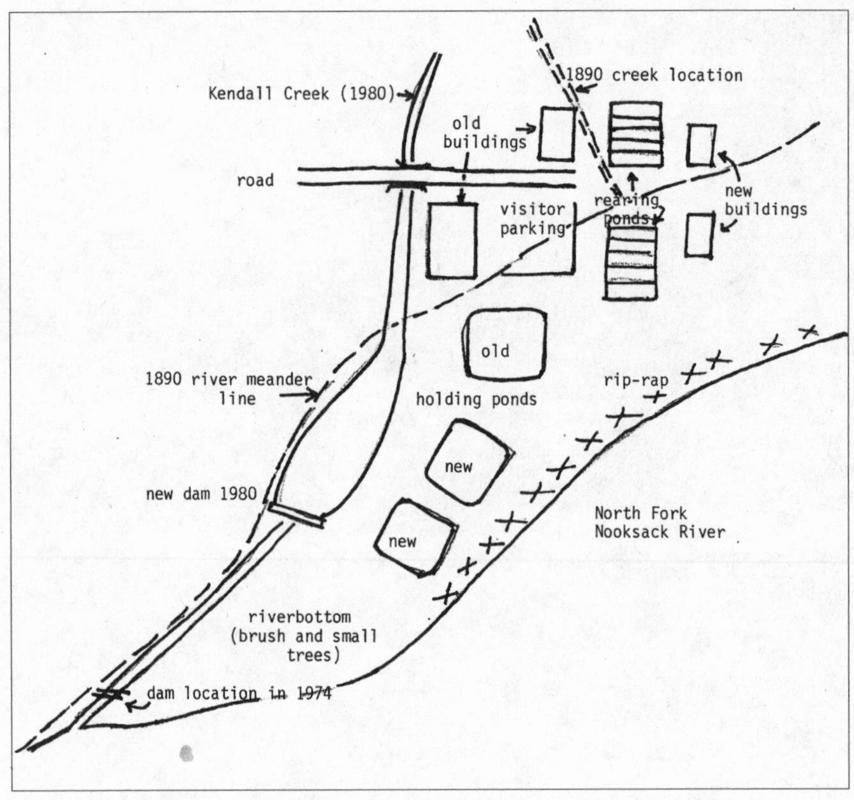

Map 16 *Locations of historical and recent buildings, fish hatchery ponds, and river at place 100 Xwkw'ö́l7oxwey. Sketch completed following a field visit with the Nooksack elders.* (A. Richardson field notes, 31 July 1980)

smokehouse, which was standing around 1905, was probably located near the old hatchery buildings, just east of the present creek channel (see Map 16). Also see place 101 Q'oyó7ts.

100A. Xwmó̲lsemelhp Kendall Creek. **Map 15**

<**Xwmó̲lsemelhp**> "Hoo-máhl-so-mep ~ Hoo-máhl-so-mel" (BS). The name <Xwmó̲lsemelhp> derives from <xw-> *always* + <mó̲lsem> *swamp blueberry, marsh blueberry* + <-elhp> *tree, bush*, thus ***always marsh blueberries.*** Place name 59 has the same etymology.

The Northwest Boundary Survey materials include the following: "Hoo-máhl-so-mep creek which empties into the north branch of the Nook-sahk river ... the Koh-yootl village at its mouth" (Gardner 1857b). This is clearly Kendall Cr., and the name "Hoo-mahl-so-mep" is handwritten at this location on the manuscript map. The wet areas drained by Kendall Cr. would likely have supported blueberry bushes and formed the basis of the place name, perhaps referring to the upstream area, since Xwkw'ól7oxwey (place 100) is the name for the mouth of Kendall Cr.

100B. Layélhcho7 Area on Kendall Creek by lakes. **Map 15**

<**Layélhcho7**> "Lajecho" (BS-Custer). "Lajecho" looks similar to Halkomelem <lóyéxwa> in some ways but that means *do I have to? does one have to?* and so is not a believable etymology. The "j" is probably Custer's use of German "j" to represent a "y" sound, which would give a Nooksack root <lay> ***fir bark;*** if Custer missed the <lh> sound in the Nooksack suffix <-élh-cho7> *dirty or unclear water* (see examples in place 81A), <lay> + <-élhcho7> would mean *fir bark (unclear/dirty) water,* which could be a description of the area on Kendall Cr. by those lakes. Another, less likely etymology would put together the same root <lay> *fir bark* + <-ich> *in back; on the back* + <-xw> *circle, in a circle* or a possible <-ow> if cognate with Halkomelem <-aw> *on top of itself.* The first explanation seems much more likely.

This place name is known only from a sketch in Henry Custer's reconnaissance book "Season 1859 Book no. I" (RG 76, E 202). "Lajecho" is placed near two lakes now called Sprague L. and Kendall L., located two to three miles upstream from the mouth of Kendall Cr. The marshy area surrounding these lakes is perhaps the basis of the name "Hoo-máhl-so-mep creek" applied to Kendall Cr. in some of the Boundary Survey records (see place 100A).

---

101. Q'oyó7ts Village at the mouth of Kendall Creek. **Map 15**

<**Q'oyó7ts**> or <Kweyó7ts> "Koh-yooth" (BS), "Koh-yootl" (Gardner 1857b). Probably [qoyuθ] or [q'oyuθ] or [kweyuθ] or [kw'eyuθ] reflect the Halkomelem-accented Nooksack in the Boundary Survey citation here; no stress is shown, so it could be

on either syllable; the final [Θ] in unaccented Nooksack is [¢] and shows Nooksack <-ó7ts ~ -ó7tsin> /-óʔc(in)/ [-óʔc(in) ~ -úʔc(in)] *(in/at the) mouth* (cf. /-á·Θəl/ *in/at the mouth* in Halkomelem), or Nooksack <ó7ts> /-óʔc/ *edge* (cf. /-á·Θ/ in Halkomelem). If the first consonant is glottalized, the root may be cognate with Upriver Halkomelem <kw'iy ~ kw'ey> *climb, ascend* or, more likely, <q'oy> *die* (Nooksack <q'oy> /q'oy/ *die*); the second root would yield a meaning for the place name like ***die at the edge*** or *die at the mouth,* which could be appropriate for a salmon spawning ground such as this site (one place in BC, in Stó:lō territory, was named like this in Upriver Halkomelem, after the fact that spawned-out salmon were frequently found dead in the area in great numbers). So the Nooksack place name was most likely <Q'oyó7ts> or <Q'oyú7ts> with a Halkomelem accent variant <Q'oyúth ~ Q'oyóth>. The Gardner version with final "tl" may reflect an alternative suffix or more likely an error, since the village was at the mouth of the creek and Nooksack <-ucin ~ -uc ~ -ó7ts ~ -ó7tsin> means *mouth.* Possibly compare place 58.

This village is shown on the Boundary Survey manuscript map on the west side of the mouth of Kendall Cr., the location of the Nooksack village of Xwkw'ól7oxwey. Although this village may not have been permanently occupied when visited by the Boundary Survey in 1857, it was an important seasonal site with large permanent buildings (see place 100).

---

102. P'eq'ósiy Maple Creek. **Map 15**

<P'eq'ósiy> "Pekosie" (Baker 1900). See place 104 for etymology, ***white-face-place.***

Published lists relating to the 1857-62 Boundary Survey (Baker 1900) include "Pekosie" as the name for both Silver L. and Maple Cr., which flows from it (see place 103). The field report refers to this creek as "the Pekosy" and describes an Indian trail that follows it and was "said to lead from the Nooksahk river to the Sweltcha Lake, via the Pekosy Lake" (Custer 1859). "Sweltcha Lake" was Cultus L. in BC (Upriver Halkomelem <swíylhcha>). The Nooksack fished for dog salmon at the falls of Maple Cr., near the town of Maple Falls (Richardson 1974, 68).

---

103. P'eq'ósiy Silver Lake. **Map 5**

<**P'eq'ósiy**> "Pekosie" (BS). See place 104 for etymology, ***white-face-place.***

This lake is named "Pekosie" on the 1857-62 Boundary Survey manuscript map and in published records of the Boundary Survey (Baker 1900), which also applies "Pekosie" to Maple Cr. (place 102). The form "Pekosy" is applied to the lake on the field map 19-2 and in the field report (Custer 1859). Silver L. was on a main travel route between the Nooksack and Chilliwack areas, linking the North Fork (four miles to the south) with Cultus L. (five miles to the northeast). Three Indian canoes were found at the bottom of the lake around 1974 or 1975, clearly documenting Indian use of the lake for travel. The Nooksacks may have had a longhouse at Cultus L., or at least people living there spoke Lhéchelesem (AR interview with Ella Reid, 1 July 1975) (also see place 139).

---

104. P'eq'ósiy Red Mountain. **Map 5**

<**P'eq'ósiy**> "Pe-ko-sie" (BS). There are several active lime quarries on Red Mountain; this suggests a possible etymology: /p'əq'-ós-iy/ ***white-face-place*** after natural exposures of white limestone on the mountain; it would require a mixture of Halkomelem (/p'ə́q'/ *white* vs. Nooksack /kʷə́q'/ *white*) and Nooksack ([ós] /-ós/ *face* vs. Halkomelem /-á·s ~ -əs/ *face,* and Nooksack /-iy/ *place*), but both languages were spoken at Cultus L. five miles N of Silver L.; indeed, the two roots are very close in shape. Just such a place name is attested already in Halkomelem, /ləxʷ-p'ə́-p'əq'-əs/ *always-many little-white-face,* a mountain between Yale and Hope, on the W bank of the Fraser R., so named because it has white mineral deposits visible in many places (some are mined). Lakes and rivers are often named after the largest nearby mountain in Halkomelem and prob. also in Nooksack, thus place 102 and place 103.

This mountain rises abruptly to the west of place 103 Silver Lake, and extends five miles to the southwest to near the community of Kendall. The form "Pe-ko-sie" for Red Mountain is from the 1857-62 Boundary Survey manuscript map. One field report (Gardner 1857b) uses the form "Pe-kó̱h-sai."

---

105. Q'iysú7ts Bald Mountain. **Map 5**

<Q'iysú7ts> "Kaisoots" (BS), "Kaisootst" (Baker 1900), "Ka˙i-sootst, Kaisoots't, Casuts, Casutz, Kasutz" (BS-Custer). Poss. has Nooksack [-.úʔc] /-óʔc/ *edge* (cf. /-á·Θ/ in Halkomelem). Possibly <Q'eysu7ts> or <Q'o̲yso7ts> or <Q'iysu7ts> or <Q'iyso7ts>. There is no plain [k] in Nooksack and with the next vowel apparently unrounded [e] /i/ <i> the first consonant cannot be labialized <kw>, <kw'>, <qw>, or <qw'> since the rounding would be reflected by the BS in a following rounded vowel. Thus, the first consonant must be <q> or <q'>, precisely the sounds that cause Nooksack (and Halkomelem) /i/ to be pronounced with allophone [e] as the spelling indicates. The root could be as in Nooksack <q'íys-in> *tie s-th together* (GA:LG), cognate with Upriver Halkomelem root <q'eys> as in <q'éyset> *tie something,* or could be cognate with Lushootseed root /q'is(i)-/ *uncover in order to look at it; uncovered* (Hess 1976, 469, 404), or could be entirely unconnected. If there is such a connection, **<q'iysú7ts>** would mean *tie the edge* or ***uncovered edge*** and <q'eysú7tst> would mean *tie something on the edge* or *uncover it on the edge;* because the form and literal meaning are unclear, it is unclear whether this might be related to the story of how the Nooksacks saved themselves in the great flood by tying their great canoe to a mountain still above the floodwaters. The Lhéchelesem story of the flood should be checked to see whether the mountain in that legend is located near this mountain. Or if the *uncovered* etymology is correct, the name could refer to the uncovered or bald look of the mountain, making this perhaps more likely.

This small mountain with an unforested top is located north of Boulder Cr. and Canyon Cr. on the North Fork two miles south of the border. No specific Nooksack use of Bald Mountain is known, and the Indian name is known only from the 1857-62 Boundary Survey materials and the published list of elevations (Baker 1900, 46), where it is written "Kaisootst." The additional variants "Ka·i-sootst," "Casuts," "Casute," "Kaisoots't," and "Kasutz" are found in the field materials of Henry Custer (Majors 1984, 31, 38, 39, 43).

105A. "Tah-ho-léh-uk" A branch of the North Fork Nooksack River upstream from Kendall Creek, possibly Boulder Creek.

"Tah-ho-léh-uk" (BS). There are several possible realizations of this in the Nooksack orthography. <To̲xwelíqw>, <T'ex̲elíqw>, or <T'eqw'elíqw> seem the most likely, although <T'ex̲w̲elíqw>, <Taxwolíqw>, <To̲x̲welíqw>, and <Tax̲wolíqw> are also possible. The combination "éh-uk" is certainly the Nooksack suffix <-íqw> ***top of head, hair; fish*** (as in Halkomelem <t'x̲emíqw> *six fish*), which is often pronounced with [-íᵊqʷ], due to the schwa transition needed to get from high front vowel [i] to uvular consonant [qʷ] (see also place 60 and place 127). The initial "t" could be either <t> or <t'> since glottalized consonants are not transcribed differently from plain ones in Boundary Survey materials. The "h" could be an <h> but since there are almost no roots in Nooksack that end in <h>, it is more likely <x̲>, or <xw> or <x̲w> (since following "o" often indicated a labialized consonant either followed by <e> or <o>). Most likely the root is Nooksack <t'ex̲> ***branch, spread apart*** (as in Nooksack [st'ə́x̣əs] (LT:LG) *fork of tree,* Halkomelem /s-t'ə́x̣/ *fork of creek, fork of tree*) or <t'(a)qw'-> (as in Nooksack [t'q'ʷə́nɛ] <t'qw'-éna> *to break loose from mooring (of canoe or watercraft)* (PF:GS, NKF 2.1499) (where <-ena> means *on the side of the head* with a geographic extension perhaps meaning *on the side*). Upriver Halkomelem has a root <t'oxw> that seems appropriate for a branch of a river; it may have a cognate in Nooksack and is shown in Galloway's *Dictionary of Upriver Halkomelem* (2009) as:

> <**t'óxw**>, free root //t'áxʷ//, DIR /'*go down(hill) to the water, go towards the river'*/, WATR, syntactic analysis: adverb/adverbial verb, attested by Deming (4/17/80), EB (5/25/76), other sources: ES /t'áxʷ/ *downhill, toward water,* for example: <**le t'óxw.**>, //lə t'áxʷ//, /'*He went towards the river.'*/, attested by EB.

Halkomelem also has a root <toxw-> *drag hehind,* which seems less likely. With the root <t'ex̲> + <-el> ***come, go, get, become*** + <-iqw>, the literal meaning of <T'exelíqw> would be *become spread apart at top of the head;* with root <t'(a)qw'> + <-el> *come, go, get, become* + <-iqw>, the literal meaning of <T'eqw'elíqw> would be *become broken loose at the top of the head* or perhaps even *fish become broken loose.* With root <t'oxw> plus the same suffixes, the literal meaning of <T'o̲xwelíqw> would be *go downhill towards the river at the head* or even perhaps *fish go downhill towards the river.* These three seem appropriate for a branch of a river; in Nooksack, as in Halkomelem, one can speak of the head of a river using this suffix.

This name is known only from "Field Notes 1858 of Joseph S. Harris" (RG 76, E 200). On folded blue paper in the back of the book, perhaps in George Gibbs's handwriting, is a short list of place names, including: "Tah-ho-léh-uk a branch of Nootsahk." In the context of this list, the name refers to a tributary of the North Fork upstream from Kendall Cr., but it is unclear where to show this on the map without more information. One possibility is Boulder Cr., which flows off Bald Mountain and carries boulders and other debris in frequent floods. Boulder Cr. is also the largest tributary of the North Fork with no known Native name.

---

106. "Cowap" Canyon Creek on the North Fork Nooksack River. **Map 5**

"Cowap" (BS). Poss. one syllable since not syllabified, poss. <Qwap> /q^{w}ǽp/ comparable to the Halkomelem place name /s-q^{w}ǽ·-p/ *(nominalizer)-get hole-in dirt, ground,* the name for a morainic lake near summit of Cheam Peak (on its S side) and also for Chipmunk Cr., which has its source in the lake. Canyon Cr. has several such morainic lakes as sources (for tributaries Kidney Cr. and Whistler Cr. on Church Mountain, Church L., Bearpaw Mountain L., and Canyon L., the first source of Canyon Cr. near Excelsior Peak). <Qwo7áp> is another possibility with Nooksack root <qwo7> *water* plus <-ap> *in the ground, dirt.*

This creek is named "Cowap" in the 1857-62 Boundary Survey maps and reports, and is a major northern tributary to the North Fork. Jeffcott (1964, 8) states that the area on the downriver side of the mouth of Canyon Cr. was a "stopping place for hunting parties," and gives the name "Na-e-wha-quam" (place 107) to the site. Dog salmon and silver salmon were probably also caught at the mouth of this creek (Richardson 1974, 68).

---

107. "Na-e-wha-quam" Camp at the mouth of Canyon Creek on the North Fork Nooksack River. **Map 5**

"Na-e-wha-quam" (PJ). Possibly something like <Ne7íxweqwem> or <Níx̲weqwem> or <Níxweqwem> or <Níqweqwem> or <Níx̲weqwem> or <Nexwxwóqw'em> or <Nuxwxwó̲kw'em>, etc. Of these, several may have plausible literal meanings: <Nexwx̱wó̱qw'em> *always sawbill duck (place to) get/have,* with <nexw-> *always* + Halkomelemized <x̱wó̱qw'> *sawbill duck* + Nooksack <-em> *(place to) get/have* (Nooksack has <x̱woqw'> *sawbill duck,* which would yield a form <Nexwx̱wóqw'em>, quite possible if the PJ <a> in the second syllable is wrong, as PJ is the least accurate transcriber); <Nexwxwó̱qw'em> or <Nexwxwóqw'em> *always snore place;* <Níqweqwem> *nod the top of one's head down/nod the top of the head down place to have/get;* <Niqweqwem> *soft (of mossy ground) on the head place to have/get.* In some of the possibilities, <-eqw> could be an unstressed Halkomelemized version of Nookesack <-íqw> *on top of the head, hair* and <-em> *middle voice, do to one's own,* or in the last four, the most likely ones, Nooksack <-em> *(place to) have/get;* more investigation of possible Nooksack roots like <ixw>, <ixw>, <nixw>, <nixw>, <ne7ixw>, <ne7ixw>, <xwoqw'>, <xwokw'>, <x̱woqw'>, <x̱wokw'>, <xwoqw>, <xwokw>, <x̱woqw'>, and <x̱wokw'> may provide further possibilities, as any of these are possible here, since neither PJ nor BS show postvelar/uvular consonants differently from velars and usually do not show glottalized stops differently from plain ones. Nooksack <níqw-em> *soft (e.g., of a pillow or mossy ground)* (GA), or Nooksack <xwóqw'em> *to snore* or Nooksack <níqweqwem> *nod the top of one's head down* (compare Upriver Halkomelem <liqwesem> *nod one's head*). The meanings of these (*soft [of pillow/mossy ground], snore, nod one's head down*) might be relevant to mountain goat hunters stopping to rest or sleep. The *snore* possible etymology would require prefix <nuxw-> *always; people of.* A cognate with Halkomelem <le7á-> *facing away, on opposite side,* with Nooksack <n> for Upriver Halkomelem <l> as often happens, might also be possible. None of these is confirmed; they are just possible etymologies.

This name is known only from Jeffcott (1964, 8). See place 106.

---

108. Sháwaq Church Mountain. **Map 5**

"Show-ak" (BS), prob. **<Sháwaq>**. The name appears to be similar to Nooksack <sháwaq> (PA:SJ) /šǽwæq/ *wild carrot* (prob. wild caraway, *Perideridia gairdneri*), but this has not been identified as the meaning of the place name in documents found so far. The carrot etymology may be more likely, since the mountain has a sharp peak that might resemble a carrot; it could also be that wild carrots grew on the slopes.

This mountain consists of a high rocky ridge about four miles long, paralleling the North Fork on the north side between Glacier Cr. and Nooksack Falls. This is one of the most accessible areas of high country from the North Fork, and is known as a place where Nooksack people used to get mountain goats. The Indian name is known only from the Boundary Survey materials. The form “Sowack” appears in the field report (Custer 1859) and on the field map (Series 69, Map 19-2), with “Show-ak” on the Series 68 manuscript map.

---

109. Nuxwt’íqw’em Glacier Creek(?). Map 5

<**Nuxwt’íqw’em**> or <Nuxwt’íqw’um> “Noo-téh-a-kwoom” (BS), certainly /nox^{w}-t’íq’^{w}əm/ meaning ***always-murky*** as in place 95. The “a” reflects the schwa glide transition from /i/ to /q’^{w}/.

“Noo-téh-a-kwoom” is used to name Glacier Cr. on the 1857-62 Boundary Survey manuscript map, from which the Middle Fork is entirely missing. “Indian Nomenclature” (Gibbs 1857-61) describes “Noo-téh-a-kwoom” only as a “branch of Nooksack.” The published Boundary Survey material in Baker (1900) does not include this name, but has “mouth of Noochsakatsu, South Branch” at the precise elevation and location of the mouth of Glacier Cr. (see place 110). The name “Noo-téh-a-kwoom,” or <Nuxwt’íqw’em>, could certainly have been used twice, but in this case it appears that the Boundary Survey manuscript map is in error. No one from the Boundary Survey visited the Middle Fork. Henry Custer thought he had reached the Middle Fork in June 1859, when he was at the mouth of Glacier Cr., but he named the stream “Nuschechaze” (see place 110).

---

110. Nuxwchx̲áchu Glacier Creek. Map 5

Prob. <**Nuxwchx̲áchu**> “Noochsakatsu” (Baker 1900), “Noochsehatso, Noochtsa-hatche, Nuschechaze” (BS-Custer field notes). Prob. has <nuxw-> /nox^{w}-/ prefix and <ch- ~ ts-> *have*. Prob. <Nuxwchx̲áchu ~ Nuxwtsx̲ácho(7)> ***always has a lake*** with root <x̲áchu7 ~ x̲ácho7>, which is the Nooksack word for *lake*. The last two Custer transcriptions may have final "e" showing a further suffix on some versions, Nooksack <-ey> *place,* i.e., *always has a lake place;* Custer was Swiss-German and "ch" usually has its German value <x> after back vowels like <u> or <o>, as here. The third version, however, also has a "ts" after the "ch," which indicates a further suffix, Nooksack <ts->, the Halkomelemized version of <ch-> *have, get.* The form "Noochse-hatche" appears in Custer's field report (1859), and "Noochtsa-hatshum" on the field map (Series 69, Map 19-2), with the additional form "Nuschechaze" in Custer's field notebook (RG 76, E 202). There is no lake of any size in the Glacier Cr. drainage now, but there may have been one in the past formed by a landslide or glacial ice blocking the creek. A rough sketch map with the Boundary Survey materials (Series 69, Map 43) does show lakes on what is probably Glacier Cr.

Glacier Cr. is a major stream draining from Mt. Baker. As the first direct route to Mt. Baker from the North Fork, it was probably followed frequently by Nooksack people.

---

111. "Tchahko" Maple Creek. **Map 5**

"Tchahko" (BS), "Shako" (BS-Custer). The word may be a single syllable with labialized velar or postvelar, so possibly Nooksack <chokw> *far* (GA) or Upriver Halkomelem <chókw> *far* or <ch'áxw> *quiet,* or any of the consonants could be glottalized (eight possibilities), and there could be a suffix <-ow>. The first (or only) vowel could be either <o̲> /a/ (Halkomelem accent for <o> /o/), or perhaps <a> since the Boundary Survey orthography has no consistent way of showing <a> /æ/. The Lushootseed cognate with the Nooksack and Halkomelem words for *far* (Upriver Halkomelem <chó:kw> /čá·kʷ/) is /čaʔkʷ/ *seaward, towards the water.* Upriver Halkomelem also has <ch'áxw> *quiet, silent (after noise).*

Custer's field notebook, "Sketches and bearings taken during the Summer of 1859" (RG 76, E 202), includes the following: "Crossed little Stream coming from the North, Shako coming from the Sowack." "Shako" is clearly a variant of "Tchahko," and "Sowack" is Church Mountain (place 108), located north of the North Fork. Custer's party left its camp across from the mouth of Glacier

Cr. at 7:00 AM, and after moving slowly on steep slopes, reached this creek at 9:52. When the bearings in the field notebook are followed on Custer's "Plot of the Nooksack River" (Series 69, Map 44), this is definitely Maple Cr., which enters the North Fork 1½ miles above Glacier Cr. Custer would have travelled almost 3 miles from his camp to reach the upstream location where he crossed the creek. Both the 1857-62 Boundary Survey manuscript map and the published list of elevations (Baker 1900, 46) use "Tchahko" for a small creek supposedly entering the North Fork from the south 3 miles above Glacier Cr., which conflicts with Custer's location to the north. Also, at or near this location there is no creek south of the river large enough to be placed on recent maps, so these sources are almost certainly in error.

111A. Sháwaq Coal Creek. Map 5

"Sowack" (BS-Custer). Probably from <**sháwaq**> *carrot* as in place 108.

A creek entering the North Fork from the north a short distance upstream from "Shako" (see place 111). Custer crossed this creek 28 minutes after crossing "Shako." From Maple Cr. to Coal Cr. at the base of Church Mountain away from the river is a short distance, easily travelled in this amount of time.

111B. Q'élep'eqs Deerhorn Creek. Map 5

"Kalupokus" (BS-Custer). Probably <**Q'élep'eqs**> ***twists around itself on a point*** (<q'el-> *twist* + <-(e)p'> *on itself* + <-eqs> *on the nose, point of land*).

Custer's party crossed "Sowack" creek at 10:20 AM, then crossed an unnamed creek coming from the north at 11:20, and reached "Kalupokus Creek from the north" at 1:15. Another creek coming from the north was crossed at 1:40, and camp was made at 4:00 a short distance downstream from the mouth of Wells Cr. on the north bank of the river. When the entire day's travel by Custer's party as detailed in his field notebook is considered with Map 44, "Kalupokus" is almost certainly Deerhorn Cr. The creek crossed at 1:40 would be Fossil Cr. and the one crossed at 11:20 is Lookout Cr. Modern names for creeks in this area are from US Geological Survey 7½′ Glacier and Bearpaw Mountain quadrangles, 1989 provisional edition.

111C. "Bakhum" Wells Creek. **Map 5**

> **"Bakhum"** (BS-Custer). Poss. compare Lushootseed /bák'ʷam/ *move rapidly* or Lushootseed /báqʷu7/ *snow* or possible cognates of Upriver Halkomelem <póx̱w> *blow spray* or <p'óqw'em> *foam* or, less likely, <p'ékw> *float* or <pókw'em> *plant fuzz (or light snow that resembles it) blows.* None of these is confirmed, but those with meanings connected to water or rapid motion seem most likely. Nooksack Falls is adjacent to the mouth of Wells Cr. and may account for the spray.

This name is known only from Henry Custer's field notes for 14 June 1859 (RG 76, E 202), where it clearly applies to Wells Cr.; strangely, it is not used on the Boundary Survey maps that clearly show the creek. Wells Cr. is a major tributary entering the North Fork from the south, just below Nooksack Falls.

111D. Lháwos Creek entering the North Fork Nooksack River from the north. **Map 5**

> "Klauss" (BS-Custer). The most likely Nooksack language interpretation of this name is a place name beginning with either <tl'> or <lh>, which are often spelled as "kl" by explorers of European descent (since neither sound exists in European languages). This could lead to any of the following possible combinations in Nooksack: <Tl'aws>, <Tl'awos>, or <Tl'awels> *bark (of dog)* in Halkomelem, or <Lhaws> or **<Lháwos> *heal the face*** from Nooksack root <lhaw> *heal* + <-os> *face,* or even poss. with a root cognate to the one in Halkomelem <shxwtl'os> *loud* – although one has not been found so far. Sometimes creeks or ponds were named for their healing properties, so <Lháwos> may be the most likely of the possibilities, but no such literal meaning is attested for the place name. It is doubtful that the name refers to a German on the survey crew named Klauss (if such a person existed), since no such person is named in the Boundary Survey materials.

Henry Custer's field notebook, "Sketches and bearings taken during the Summer of 1859" (RG 76, E 202), has a reference to "Klauss Creek coming from the North," opposite cliffs on the south bank. Based on this notebook (the only record of this name) and his route plotted on Series 69, Map 44, this is a stream entering the North Fork one mile upstream from Nooksack Falls, directly south of the site of Excelsior Lookout.

---

112. Spelhpálhx̲en Meadows at the foot of Mt. Baker. Map 5

<**Spelhpálhx̲en**> [spəɬpǽɬx̣ən] (WS:GS; PFM), /s-pəɬ-pǽɬx̣ən/. *(Nominalizer)-plural (many)-prairie, meadow* or ***many meadows*** from Nooksack <s-> *nominalizer* + <C_1eC_2-> reduplication (copy the first consonant of the root, add <e>, copy the second consonant of the root, prefix to root) *plural/many* + stem <palhx̲en> meaning *prairie/meadow* (itself from root <palh> *wide* + <-x̲> *all around* + <-an> *place.*

These lower-elevation (4,500 to 5,500 feet), more sheltered meadows are where people camped. Each family had its own camp where it dried meat and berries (Wayne Suttles interview with George Swanaset, 26 April 1950). These meadows could be reached from either the North Fork or the Middle Fork. Many berries would have been available in and near these lower meadows, as well as on higher slopes.

---

113. Kwelshán The high open slopes of Mt. Baker. Map 5

<**Kwelshán**> [kʷəlšǽ·n] (WS:GS; BG:LG, BG:EF), /kʷəlš-ǽn/. ***Shooting place*** (WS:GS) or *shoot (with bow and arrow)-(transitivizer)* from Nooksack /kʷə́lə́š/ *to shoot (with bow and arrow)(later with gun)* + /-ǽn/ *place,* or, less likely, instead /-Vn/ *transitive (do on purpose to s-th);* this is likely the source of the names for Mt. Baker in the neighbouring languages: Halkomelem /kʷəlxʸ-ɛ́·lxʷ/ (Halkomelem /kʷə́lə́xʸ/ *to shoot [with bow and arrow, later with gun]*) and Lummi /kʷəlšɛ́n/. The US Forest Service and other non-Indian sources often cite the Indian name or Nooksack name for Mt. Baker as "Koma Kulshan"; this may be Nooksack [kʷómæ kʷəlšǽ·n] /kʷómæ kʷəlšǽn/ *go up high or way back in mountains shooting place* from [kʷómæ] /kʷómæ/ *go up high or way back in mountains* (BE:GS, BG:LG), prob. a phrase rather than the proper name.

This place name is described by George Swanaset as "the slopes clear of underbrush where they hunted" (Wayne Suttles interview, 26 April 1950). There

Photo 29 *Place 113 Kwelshán (*shooting place*), the high open slopes of Mt. Baker, important for hunting. Lower slopes in the photo could include place 112 Spelhpálhx̲en (*many meadows*), where family groups camped. View south from the viewpoint at the end of Glacier Creek Road. 3 September 1980.* (Photo by B. Galloway)

are extensive open slopes surrounding Mt. Baker between the treeline at about 5,000 feet and permanent snow, ice, or steep rock at about 7,000 feet. A small part of this terrain is shown in Photo 29. The animals hunted in this area were primarily deer, elk, and mountain goat, and, to a lesser extent, bear and perhaps marmot and grouse. Some outsiders, such as the Thompson, were rigidly excluded from hunting mountain goats in this area (Coleman 1869), although Upper Skagit people freely hunted the south and east slopes of Mt. Baker, and others may have hunted on the north and west slopes with Nooksack relatives. Cognates of Kwelshán are used as names for Mt. Baker in Chilliwack Halkomelem (<Kwelxá:lxw>) and the Lummi dialect of Northern Straits Salish (<Kwelshán>). These names are the source of "Kulshan," which is frequently used by non-Indians as the Indian name for Mt. Baker. See also place 115 "Teqwúbe7."

Photo 30 *Place 114 Kweq' Smánit* (white mountain*), Mt. Baker, especially the glacier-covered top. View from the end of Glacier Creek Road. 3 September 1980.* (Photo by B. Galloway)

114. Kweq' Smánit Mt. Baker. Map 5

<**Kweq' Smánit**> [kʷə́q' smǽ·nɪt] (WS:GS; BG:LG), /kʷə́q' smǽnit/. Mt. Baker, especially the glacier-covered top (above 7,000 feet). ***White mountain*** from Nooksack <kweq'> *white* + <smánit> *mountain.*

This name refers specifically to the steep summit of Mt. Baker above 7,000 feet, which is almost entirely covered by glaciers and therefore white at all seasons of the year, as can be seen in late summer in Photo 30. This mountain is visible throughout the Nooksack area and a great distance beyond. Mt. Baker and the surrounding mountain area are important in Nooksack religious beliefs and practices, and traditionally were an important source of wealth from mountain goat wool and an important source of food from meat and berries. In 1980,

Photo 31 *This photo taken at the end of Glacier Creek Road shows, from left to right, Ernie Paul, Helen Paul holding tart mountain blueberry (léth'ilets), unknown person, Allan Richardson, Esther Fidele, and Louisa George holding sweet mountain blueberry (xwíxwekw'). In the background is place 114 Kweq' Smánit, Mt. Baker. 3 September 1980.* (Photo by B. Galloway)

the elders we worked with remembered the names of different species of mountain blueberries (see Photo 31).

---

115. Teqwúbe7 Skagit name for Mt. Baker. **Map 5**

"Te-kómeh" (BS), Lushootseed /təqʷúbəʔ/ <təqʷúbəʔ> ***any snow-capped mountain*** (Hess 1976, 424, has root /qʷú/ *water;* the writing system used for Lushootseed is the IPA [International Phonetic Alphabet]). The term is probably a loan into Nooksack from Lushootseed, since Lushootseed <b> is pronounced <m> in Nooksack and Lushootseed <u> is pronounced as <u ~ o> in Nooksack, and since the final "eh" could be the Nooksack suffix <ey ~ iy> *place;* thus, the Nooksack pronunciation of the Lushootseed name would be the BS form cited or <Teqwómey>.

This name for Mt. Baker is used on the Boundary Survey manuscript map and in "Indian Nomenclature" (Gibbs 1857-61). "Te-ko̲-meh" is equivalent to T'kóba, the Skagit name for Mt. Baker (Collins 1974, 257). Similar forms are used by other Lushootseed-speaking groups to refer to high, snow-covered peaks in general or specifically to Mr. Rainier, hence the name Tacoma (Clark 1953, 26-28).

"Tuk-we-sallie" (BS) is another name for Mt. Baker written in lightly on the Boundary Survey manuscript map. This is apparently taken from one of the sketch maps by Teosaluk (Series 69, Map 26), which has "Tuk-wesállie" for Mt. Baker. This additional name could be Nooksack with <-áli> /-ǽli/ *container of* or <-áli> /-ǽli/ *people*. Some possible roots or stems are Nooksack <ts̓okwsáli> *seven people* (as with the multiple peaks of Mt. Cheam, which were a mother and three daughters and a dog, all turned to stone by the Transformer, this could refer to seven of the peaks of Mt. Baker, major and minor, and have a similar origin), Nooksack <t̓okw'> *(go) homeward*, <teqw'>, the root in Nooksack <téqw'teqw'> *stuck in mud* (possibly transcription errors since the Upriver Halkomelem cognate root is <t̓ekw> *stuck in the mud;* see also <t̓ékwt̓ekw> *muddy*). Alternatively, "Tuk-wesállie" could be from the Thompson language spoken by Teosaluk, who gave names in this part of the map and to the north and northeast of Mt. Baker.

---

116. "Pút-lush-go-hap" Tomyhoi Peak. Map 5

"Pút-lush-go-hap" (Baker 1900), "Putlatchgohap ~ Putlashgohap." Most likely something like <Putl̓élhcho7xap>, Kuipers (2002, 74) has Proto-Salish */p'uƛ'/ *to come, come to an end, come out (of the bush),* which would become <putl'> in Nooksack, + Nooksack <-élhcho7> *water* + Nooksack (and Upriver Halkomelem) <-x̲> *all around* + Nooksack (and Upriver Halkomelem) <-ap> *in the dirt, at the bottom;* thus, the literal meaning if this form is correct would be *water coming (to an end/out of the bush) all around in the dirt/at the bottom.* Poss. <Pétl'ushkwohap>, or the <kw> could be <qw> or either of them could be glottalized, as could <p>; the <h> is most likely <x̲> instead. The final <ap> may be a Nooksack suffix for *rump* or for *dirt.* See place 117 also, where the same name appears with an alternate form, "Páp-loshe-ko," which shows reduplication added and no <(h)ap> suffix; it also shows the second vowel as Nooksack <u ~ o>, and the last vowel may either be <-ow> or merely show the rounding for the final consonant <kw>, <kw'>, <qw>, or <qw'>.

This peak is located immediately to the west of Tomyhoi L. (place 117), also named "Put-lush-go-hap." It is among the highest peaks in the area, and visible from much of the upper North Fork Nooksack R. area, although in the Chilliwack drainage. Custer (1859, 19-20) clearly designates the present Tomyhoi Peak as "Putlatchgohap peak," then "Putlashgohap mountain," describing it in detail and locating it precisely between the branches of "the Tumeahay," Tomyhoi Cr. "Put-lush-go-hap Mountain" is mistakenly used for peaks east of Tomyhoi L. in Baker (1900, 46-47), which gives the summit the location of American Border Peak but the elevation of Mt. Larrabee. Custer (1859, 25) includes American Border Peak and Mt. Larrabee as part of "the Tumeahay Mts," a name that more properly applies just to Mt. McGuire (see place 117A below).

116A. "Pa-ah" Tomyhoi Peak. Map 5

"Pa-ah" (BS-Custer). No clear Nooksack root has been found as a possibility here. One could compare Upriver Halkomelem root <pax-> *spread apart* or <poh-> *blow* or <poxw> *blow spray (as an Indian doctor to cure)* as the closest matches in sound so far, and Tomyhoi Peak has two peaks spread apart from each other. Another interpretation of the original transcription is <pa7ax> or <pa7x> or <po7ox>, since a hyphen between vowels in Boundary Survey materials usually indicates a glottal stop ([?] <7>). This could point to a Nooksack cognate <pa7x> *spread apart* if it exists, or in the direction of an entirely different root in Nooksack, but one that has not yet been identified.

This name for Tomyhoi Peak appears twice in Henry Custer's "Sketches and bearings taken during the Summer of 1859" (RG 76, E 202).

116B. Shále7 Sasq' Tomyhoi Peak. Map 5

Prob. <**Shále7 Sasq'**> "Shälusäsk ~ Shäla Säsk" (BS-Custer). Custer used German <ä> here, which is pronounced as the <a> /æ/ in English <hat> and is the equivalent of Nooksack <a> /æ/. The name could be from Nooksack <shále7> *penis* and Nooksack <sasq'> *split* (see Upriver Halkomelem <sxéle> *penis* and

> <seq'át> *split something;* thus, the name prob. means ***penis split.***) This could describe a mountain with two or more sharp peaks, and Tomyhoi Peak does have a sharp summit with two small split-apart summits.

This third name for Tomyhoi Peak appears together with the other two (see place 116 and place 116A) on a sketch by Henry Custer in the field notebook cited in place 116A.

---

117. "Put-lush-go-hap" Tomyhoi Lake. **Map 5**

> **"Put-lush-go-hap"** (BS), poss. "Páp-loshe-ko" (BS-Teosaluk); see place 116.

This large lake is located at the head of Tomyhoi Cr. (US) or Tamihi Cr. (BC); the creek is a tributary of the Chilliwack R. and is named in Halkomelem <T'amiyahó:y Stótelew> /t'ɛmiyɛ-há·y státələw/ *deformed human, hermaphrodite-finish creek* from the name for adjacent Mt. McGuire (see place 117A). Tomyhoi L. is just four miles from the North Fork Nooksack R. and only one mile from the drainage divide; it is therefore likely that Nooksack hunters knew of and visited this lake. This place name is included in the Boundary Survey maps, field reports, and published lists.

117A. T'amiyehó:y Mt. McGuire. **Map 5**

> Nooksack <**T'amiyehóy**> /t'æmiyɛ-hóy/ and <**T'amiyehó:y**> /t'ɛmiyɛ-há·y/ the Upriver Halkomelem name for Mt. McGuire, sources of the names Tomyhoi (in Washington) and Tamihi (in BC) on English maps and of the spelling by Custer (1859) of "the Tumeahay" (19-20), Tomyhoi Cr., as well as of "the Tumeahay Mts" (25), a name that more properly applies just to Mt. McGuire. The interesting thing is that in the English spelling used in place names on the US side of the border (Tomyhoi), "-hoi" matches the Nooksack language root /hoy/ <hoy> *finish, end,* corresponding to the "-hi" Canadian version, which matches the Upriver Halkomelem root <ho:y> /ha·y/ *finish, end.* The root in both is <t'ámiye> *hermaphrodite baby, deformed baby,* since Mt. McGuire is the place where the Stó:lō left these babies to "finish" or die, thus ***deformed baby finish.***

Mt. McGuire is close to the Chilliwack R., but is connected by a high ridge to American Border Peak and then to Mt. Larrabee, which is close to the Nooksack drainage. Custer (1859, 25) includes American Border Peak and Mt. Larrabee as part of "the Tumeahay Mts." This same extended use of "Tumeahay Mts" also occurs on a field map (Series 69, Map 19-2) and the manuscript map (Series 68, Folder 1, Map 1) of the Northwest Boundary Survey.

---

118. Yi7íman Goat Mountain. **Map 5**

> **<Yi7íman>** or **<Yi7imán>** "Yeh-mann" (BS) or <Íman> "E-maan" (BS-Teosaluk). Probably [(yiʔ)ímæn] or [(yiʔ)imǽn] or [(y)imæn] or [(y)ɛmæn]; stress could be on the root or suffix. Prob. compare Nooksack root <im-> *step* (as in Nooksack <ímash> *walk;* Nooksack <-ash> *upright*) and suffix <-án> or <-an> *place,* thus <Íman> if the name Goat Mountain in English refers to there being many goats on the mountain, as goats are known for stepping and jumping carefully all around steep mountains and may also have been hunted there (a ***place to step***), or the mountain may have been a marker for a trail. If there was an initial <yi->, it would be Nooksack <yi-> *travelling by means of,* so <Yi7íman> or <Yi7imán> ***place for travelling by step***.

This mountain is located north of the North Fork to the east of Swamp Cr. "Yeh-mann" is clearly used to name Goat Mountain on the Boundary Survey manuscript map (Series 68, Folder 1, Map 1) and the final "Map of the Western Section" (Series 66), with the form "Yeman" being used to name Goat Mountain in Custer's field report (1859). One of the two Teosaluk maps (Series 69, Map 26) has "E-maan" in this general area. Goat Mountain is a prominent peak in the upper North Fork area, and is a likely place for hunting mountain goats.

118A. Yi7íman Ruth Creek. **Map 5**

> **<Yi7íman>** or **<Yi7imán>** "Yéman ~ Yehmáan" (BS-Custer). Same etymology as in place 118. The transcriptions here seem to show that the stress was on either vowel. Creeks were frequently named after the nearby mountain that they came from.

This major tributary of the upper North Fork flows between Goat Mountain and Mt. Sefrit. "Yéman" is used to name Ruth Cr. in Custer's field notebook (RG

76, E 202), and the form "Yehmáan" is applied to this creek on the field map (Series 69, Map 19-2).

---

119. Spelhpálhx̱(en) Bogs on the upper North Fork Nooksack River. **Map 5**

> "Spespaas ~ Spispach ~ Spispasch" (BS). Prob. has (*nominalizer*) and *plural (many)* reduplication. Most likely (esp. in light of the third BS form) **<Spelhpálhx̱>** from **<Spelhpálhx̱en>** ***many prairies/meadows*** with same etymology as place 112. Poss. instead, but much less likely (and with no confirmation from the location), compare Nooksack <spetspáts> *many bears* (and in Halkomelem-accented Nooksack <ts> ~ <ch> since these sounds vary freely in Upriver Halkomelem).

One of the Boundary Survey reconnaissance books (RG 76, E 202) states: "Name of 2 prairie like marshes Spispasch." The accompanying sketch map, reproduced here as Map 17, places these at the foot of Goat Mountain in the North Fork valley between Swamp Cr. and Ruth Cr. There are two open bogs in this area today. One of the Teosaluk maps (Series 69, Map 26) has "Spes-paas" for a lake, near a second lake, draining towards the Nooksack R., which can be interpreted as the same marshy areas, or possibly as Twin Lakes. "Spespaas" is used to name Swamp Cr. on the 1857-62 Boundary Survey manuscript map, although this is in conflict with other sources (see place 120).

---

120. Nuxwhóchem Swamp Creek. **Map 5**

> "Nuquoichum" (Baker 1900). Prob.**<Nuxwhóchem>** /noxʷ-hóčəm/ *always-water* or, much less likely, poss. root <qw'oy-> *die,* or <qwoy->, <kwoy->, or <kw'oy-> if such exist in Nooksack. Upriver Halkomelem has similar roots <qw'ey-> *shake* and <qwá:y> *scorched, blackened* as in <qwáychep> *red-hot ashes,* which itself may be the cognate to the place name if there had been forest fires near the creek and if the final "m" were mistranscribed for "p."

The published list of elevations along the 49th parallel (Baker 1900) includes the name "Nuquoichum" for a creek that is almost certainly Swamp Cr. Custer (1859) clearly names Swamp Cr. as "Naquoicha Creek," with two lakes at its

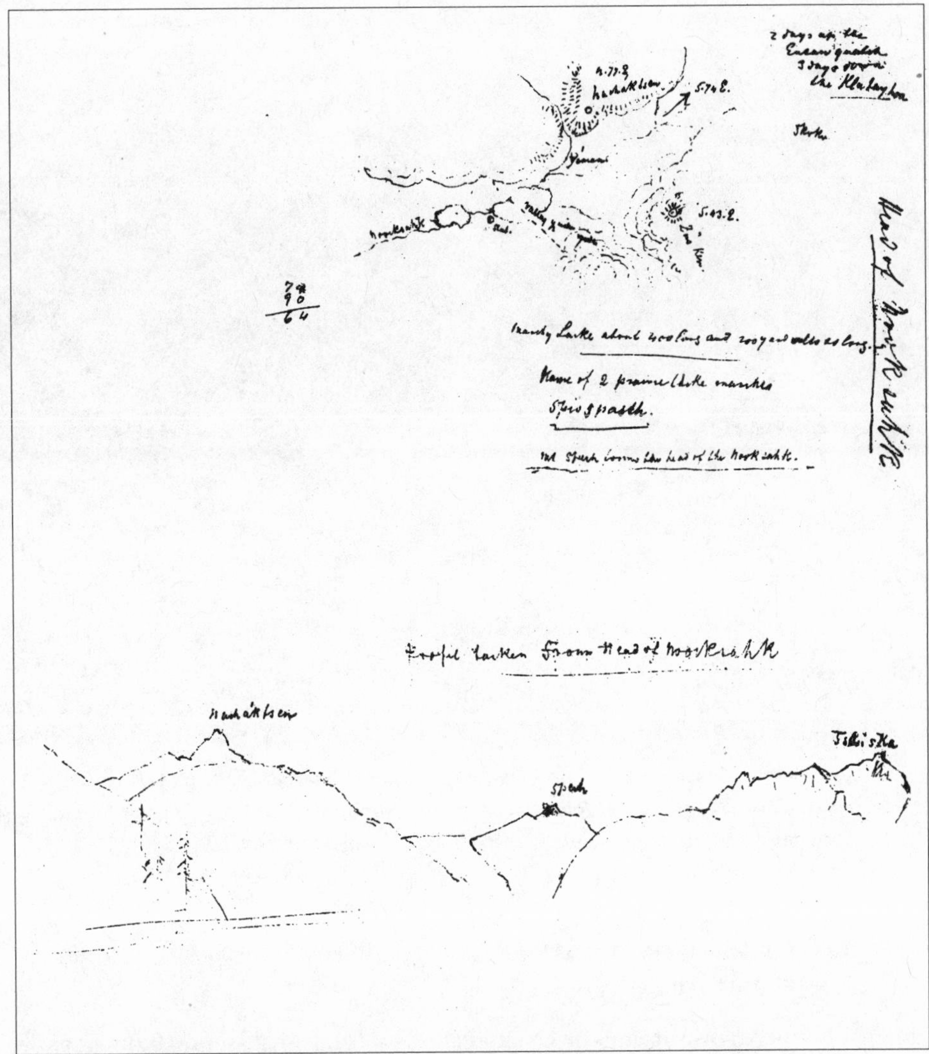

MAP 17 *"Head of Nooksahk" sketches of Henry Custer, June 1859, from his field notebook "Sketches and bearings taken during the Summer of 1859."* (United States Northwest Boundary Survey, RG 76, E 202: Reconnaissance Books, 1857-63)

headwaters on the divide between the Nooksack R. and Silesia Cr. drainages. This creek drains Twin Lakes and is a northerly tributary entering the North Fork ⅓ mile above the last Mt. Baker Highway bridge. The junction of Swamp Cr. and the North Fork is shown in Photo 32.

Photo 32 *Place 120 Nuxwhóchem (*always-water*), Swamp Creek, and place 121 Nuxwsx̲átsem (*always-lake-place*), North Fork Nooksack River above Swamp Creek. View southeast, upstream, with Swamp Creek entering river from left. 23 July 1981.* (Photo by B. Galloway)

121. Nuxwsx̲átsem (or Nuxwsx̲étsem) North Fork Nooksack River above Swamp Creek. **Map 5**

<**Nuxwsx̲átsem**> or <Nuxwsx̲étsem>, "Nuks-hah-sum" (BS), "Noots-háh-tsum" (BS-Teosaluk), "Ts-hah-sum" (BS). The name seems likely to be <Nuxwsx̲átsem> or <Nuxwsx̲átsam> /nox^{w}-s-x̣ácɛ-m/ or <nuxwsx̲áchu7m> /nox^{w}-s-x̣ǽčoʔ-m/ ***always-(nominalizer)-(little) lake-place to get*** from Nooksack /x̣ǽčoʔ/ <x̲ácho7> or Halkomelem /x̣ácɛ/ <x̲ótsa> *lake* or Halkomelem /x̣áx̣cɛ/ <x̲óx̲tsa> *little lake.* Another possible etymology is Nooksack *always-(nominalizer)-cold-place to get* from Nooksack <x̲étsem> *cold* plus the same prefixes and suffix <-em> *place to get.* This second etymology is possible on linguistic grounds, but doesn't make as much sense for the place named. The last

BS term, “Ts-hah-sum” could be <Tsx̲ó(x̲)tsem>, a triply Halkomelem-accented term meaning *place that has a little lake* or, without the second <x̲>, *place that has a lake.* It seems a bit vague as a literal meaning, and is also outweighed by the other two forms, the first of which was adopted on the official map of 1866.

The 1857-62 Boundary Survey manuscript map and map of the Western Section give the name “Nuks-hah-sum” to the portion of the North Fork above Swamp Cr., although the Teosaluk map (Series 69, Map 26) applies “Noots-háh-tsum” to a large creek draining the north side of Mt. Baker, possibly Wells Cr.–Bar Cr. A sketch map of unkown authorship (possibly Gibbs) found with the Boundary Survey materials (RG 76, E 223) uses “Ts-hah-sum” for a large stream draining into the North Fork northeast of Mt. Baker. The river bottom above Swamp Cr. has many sloughs and swampy areas (see place 119), and there are several mountain lakes in the North Fork headwaters, so either may be the source of the name based on the first etymology given above. For this etymology referring to lakes it seems more likely that “Nuks-hah-sum” is the upper North Fork, and not Wells-Bar Cr., which is a fast-running stream draining Mt. Baker.

---

122. Nexwx̲ex̲tsán Skagit Range, or possibly Mt. Sefrit. **Map 5**

“Nach-hahk-tsehn” (BS). Poss. <Nechx̲o̲x̲tsan> or more likely <Nexwx̲ax̲tsán> with prefix <nexw-> *always* + stem <xáxtso7> meaning *little lakes* + <-án> *place,* although this meaning is not attested for the place name. If the root instead were as in Nooksack <x̲étsem> *cold,* the name could be <**Nexwx̲ex̲tsán**> with reduplication infixed and mean *always cold place* (see place 121 also). This second meaning makes more sense for naming high mountains where there are no lakes.

Mt. Sefrit, a prominent peak south of Ruth Cr. in the upper North Fork Nooksack R. area, is clearly named “Nacháktsen” on two field sketches in a Boundary Survey reconnaissance book, “Season 1859 Book no. I” (RG 76, E 202). These sketches are included here as Map 17. Similarly, “Nach-hahk-tséhn” is used to name Mt. Sefrit in the “Profile taken from the head of Nooksahk River, June 1859, H. Custer” (Gibbs 1860). A later sketch in the same reconnaissance book uses “Nachaktsan” to name *both* Mt. Sefrit and the Skagit Range. In contrast, the Boundary Survey manuscript map places “Nach-hahk-tsehn” approximately in the area of the Skagit Range NE of Ruth Cr., with a similar placement for "Nach-ak-tsehhn" on Series 69, Map 19-2. This location is supported by the use of "Nachaktsen" for the West Fork of Silesia Cr. in Custer's field notebook "Sketches and bearings taken during the Summer of 1859," since the Skagit Range is located between upper Ruth Cr. (Nooksack drainage) and Silesia Cr. (Chilliwack drainage), and extends north between the forks of Silesia Cr.

122A. Spiw7x̲ Icy Peak, or possibly Ruth Mountain. Map 5

Prob. **<Spiw7x̲>** "Spech," "Spéh-uch" (BS). The etymology is unknown, although since Custer's native language was German, his "ch" often indicates a final Nooksack <x̲> instead of <ch>, and this would explain the "eh-uch" as a final [iᵊx̣] <-ix̲> or [íyəx̣] <-íyex̲>, or better yet /iwx̣/ <iwx̲>; the "p" could be either <p> or <p'>, but the initial "s" is probably Nooksack <s-> *nominalizer.* The most likely stem is Nooksack <spiw7> *ice* and the suffix is probably <-ix̲ ~ -x̲> *all around.* Thus, the Nooksack term for Icy Peak is probably <Spiw7x̲>, lit. ***ice all around.*** The English name notes the same feature of ice.

Boundary Survey sketch maps and profiles (RG 76, E 202), shown here as Map 17, clearly identify "Spech" as Icy Peak, directly at the head of the uppermost North Fork. The form "Spéh-uch" appears on the "Profile taken from head of Nooksahk River, June 1859, H. Custer" (Gibbs 1860). The related field report by Custer (1859) states that "Spech" lies in a triple divide, which would more correctly fit Ruth Mountain. The north and west slopes of Ruth Mountain drain into the Nooksack, the northeast slopes into the Chilliwack R., and the southeast slopes into tributaries of the Skagit R. Custer's report on his later explorations (also in 1859, but written up in 1866) uses "Spech" for Ruth Mountain, or at least a mountain he assumed was located in the triple divide when viewed from the east.

---

123. "Smámt-lek" Ruth Mountain and Nooksack Ridge. Map 5

"Smámt-lek" (BS), "Smám-at-lehk" (BS-Teosaluk). Poss. <Smámtl'eq> or <Smámatl'iq(')>, poss. root <mátl'> /mǽƛ'/ + infixed reduplication + poss. suffix <-eq> *male, penis;* poss. root cognate with Squamish /máƛ'/ *be dirty* and Upriver

Halkomelem <motl’> *blowing dirt or dust; stumped.* Or if the second <m> is a mistake for <n>, possibly <Smant-leq> with root Nooksack <smánit> *mountain* + <-le-> *plural* + <-eq> *penis,* after the shapes of the ridge tops, thus *many penis mountain.* Although Ruth Mountain is a simple smooth peak, Nooksack Ridge, which extends from Ruth Mountain to Mt. Sefrit, has a series of peaks.

This place name is shown on the Boundary Survey manuscript map roughly at the location of Ruth Mountain, and is listed in “Indian Nomenclature” (Gibbs 1857-61) as “Mtn between Chiloweyuk & Nooks.” It is also included on Teosaluk’s map (Series 69, Map 26) as “Smám-at-lehk,” located at the head of the upper Chilliwack R., which matches the location of Ruth Mountain. On the sketch map found with Gibbs’s “Indian Nomenclature” in RG 76, E 223, “Smamt-lek” is shown as a ridge going away from the drainage divide roughly in the location of Nooksack Ridge and Mt. Sefrit.

---

124. Shéqsan ~ Ch’ésqen Mt. Shuksan. **Map 5**

“T’shuskan” (BS), “Tschüska ~ Züs kan” (BS-Custer), “Tchús-kan” (BS-Teosaluk), “Shuk-san” (PJ), prob. <**Shéqsan**> /šə́q-sæn/ ~ /šə́q-sən/. Mt. Shuksan. PJ says it means *steep and rugged;* compare Lushootseed /šəq/ *high, up* (Upriver Halkomelem root /xiq-/ *lift up and out, squeeze up and out*) and /-səd ~ -šəd ~ -ša(·)d/ *foot, entire leg and foot* (/-sən, -šən, -ša(·)n/ in the 1850s before the sound shift of /n/ to /d/) (Hess 1976) (or the Nooksack cognate suffix, /-šən/ <-shen>; the Nooksack cognate would be similar, /šə́q-šən ~ šə́q-šæn/; /-šən/ could refer to *trail* (*on foot*), as in place 73 above (or <-shen> *foot* + <-an> *place,* with the second suffix automatically replacing the <en> in the previous suffix). If this etymology is correct, the place name would be more properly spelled <Shéqshan>. The BS forms are intriguing but do not fit the literal meaning that PJ got (steep and rugged). If the BS forms are right, the word would be something like <Ch’ísqen ~ Ts’ísqin ~ **Ch’ésqen** ~ Chésqen>; such a form is cognate to the word for *golden eagle* in closely related languages. Galloway’s *Dictionary of Upriver Halkomelem* (2009) has:

> <**ts’ésqel**>, ds //c’ə́s=qəl//, EZ [‘*golden eagle,*’ *Aquila chrysaetos*], lit. /‘(perhaps) black in the head’/, ASM [‘had a dark brown head (and

body) with a golden nape visible only at close range'], possibly root **<ts'és>** *dark brown, black* possibly root as in **<ts'ésqsel>** *"black-nose" or "smut" (a card game in which the nose is colored black on the loser),* lx **<=qel>** *in the head,* syntactic analysis: nominal, attested by Elders Group (6/4/75, 7/9/75, 2/18/76, 2/23/80), other sources: ES and JH /c'ə́sqəl/ (CwMs /c'ə́sqən/) *golden eagle,* Salish cognate: Squamish /č'ə́sqn/ *snow eagle, golden eagle,* Saanich /č'ə́sqən/ *golden eagle.*

If the Nooksack name meant *golden eagle,* it might refer to the mountain's appearance, with an eagle-like shape from some view and a dark brown top or dark brown parts. A possible solution to the two etymologies is to admit both: the *eagle* etymology for Nooksack and the *high foot* etymology for a Lushootseed name for it, perhaps also borrowed into Nooksack. (The steep slopes of Mt. Shuksan are seen in Photo 33, despite the cloud cover on the day of our visit.) The word for *golden eagle* is uncommon in Upriver Halkomelem and Nooksack; in both languages, *eagle* is more commonly known: Upriver Halkomelem has <yéx̲wela> and Nooksack has /yə́xʷəliʔ/ <yéxweli7> *eagle* (LT:SJ) and /yəxʷəléʔ/ <yexwelá7> *eagle (bald-headed or golden)* (LT or BE:LG).

The form "T'shuskan" is shown for Mt. Shuksan on the manuscript map (Series 68) and field map (Series 69, Map 19-2) of the 1857-62 Boundary Survey. The form "Tchós-kan" appears for Mt. Shuksan on one of the sketch maps by Teosaluk (Series 69, Map 26) and in one of the Boundary Survey reports (Custer 1859). The field materials of Henry Custer also include the forms "Tschüska" and "Züs Ken," both forms using his native German phonetics (Majors 1984, 72, 82). An original Nooksack name for Mt. Shuksan was apparently not recorded in the 20th century. Even so, Mt. Shuksan is considered to be within Nooksack territory, and was used as the easternmost point of the Nooksack land claim before the Indian Claims Commission in the early 1950s. The primary Nooksack use of the Mt. Shuksan area was for hunting.

---

125. Ts'éq Creek and fish camp at Acme. **Map 5**

<Ts'éq> [c'ə́k] (Smith 1950), [noxʷθ'ə́q] (PFM), [c'ə́q] (BG:SJ), /c'ə́q/. Probably a cognate with Lushootseed /c'əq/ *fermented*

Photo 33 *Place 124 Shéqsan (*high foot*) ~ Ch'ésqen (*golden eagle*), Mt. Shuksan. View from the north on White Salmon Road. 23 July 1981.* (Photo by B. Galloway)

> ***salmon eggs*** (GA), since there was a fish camp and these salmon eggs were probably made at the fish camp; the PFM variant has Nooksack prefix <noxw-> *always,* which would give a literal meaning of *always fermented salmon eggs;* the /Θ'/ <th'> is the Upriver Halkomelem equivalent and Halkomelem-accented Nooksack for /c'/ <ts'>.

According to Sindick Jimmy (BG:SJ), this name applies to a creek from the mountains that entered the South Fork Nooksack R. at Acme. The mouth there was washed away and the creek now enters the river above Acme; many fish ran up it, and it gave its name to the fish camp there. The creek that best fits this description is an unnamed creek entering the South Fork from the west at river mile 9, directly east of the centre of Acme. Ts'éq is considered to be a village only by Smith (1950, 339), who states: "ts'ʌk. At Acme. Both the village and creek which entered the Nooksack at this point bore the same name." A frequently used camp with a fish-drying house is a more likely interpretation based on other sources (see Richardson 1974, 66). An early historical observer travelling near here in August 1860 stated: "We passed an Indian habitation and a fish weir" (Lane 1860). The trail to L. Whatcom on the route to salt water began here (Wayne Suttles interview with George Swanaset, 26 April 1950). The form [NoxʷΘ'ά·q] appears on a map made to support the Nooksack land claim (Indian Claims Commission 1950). In the early 20th century, people camped a mile below Acme and across the river from Acme on trips to fish on the upper South Fork (GC, HP). The stretch of river near Acme was fished for spring salmon from jams with spears and dip nets.

---

126. Núx̱waymaltxw Camp at the mouth of Skookum Creek on the South Fork Nooksack River. **Map 5**

> <**Núx̱waymaltxw**> [nə́x̣ʷaymɛltxʷ] (WS:GS), prob. /nə́x̣ʷæy-m-æltxʷ/ or /nuxʷ-x̣ʷǽy-əm-æltxʷ/, [nə́x̣xʷəlmɛ́·ltxʷ] (PFM), [nəx̣ʷəmɛ́ltxʷ] (WS:GS, 26 April 1950). ***Slaughter-house*** from /nuxʷ-/ *always,* /x̣ʷæy/ *die together,* /-əm/ (*intransitivizer*), /-æltxʷ/ (*building, house*); the root also appears in /x̣ʷǽy-t/ *slaughter them [kill a group].* Smith (1950) reports it as a village, with a Skagit name [daxʷəbáltxʷ], where both Nooksacks and Skagits lived, above Acme (cf. Lushootseed /ʔu-x̣ʷája-t-əb/ *several families were slaughtered,* however, with root [x̣ʷádz(a)] /x̣ʷáj(a)-/).

This place name applies to the location at the mouth of Skookum Cr., according to M. Smith (1950; informant Jack Jimmy) and Jeffcott (1964, map; informant Lottie Tom?). Wayne Suttles's interview with George Swanaset (August 1958) includes the following: "[nə́x̣ʷaymɛltxʷ] (slaughter-house) a hunting camp of the [nəxʷ ʔíəm] people, toward Wickersham." This does not necessarily exclude the Skookum Cr. location, but does make the location of Núx̱waymaltxw uncertain. The mouth of Skookum Cr. was definitely an important camp area while people were fishing and drying spring salmon. In August 1860, F.F. Lane observed an "Indian encampment" in this area occupied by "about a dozen" people and containing "Indian lodges," including an "old winter house" (Lane 1860). The last item can be interpreted as a well-built cedar plank structure, not necessarily as evidence of winter occupation.

---

127. Lahíw7 Camp area and fishing site on the South Fork Nooksack River above Skookum Creek. **Map 5**

<Lahíw7> [læhíwʔ ~ letx̣éyuk'] (AR interview with Tom Williams, 12 June 1974). The shorter of these two names can probably be compared with Upriver Halkomelem <le> *he/they/it went* + <ahí:w> ***upstream***. The orthographic equivalent of the second phonetic transcription is <Litx̲éyuk'> but <k'> is not a native sound in Nooksack (so <Litx̲éyuq'> would be more likely) and the rounded vowel before it, <u>, probably reflects the rounding of the final consonant (to <qw'>); since the pronunciation of [e] and [ey] is a variety of Nooksack <i> /i/ or <ey> /əy/, either may be a possible spelling. Nooksack /i/ is also pronounced as [i^{yə}] before postvelars [q, q', qw, qw', x̲, and x̲w], and if the glottalization is in error, a suffix <-iqw> *top of head, hair, head of a river; fish* (as in Halkomelem <t'x̲emíqw> *six fish*) would yield <Litx̲iqw> or <Leytx̲iqw>; this seems likely since the site was a popular fishing site. The root could be Nooksack <lit-> (none found yet with this shape) with <-x̲> *all around* + <-iqw> *fish* or a root cognate with Halkomelem <t'ex̲> *to fork or branch, split unevenly* + <-iqw> *fish; head* but would require a prefix <li->, which we have not yet found in Nooksack , unless one cognate with Upriver Halkomelem <le-y-> *go by way of* (thus perhaps *go by way of a fork at the head*).

This place name was given only by Tom Williams (Richardson 1974, 67). The name was applied to an area along the northeast bank of the river ½ to 1¼ miles above Skookum Cr. where people camped and dried spring salmon, and also to the main fishing location in Dye's Canyon 1¾ miles above Skookum Cr. The fish were caught in the canyon with dip nets and spears, then taken to the scattered family camps downstream for butchering and drying. This spring salmon fishery took place in early to mid summer (around July), and included almost all of the Nooksack people. The fishing site is also known as Yúmechiy (place 128).

---

128. Yúmechiy Canyon in the South Fork Nooksack River where spring salmon were caught. **Map 5**

<Yúmechiy> [yúməči] /yóməč-iy/$_3$. ***Spring salmon-place.*** Same etymology as in place 32 and place 96.

This canyon, also known as Dye's Canyon, is 1¾ miles above Skookum Cr. at Mile 16 of the South Fork Nooksack R. (US Geological Survey map). It was the most important fishing location for spring salmon, and perhaps the most important of all Nooksack fishing locations (see place 127 Lahíw7). The South Fork is very narrow here, with rocks suitable for fishing. The "Mother Salmon" lived in a cave in this canyon, and was seen here by Sindick Jimmy's grandfather (Richardson 1974, 67).

128A. Upper reaches of the South Fork Nooksack River. **Map 5**

No distinct place name for this area is known, although it is a distinct area for resource exploitation. The South Fork as far as 15 miles above Skookum Cr. (possibly to Mile 30 of the South Fork on US Geological Survey maps) was an important fishing area. For some families, this was a preferred area for catching spring salmon, as the meat of the fish was less oily and more easily dried and stored for winter use (Sindick Jimmy, in Richardson 1974, 67). In 1860, the F.F. Lane party travelled the South Fork above the canyons and "reached an old house or shed of Indian construction, where Indians formerly had stopped" (Lane 1860). A camp was located at the mouth of Howard (Sisters) Cr. for use as a base camp on hunting trips on the slopes of the Twin Sisters Mountain. The upper South Fork was also fished by the nearby Upper Skagit people, with hunting on the Twin Sisters perhaps more limited to just Nooksack people.

---

129. Kwetl'kwítl' Smánit Twin Sisters Mountain. **Map 5**

<**Kwetl'kwítl' Smánit**> "Quik-quek Sman-ik" (PJ), [kʷə́ƛ' smǽnit] (BG:LG or EF), Halkomelem [ckʷím smǽ·lt], Nooksack poss. /kʷə́ƛ' smǽnit/ or prob. /kʷəƛ'kʷíƛ' smǽnit/. ***Red mountain*** (in both languages) because of its red appearance in summer, when the snow is gone; from Nooksack /kʷəƛ'kʷíƛ'/ *red, brown* and /smǽnit/ *mountain*.

This mountain (actually a six-mile-long ridge with two prominent peaks at the northwest end) is visible from most of the Nooksack area, and is second only to Mt. Baker in importance as a geographic feature and mountain resource area. It is said to be the wife of Mt. Baker. Animals hunted on the slopes of the Twin Sisters included bear, deer, elk, and mountain goat, with the meat cut into strips and wind dried while on the mountain (Tom Williams, in Richardson 1974, 67). Mountain goats were the most important because of the high value placed on their wool. Berries were also picked and dried in this mountain area.

129A. Samish River at Wickersham. **Map 5**

The Nooksack camped and built fish traps on the uppermost part of the Samish R. at Wickersham, a location on the trail from the South Fork to L. Whatcom, and also convenient for travel to and from the Skagit R. (Richardson 1974, 69). Paul Fetzer shows a fish trap here on his manuscript map. This location is close to Nuwhaha territory, which includes nearly all of the Samish River drainage.

---

130. X̱achu7ámish Village at the upper, southeast end of Lake Whatcom. **Map 5**

> <**X̱achu7ámix**> [x̣εčuέ·mɪx^{y}] (PF), [x̣ačuέ·mɪx^{y}] (PFM), [x̣ačuʔǽmɪx^{y}] (WS:GS; BG:LG), Skagit [sx̣ačuʔábš] (BG:LG), Nooksack prob. <**X̱achu7ámish**> /x̣æčoʔ-ǽmiš/. ***Lake-people*** from /x̣ǽčoʔ/ *lake;* [ǽmix^{y}] resembles Halkomelem /-á·məx^{y}/ *in appearance,* but the latter is cognate with Nooksack /-ómiš/ as in [qələɬó·mɪš] /qəl-əɬ-ómiš/ *ugly, bad-looking;* Skagit /-ábš/ *people* corresponds to Nooksack /-ǽmiš/, although Nooksack also has /-mix^{w}/ *people, person.*

This village was located near the site of the town of Park, probably at the mouth of the creek draining Mirror L. People from other Nooksack villages kept canoes here, which they used to travel the 12 miles to the lower end of the lake on trips to salt water. This village was only loosely affiliated with other Nooksack villages, and in some sources is considered a small independent "tribe" (Richardson 1974, 69; Fitzhugh 1858, 329). X̱achu7ámish was perhaps as closely tied to the Nuwhaha (Samish R.) people as to the Nooksack. "On Lake Whatcom were the 'Lake People,' a mixed Nooksack-Nuwhaha group" (Suttles 1954, 52). People were definitely living somewhere on L. Whatcom in the 1850s (Fitzhugh 1858, 329), although there is no evidence of occupation later in the 19th century. X̱achu7ámish is the only known settlement on L. Whatcom, and therefore was last occupied around 1860. In 1858, Henry Custer of the Northwest Boundary Survey encountered *one* Indian man living at the lake, who assisted the team in their surveys. The Boundary Survey field map (Series 69, unidentified map in folder following Map 76) shows a building ½ mile NW of a creek mouth at the SE corner of the lake, thus near the historic town of Blue Canyon. The survey team also found "an old deserted Indian hut made of split boards" on the SW shore of the lake (Custer 1858b).

130A. Lake Whatcom. **Map 5**

The Lhéchelesem name of L. Whatcom is uncertain, although the creek name X̱wó̱tqwem may have been used (see place 133). L. Whatcom was most important to the Nooksack as a route of travel to saltwater locations (see place 130). The lake also was fished for "silvers," landlocked sockeye the size of trout, called <óyqs> in Skagit (LG). These fish were caught at spawning time in the lake along the bank using traps with guides to lead fish into the trap (AR interview with Joe Louie, 31 July 1975). The 1857-62 Boundary Survey manuscript map shows a trail from the mouth of Anderson Cr. (place 78 Nuxwsá7aq) to L. Whatcom at Agate Bay on the north shore, and continuing to the town of Whatcom. The field map (Series 69, unidentified) shows just the portion coming to Agate Bay. Henry Custer travelled on this trail on 20 June 1858, and found it to be "a very rough and indistinct one difficult and tiresome to follow" (Custer 1858b). This trail would have provided another access route to salt water and to L. Whatcom for fishing or other purposes.

130B. Camp at the northwest end of Lake Whatcom. **Map 5**

This camp was used on trips to salt water, but the name and exact location are not known. "There were smokehouses at the lower end of the lake ... handy to the trail to Chuckanut" (Wayne Suttles interview with George Swanaset, 26 April 1950). Canoes were stored at this camp during trips to Chuckanut (Richardson 1974, 69). The probable location of this camp is at the outlet of L. Whatcom into Whatcom Cr., now within the city of Bellingham. Some of the Boundary Survey maps show a trail from L. Whatcom to the town of Whatcom on the north side of Whatcom Cr., although the survey team found it rough and hard to follow (Custer 1858b).

---

131. Ch'ínukw' Toad Lake. **Map 5**

<Ch'ínukw'> [č'ínʊk'ʷ] (BG:EF), /č'ínok'ʷ/ ***Thunderbird*** from Nooksack [čínʊk'ʷ] *thunderbird* (BG:EF); also cf. Skagit [sč'ídək'ʷ] *thunderbird* (BG:LG).

PHOTO 34 *Place 131 Ch'ínukw'* (thunderbird), *Toad Lake, an isolated lake north of Lake Whatcom. 3 October 1981.* (Photo by B. Galloway)

This lake, located 1½ miles north of the lower, northwest end of L. Whatcom, drains into Squalicum Cr. Toad L., also called Emerald L., is ½ mile long and ⅛ mile wide, located in an isolated area and surrounded by steep hillsides, as can be seen in Photo 34. No specific Nooksack use of this lake is recorded, although the name suggests religious beliefs and possibly religious practices related to the lake.

131A. X̲alachiséy or X̲aláchisey Squalicum Lake. **Map 12**

"Cälläshesey" (BS-Custer). "Cälläshesey" can be interpreted phonetically in a number of ways, but Custer probably used the German orthography <ä> here for the sound as in English "ash," written in Nooksack as <a>; a plain <c> could be Nooksack <q> or <x̲>, so the most likely possibilities are <Qalashesey> or

<Qalachisey> or <X̲alashesẹy> or <**X̲aláchisey**> or <X̲alachiséy>. There is a note that this is a "little cranberry marsh," but it is unclear whether this is a description of the lake or a semi-literal interpretation of the name. However, Nooksack <x̲ala-> ***mark, write*** + <-chis> ***on the hand*** + <-ey> ***place*** would account nicely for the description, lit. ***mark on the hand place*** if it referred to cranberry stains on the hands from picking them (cranberry juice is well known for leaving stains). The stress is probably on the last suffix (as in place 19 and place 46), but could also be on the second syllable (less likely on the first, and not possible on the third since the form of the suffix would be one that would be transcribed by Boundary Survey personnel as "chees" rather than "ches"). The possible forms with <Q> or <sh> are less likely, since no possible etymologies have been found for them so far.

This lake is the headwaters of Squalicum Cr., which drains directly to Bellingham Bay. The lake is near a low pass between the Anderson Cr. drainage and L. Whatcom, and was visited by Henry Custer while he was travelling on the trail following this route (see place 130A). Custer's 1858 reconnaissance book, "Reconnaissances Fort Langley trail, Trip to Sumass Whatcomb Lake & Whatcom trail 1859 [sic]" (RG 76, E 202) includes the following: "Cälläshesey, name of Lake/little cranberry Marsh." One of the Nooksack elders (GC) had heard a Lhéchelesem name for Squalicum L. but was unable to remember it.

---

132. Chúkwenet Chuckanut Creek and camp located at the mouth of Chuckanut Creek. **Map 5**

<**Chúkwenet ~ Chúkwenets**> [čə́kʷənəcʼ] (PFM), [čúkʷənət] (BG:SJ), poss. ~ [čúkʷənəc] (BG:SJ), prob. <Chúkwenet> /čókʷ-ənət/, poss. <Chúkwenech> /čókʷ-ənəč/ or <Chúkwenets> /čókʷənəc/. ***Beach or tide goes way out*** from /čókʷ/ *be distant, far away;* /-ənəč/, if correct, would be *(at the) bottom.* Said to be a Nooksack language term meaning *little bay* (Nooksack Tribe of Indians, 1924, 54; see the quote under place 133); this makes the above interpretation most likely. Suttles recently (2005, shortly before his death) proposed an alternative analysis, with the word being in Northern Straits Salish and the root <cheqw> meaning *burn* (cognate with

Photo 35 *Place 132 Chúkwenet (*beach or tide goes way out*), Chuckanut Bay with camp location in centre near houses. The creek mouth is just beyond the houses. 11 September 1980.* (Photo by B. Galloway)

> Nooksack and Halkomelem <yeqw> *burn*) that would yield a spelling <Chéqwenet(s)>; both may have existed.

This was the most important Nooksack camp used during clam digging, gathering of other shellfish, and saltwater fishing (Richardson 1974, 69). The camp location is at the north end of Chuckanut Bay at the mouth of Chuckanut Cr., in a neighbourhood of Bellingham known as Chuckanut Village, the area shown in Photo 35. There is a shell midden on the north side of the creek mouth close to the bay, and another midden south of the creek mouth on higher ground. Nooksack use of this area was limited after around 1900 until the increase in saltwater fishing under the 1974 Boldt Decision, *United States v. Washington,* 384 F.Supp. 312 (W.D. Wash. 1974), which set Washington Indian fishing quotas as up to 50% of all fish harvested.

132A. Samish Bay. **Map 5**

The shoreline of Samish Bay from Chuckanut Bay to Samish Island was used to a limited extent by the Nooksack for clam digging and fishing (Richardson 1974, 69). This area would mostly be considered the territory of the Samish or the Nuwhaha (Suttles 1951, 5, 42). No Lhéchelesem name is known for Samish Bay.

132B. Xwsísel7echem Fairhaven and possibly Padden Creek. **Map 5**

This place name, [xʷsísəl'əč əm], is in Suttles's notes under a list of Lummi place names, and he notes that it comes from <sí7lich> ***find salvage, as a drifted canoe.*** This etymology seems quite firm for the root. Although this seems similar to the root in place 135F, it is probably a different root, with a glottalized <l'> or <l7> in the root. The prefix is as in Nooksack <(no)xw-> *always, people of;* the first suffix is cognate with Nooksack <-ich> and Halkomelem <-ech> ***in back,*** and the suffix is cognate with Nooksack and Halkomelem <-em> ***place, place to get.*** Confirming that this is a Straits name (or Straits version of the name) is the fact that there is an infix <-se-> meaning ***(continuative aspect), -ing,*** which Nooksack lacks; also confirming that this is a Straits name instead of a Nooksack name is the Nooksack cognate, given in the Halkomelem-accented form by George Swanaset to Paul Fetzer (NKF 2.1529), [θí·lec] (<thí:lats>) *to find* and plural [θəlθí·lɛc] (<thelthí:lats>) *to find many things;* the less accented forms would be Nooksack <tsí7lech> and <tseltsí7lach>. Thus, the literal meaning of the place name is ***place of always finding salvage in the back (e.g., as of finding a drifted canoe).*** Another attestation of this place name is by Dora Solomon, who gave it as a Lummi name, [xʷsísəlʼčəm] <Xwsísel7chem>; this is reported by George Adams, whose first wife was a granddaughter of Dora Solomon.

The following summary regarding Xwsísel7echem is based on notes compiled by Wayne Suttles (unpublished materials):

> August Martin said there was a little creek here, whose name he didn't know; it runs up to the Larrabee school. Lummi lived around here in summer, but it's too rough and wild in winter. Dan Harris also lived around here. August also didn't know the name of

> Padden Lake and couldn’t say who owned it. But the Lummi used to fish the mouth with harpoons and gaff at low tide for dog salmon only. J.P. Harrington gives [xʷsísiličam] as *West Bellingham.* Gibbs 1863 gives “Sis´lit-chum” as the *Thomas claim.*

This place name was used for the site of the historic town of Fairhaven (now part of Bellingham) and possibly for Padden Cr., which enters Bellingham Bay at Fairhaven. Xwsísel7echem is in the area that the Nooksack people used on visits to salt water, but it has not been confirmed as a Nooksack name. Early historical records include the forms “Sis´lit-chu̲m”(Gibbs 1863) and “Sus-lichm” (Series 69, Map 12-2, Northwest Boundary Survey).

---

133. X̲wó̲tqwem Whatcom Creek and camp at mouth of Whatcom Creek. **Map 5**

> <**Xwó̲tqwem ~ X̲wó̲tqwem**> [x̣ʷá·tkʷəm] (PF), [x̣ʷát’qʷʊm] (PFM), [xʷá·tqʷəm ~ x̣ʷá·tqʷəm] (BG:LG, BG:EF, others), /xʷátqʷəm ~ x̣ʷátqʷəm/ ***sound of water splashing or dripping fast and hard*** (= Nooksack [xʷá·tqʷəm ~ x̣ʷá·tqʷəm] *sound of water splashing or dripping fast and hard*); cf. also Halkomelem /xʷátqʷəm/ *sound of water splashing or dripping fast (loud waterfall or hard rain)* and Lummi (GA) <x̲wót’qwem> [x̣ʷát’qʷəm] *bubbling, sizzling, fizzing,* possible connection with Lushootseed root /xʷít’- ~ xʷt’-/ *fall/drop from a height* as in /s-xʷət’/ *waterfall* and /ʔu-xʷít’-il/ *fall (from a high place).* Hess 1976, 564, gives a possible connection with Sechelt and Mainland Comox /x̣ʷax̣ʷát’q’ím/ *thunderstorm?* The Nooksack <o̲> (instead of <o>) is probably Halkomelem and Straits influence (since */u/ from their parent language has become /a/ in both but lowered to /o/ in Nooksack [with [u ~ o] allophones]); the Lummi, Lushootseed, and PFM attest to a possible <t’> in the place name instead of plain <t>, although all other attestations give <t>.

Whatcom Cr. drains L. Whatcom and has a series of falls near the lake and falls again at its mouth above tidewater, which are shown in Photo 36. The area on the northwest side of the mouth of the creek was the location of a Nooksack camp, with a house used by people getting saltwater foods (Wayne Suttles interview of Agnes James, 13 August 1952). This was the base for fishing and shellfish gathering on Bellingham Bay (Richardson 1974, 70). X̲wó̲tqwem was reached by way of the lower river, from L. Whatcom, or by the trail from place

54 Kwánech (see place 51 Nek’iyéy). The importance of this overland route was emphasized in a petition to the United States Congress in 1924 (Nooksack Tribe of Indians 1924, 54):

> Where the city of Bellingham now is there was a place where the Nooksacks used to reach the salt water from the camps upon the Nooksack River, a trail coming out at Whatcom, which in the Nooksack tongue means falling water. From this point they used to go down the beach at Chuckanut which is a Nooksack word meaning Little Bay. At Chuckanut and at Whatcom they used to dig clams, which they likewise dried and which kept indefinitely for food.

The town of Whatcom was established on the same site in 1852, using an Anglicized version of the Indian name. The area of the early town of Whatcom is now known as “Old Town” Bellingham. The site of the original X̲wó̲tqwem is within or near the block bounded by D, E, Astor, and Bancroft Streets.

133A. Bellingham Bay. Map 5

Areas on the north and east shores of Bellingham Bay, especially near X̲wó̲tqwem (place 133), were frequently used by the Nooksack, primarily for clam digging. Despite this use of the area, no Lhéchelesem name for Bellingham Bay has been recorded.

---

134. Nuxwkw’ól7exwem Squalicum Creek. Map 6

<Nuxwkw’ól7exwem> “No-cal-la-chum” (BS), “Squall-i-cum” (PJ), Lummi [xʷkʼʷálʔəxʷəm] (Suttles 1951, 39), prob. Nooksack <Nuxwkw’ól7exwem ~ xwkw’ól7exwem ~ skw’ó̲l7exwem> /noxʷ-kʼʷólʔəxʷ-əm ~ xʷ-kʼʷólʔəxʷ-əm ~ s-kʼʷálʔəxʷ-əm/. ***Always-dog salmon-place to get*** in both Nooksack and Lummi; the Lummi is poss. borrowed from the Nooksack name because originally the Lummis did not occupy the mainland. From Nooksack <nuxw-> *always* + <kw’ól7exw> *dog salmon* + <-em> *place to get.*

This creek, which enters Bellingham Bay about 1½ miles NW of Whatcom Cr. and drains a large area north of L. Whatcom, was fished for dog salmon by the Nooksack. The trail from Kwánech to X̲wó̲tqwem via Ten Mile Prairie (see place 51 Nek’iyéy) crossed Nuxwkw’ól7exwem about 1¾ miles above its mouth at a small falls. These falls are east of Meridian Street in Cornwall Park,

Photo 36 *Place 133 X̲wó̲tqwem (*sound of water splashing or dripping fast and hard*), Whatcom Creek with falls at its mouth, source of the word "Whatcom." 11 September 1980.* (Photo by B. Galloway)

Bellingham, where the creek drops over a sandstone outcrop with a fall of about three feet. The Telegraph Road, which was constructed along the route of the Indian trail, crossed Squalicum Cr. here, according to a plaque at the site and Jeffcott (1949, 197-99). Jeffcott (1949, 197-98) also mentions Indian dog salmon fishing at the Squalicum Cr. falls. Considering the trail location and the preference for falls as fishing sites, this is the most likely site used by the Nooksack.

---

135. Tl'aqatínus Prairie and bluff at Fort Bellingham. **Map 6**

> **<Tl'aqatínus>** ~ <Tl'eq(a)tínes> "Klik-a-téh-nus ~ Klik-a-tin-us" (BS). The root could be Nooksack /ƛ̓ǽqæt/ <tl'áqat> *long,* but the etymology is uncertain. Prob. <Tl'eqtínes ~ Tl'aqatínus> with <-ínwes ~ -ínus ~ -ínes> *chest,* i.e., *long chest* (the suffix can also mean *bluff* when applied to land features, i.e., ***long bluff***), although there is no literal meaning given in the documents. A root <tl'iq> or <tl'iq'> is also possible if it exists in Nooksack. Lummi has a version of this name, <Tl'eqtínes>.

This place name is found in two places in the 1857-62 Boundary Survey records: in "Indian Nomenclature" (Gibbs 1857-61), it is listed as "Prairie at Military Station" and is placed on the manuscript map between the mouth of the Nooksack R. and the town of Whatcom. Another Gibbs place name listing (Gibbs 1853?) includes: "Klik-a-teh-nus – Prairie at the Mily. Station." The only military station in the area was Fort Bellingham, established in 1856 close to the bluff (the chest?) overlooking Bellingham Bay 3½ miles NW of Whatcom on "the only open land in the area" (Edson 1968, 58). The Howard E. Buswell Collection at the Center for Pacific Northwest Studies, Western Washington University, Bellingham, includes a listing of Lummi place names with the variants "Kluk-tin-us" and "Click-a-tin-us" for the Fort Bellingham prairie (Box 6, Folder 2). This prairie is indicated today by an area of rich dark soil surrounding the Fort Bellingham site, which is occupied by Smith Gardens, a commercial nursery. George Adams heard this name referring to the bluff from Lummi elders Agatha McCluskey and Al Charles.

135A. Xw7élhqoyem Sq'eláxen name for camp at Lummi. **Map 6**

> **<Xw7élhqoyem>**, /xwʔə́łqayəm/ (Suttles 1951). Nooksack has prefix /xw-/ <xw-> *always,* root /ʔə́łqæy/ <7élhqay> *snake,* and suffix /-əm/ <-em> *place to get,* which give the etymology

meaning ***place where there's always snakes.*** The only difference between the form Suttles gives and the Nooksack pronunciation is the Sq'eláx̱en second vowel /a/, which in Nooksack would be transcribed as /a/ <o̱> since Nooksack has /æ/ <a> in the word for snake, not /a/ <o̱>, a sound largely absent from Nooksack except for Halkomelem-accented varieties. In the purer Nooksack varieties, /o/ <o> occurs, corresponding to this sound in most words. This difference may be a clue as to whether the Sq'eláx̱en language was closer to or was a variety of Straits or Lushootseed, or something different.

The Nooksack had a stopover camp at the Bellingham Bay mouth of the river, "at Lummi," which they used when travelling to and from saltwater locations (Richardson 1974, 70). The location of this camp is uncertain, although at or north of Fish Point on the west side of the delta is a good possibility. The Sq'eláx̱en village of Xw7élhqo̱yem (*place where there's always snakes*), occupied prior to 1820, was located just north of Fish Point (Suttles 1951, 39-40), and in 1861 "Old Lummi Village" was established on the same site (Suttles 1954, 58-60). Nooksack use of this site would have been between the times of these two non-Nooksack occupations. There is uncertainty about Nooksack access to the entire river mouth area at the time the Sq'eláx̱en villages were occupied, especially considering the emphasis placed on use of the L. Whatcom route and the overland trail to salt water. Beginning around 1820 and continuing after 1861, the Nooksack travelled to Bellingham Bay via the lower river. After 1861, a camp at the mouth of the river would probably have been away from "Old Lummi Village," perhaps near the present Lummi church or near Marietta, on the east side of the delta.

135B. Nuxws7áx̱wom Cherry Point. Map 5

"Nook-sack-um" (PJ). Most likely <**Nuxws7áx̱wom**> ***place to always get butter clams,*** from <nuxw- ~ noxw- ~ nexw-> ***always*** and stem <s-7áx̱wo> ***butter clam(s)*** and ending with <=em ~ m> ***place to have or get.*** The form "Nook-sack-um" is from Jeffcott (1949, 55; 1964, map) and is Nooksack (since the vowel is wrong for the word for "butter clams" in Lummi), although Jeffcott states: "NOOK-SACK-UM – the Lummi name for Cherry Point" (1949, 55). George Swanaset Sr. stated: "I thought he meant that place right there ... they called it 'Nooksack' ... It was told to my father Dan Swanaset from his father George Swanaset" (AR

> interview with George Swanaset Sr., 29 May 1997; Sr. is needed since the grandson uses it to distinguish himself from his son, George Swanaset Jr.). The Boundary Survey manuscript map, which has Straits Salish forms for nearby locations, has "Pt. Hul-léch-tan" for Cherry Point (compare Nooksack <x̲el> *mark, write, paint,* + <-ex̲> *all around,* + <-tan> *device, something that is,* thus **<X̲eléx̲tan>** ***something marked/painted all around***); whereas a recent Lummi source shows the name for Cherry Point in the Lummi language as [čiəx̣əm] (Nugent 1980, 36) (compare Lummi <chix̲> ***red elderberries*** (GA) + <-em> ***place to get***), thus **<Chíx̲em>** ***place to get red elderberries*** (using the Nooksack orthographic equivalent for the Lummi name).

The Nooksack had a camp above the beach to the east of Cherry Point, west of Gulf Road. According to George Swanaset Sr., tidal traps were constructed here to capture crabs, clams were dug, and fish were caught (AR interview with George Swanaset Sr., 29 May 1997). The large and rich archeological site 45WH1 is also located just east of Cherry Point.

135C. Shts'á7wex̲ [N. Straits Salish] Birch Bay and location on the south side of the bay. **Map 5**

> **<Shts'á7wex̲>** [N. Straits Salish]. This name for Birch Bay is based on Suttles (1951, 32) and appears to be the same as "Tsaó-wuch" on the 1857-62 Boundary Survey manuscript map. Compare Lummi <sts'á7wex̲> *rafted canoes* (GA), since Semiahmoo and Lummi are both dialects of Northern Straits Salish. In notes on Semiahmoo place names compiled by Wayne Suttles in the late 1940s and early 1950s, [šcʼə́ʔwəx̌] (= our <Shts'á7wex̲>) meant ***quaking bog*** and was a site on Birch Bay, according to Julius Charles, and was noted by Gibbs as what we would write as <Sts'á7wex̲> and by John P. Harrington as what we would write as <Lhts'á7wex̲>, the site of the village of the <X̲elxwéleqw> people. Gibbs (1863) has "Tsáu-wukh. Site on Birch Bay."

Birch Bay is within traditional Semiahmoo territory and was probably rarely used in early times by the Nooksack, except by families with Semiahmoo relatives. Birch Bay was the location of one or more Semiahmoo villages that were occupied until around 1850 (Suttles 1951, 29, 31). Notes found with the "Map of Lummi Territory" in exhibits A-2 and D-2 from a 1927 US Court of Claims case, *Duwamish et al. v. United States of America* (79 C. Cls. 530), list three villages on Birch Bay (Tsa-wock, on the south side of the bay where Terrell Cr. comes out of the uplands; She-kwan, in the middle of the bay near the corner of Alderson Road and Birch Bay Drive; and Mum-ma-lackan, on the north side of the bay at Cottonwood Beach). Shellfish gathering and fishing at Birch Bay were important to the Nooksack in the late 19th and early 20th centuries (Richardson 1974, 70). Clam digging by Nooksacks at Birch Bay is attested to by local historians R.E. Hawley (1971, 35) and P.R. Jeffcott (1964, 65 and map), with an established trail from the Nooksack R. at the mouth of Bertrand Cr. Jeffcott states (1964, 65): "This might well have been called the clam trail, for every year, in the summer, the Nooksacks trod that route to dig and dry their winter supply of the big clams, so prevalent in the tide flats at that location. There, they occupied two villages during the claming [sic] season, known as Quahn, on the north side of the Bay, and Mo-loc-a-na on the south side."

Jeffcott's place names correspond to place 135D and place 135E, but the locations are incorrect. The location for Shts'á7wex̱ on the south side of the bay where Terrell Cr. comes out of the uplands is within Birch Bay State Park and is an archeological site designated as 45WH009.

135D. Shkw'em Camp location on Birch Bay at the mouth of Terrell Creek, and Terrell Creek. **Map 5**

> Jeffcott gives "Quahn," but a more accurate version appears in the notes of Wayne Suttles. If the Jeffcott spelling were accurate, one might compare Nooksack <qwá7an> /qwǽʔæn/ *mosquito* and Lummi <qwó̱7o̱n> /qwáʔan/ *mosquito*, since there are swamps nearby. The notes found with the "Map of Lummi Territory" in exhibits A-2 and D-2 from the 1927 US Court of Claims case *Duwamish et al. v. United States of America* list She-kwan, as a village on the middle, east side of the bay. If the final "n" in "She-kwan" were a misreading for "m," the name would be "She-kwam," which would be similar to a Semiahmoo name for Terrell Cr. given by Julius Charles to Suttles as what would be in Nooksack orthography <Sqwém>, said to mean lit. ***swim;*** Suttles, however, follows this with [šk'ʷəm], <shkw'ém> in the Nooksack orthography, and puts a question mark after it, explaining that the name of the place comes from a word meaning *swim:* "The name comes from the fact that some

children were once swimming here when they were caught by the ogress [c'əw'x̌éləč]" <Ts'ew'x̲álech>. "She carried them off in a basket on her back, roasted them, and ate them (Julius Charles)." The Nooksack word for ***swim*** is attested as **<shkw'em>** by George Swanaset in the card files of Paul Fetzer (PF:GS, NKF 2.192), which matches the form exactly. A form in Nooksack ending in /-an/ is possible if <-an> *place to* replaces the suffix <-em> 'intransitive', on root <shekw'- ~ shkw'-> 'swim', yielding a Nooksack form <Shkw'an> *place to swim*. The Lummi and Saanich form for *bathe* is [sák'ʷəŋ] (<sókw'eng> in the Nooksack orthography); this last form is a poor match for the place name, which shows that the name may be a Nooksack-language name as well as a Semiahmoo name.

This name refers to a camp used while digging clams, located on the north side of the bay, according to Jeffcott (1964, 65 and map); see place 135C. All other sources locate this place to the south. The Boundary Survey manuscript map has "Shkwaán Cr" for Terrell Cr. Similarly, Suttles's field notes have [sqwəm] for Terrell Cr. The "Map of Lummi Territory" has "She-kwan" as a village located at the mouth of Terrell Cr. on the east side of the bay. This is near the corner of Alderson Road and Birch Bay Drive, where the archeological site 45WH010 is located.

135E. Meláx̲en Camp location on the north side of Birch Bay. **Map 5**

Jeffcott has "Mo-loc-a-na"; notes found with the "Map of Lummi Territory" in exhibits A-2 and D-2 from the 1927 US Court of Claims case *Duwamish et al. v. United States of America* list "Mum-ma-lackan" as a village on the north side of the bay. The most accurate rendition of this place name is given in the Semiahmoo place names compiled by Wayne Suttles, as [məléx̌ən] (**<Meláx̲en>** in our Nooksack orthography, for comparison). The names of Lucy Celestine and her sister came from there, according to Lucy. Perhaps compare cognates with Upriver Halkomelem root <mel- ~ mal- ~ mol-> ***mixed up*** or the root in Nooksack <malaq-nít> *forget* + Nooksack <-eláx̲en> *arm, wing, enclosure, side*. This version of the name might mean ***mixed up enclosure, mixed up side;*** if so, the name could have arisen through a mixture of peoples or of languages spoken at the camp by clam diggers, but there is no confirmation of this theory. The version from the 1927 map, “Mum-ma-lackan,” confirms the suffix and has reduplication of the root, and so would be <Memeláx̱en>, with *continuative aspect (-ing)* (if Semiahmoo or Halkkomelem) or *diminutive plural* (if Semiahmoo, Nooksack, or Halkomelem). The literal meaning of such a name in Halkomelem would be *mixing up enclosure/side* or, more likely, ***little mixed up enclosures.*** If the Jeffcott rendering were more accurate, the root could be as in Nooksack <malaq-> instead, and the suffix could be Nooksack <-an7 ~ -ani7 ~ -ana7> *ear* (and if <-an7> there is still room for the final suffix <-ey ~ -iy> *place*), i.e., in Nooksack it could be *forget in the ear place,* referring perhaps to the same idea of language mixture of the clam diggers. Jeffcott's transcriptions are the least accurate in most cases, however, and the Suttles transcriptions are usually the most accurate of all transcriptions before 1960.

This was a camp used while digging clams, located on the south side of the bay, according to Jeffcott (1964, 65 and map); see place 135C. The “Map of Lummi Territory” shows a village of “Mum-ma-lacken” on the north side of the bay in the area of Cottonwood Beach. Suttles's field notes include “məléx̌ən. The Semiahmoo village on Birch Bay nearest Blaine.” This could be the same location, but other possibilities should be considered, since no archeological materials are known at Cottonwood Beach. Further to the west, in the area of Birch Bay Village, is a large, deep archeological site, 45WH011. A shallow site, 45WH067, is located to the southeast, south of where Harbor View Road reaches the bay (Alfred Reid, personal communication).

135F. S7ílich [N. Straits Salish] The butt or bluff of Semiahmoo Spit. **Map 5**

<S7**ílich**> [N. Straits Salish]. This spit is named “Séh-litsh” on the 1857-62 Boundary Survey manuscript map, and is given as [sʔílič] by Suttles (1951, 30). The Lummi word for Point Francis is <síles>, which means *rising up* (GA), and an etymology for this place name in Lummi is root <sil-> ***rising up*** + suffix <-ich> ***in back*** (GA). (Lummi is relevant here since it is a dialect of Northern Straits Salish.)

Semiahmoo Spit, also called Tongue Spit, separates Drayton Harbor from Semiahmoo Bay west of Blaine. The chief Semiahmoo village was located at the butt of the spit. The Semiahmoo people abandoned this site and the Drayton Harbor area following the establishment of the Lummi Reservation and the surveying of the International Boundary in the 1850s (Suttles 1951, 29-30). The Semiahmoo people were given the choice of going to the reserve at White Rock, BC, or to the Lummi Reservation in Washington; there are Semiahmoo descendants at both places today. As with Birch Bay, use of the location by the Nooksack prior to 1850 would have been limited. In the historical period, including the early 20th century, clams were dug and dried in great numbers here, flounder and sole were caught and dried, and ducks were hunted and their meat dried (Richardson 1974, 70).

The following three place names were recorded, but their locations are uncertain, so they are not included on the maps. The first two are probably alternate names for known places, while place 138 is a mystery.

136. Kw'ól7oxwilh Camp with plank houses; location uncertain.

<**Kw'ól7oxwilh**> [k'ʷó·loxʷɪɬ] (PF:LG), poss. /k'ʷólʔoxʷ-iɬ/ or /k'ʷólʔoxʷ-əɬ/. The root means ***dog salmon;*** suffix *in the past* or *offspring* (if <-iylh>). See also place 100.

This place consists of four or five smokehouses for drying dog salmon, belonging to Sumas and Nooksack people (PF). The location is uncertain, but the description matches place 100 Xwkw'ól7oxwey.

137. Mó̲qwem Bog and perhaps village near Lynden.

<**Mó̲qwem**> [má·qʷəm] (PF; WS:GS), /máqʷəm/. ***Sphagnum bog/cranberry marsh,*** poss. a Halkomelem word, /má·qʷəm/ *sphagnum bog; Labrador tea.*

On a list of villages (Fetzer 1951b, 1-2), this place is close to <Chítmixw> /čítmixʷ/ (see place 34) and <Smátentsut ~ Smátentsot> /smǽtəncot/ (place 35), poss. the same prairie as <Kw'elástem7ey> /k'ʷəlǽstəmʔiy/ (place 34). Alternatively, Paul Fetzer's manuscript map shows [má·qʷəm] as a village at the location we have given Lhchálos (place 29), and places Lhchálos where we have located Chmó̲qwem (place 28).

138. Núxwilmet Location uncertain.

<**Núxwilmet**> [núxʷilmət] (BG:EF). A place name of unknown location, said to mean ***clear water;*** it has /noxʷ-/ ***always,*** but Nooksack has <íyem> for *clear water* (see place 92) with <y> instead of <l>; the stem could instead be cognate with Upriver Halkomelem <**í:lá:mt**>, //ʔí·lɛ́·m=T//, *carry s-th on one's shoulder, portage a boat,* i.e., ***always portage.***

The following are three probable Nooksack place names attested only by Halkomelem speakers in BC, but attested by one of them as Nooksack names.

139. Stótelew Hatchery Creek and village at the mouth of Hatchery Creek. **Map 5**

<**Stóteḷew**> ~ <Stútelow> [stútəlo] /stótələw/. ***Little creek*** from Nooksack /stótələw/ *little creek,* not from Halkomelem /státəlo(w)/ *little creek,* but given by Mrs. Amy Cooper (AC), a Halkomelem speaker. The word for *river* in Nooksack is <stúl7aw7> (BE:SJ). *A Stó:lō–Coast Salish Historical Atlas* (Carlson et al. 2001, 139, 149) has Stótelo, Hatchery Creek, translation 'small creek, narrow stream'; 'little creek.' The latter is the Halkomelem name. The first vowel in the Nooksack name is as in English "so"; the first vowel in the Halkomelem name is as in English "ma" or "pa." This is a consistent correspondence between Nooksack and Halkomelem. Only a small number of words or place names have the latter sound in Nooksack, often from Nooksack with a Halkomelem accent, or perhaps Nooksack undergoing the same sound change as Halkomelem already did but in only a small number of words.

Hatchery Cr. is a tributary of Sweltzer Cr., which drains Cultus L., in BC. <Stútelow> is also used to name the village at the mouth of Hatchery Cr.; this village had both Nooksack and Stó:lō residents and was bilingual. Mrs. Ella Reid, a Nooksack, also confirmed that Nooksack was spoken in a village at Cultus Lake (see place 103), and this is the only attested village.

Speakers of Nooksack or of a language midway between Nooksack and Halkomelem, called <Ch'élexwoqwem> [č'ɔ́ləxʷɔqʷəm] by Dan Milo, lived in the Chilliwack R. valley above Vedder Crossing before Halkomelem speakers from the Fraser R. came to the area (Galloway 1985). AC reported to Galloway that several place names survived from the pre-Halkomelem period, two of which were in Lhéchelesem. We have designated them as place 140 and place 141.

140. St’ept’óp Ryder Lake and Ryder Creek. **Map 5**

<**St’ept’óp**> [st’əpt’ó·p]. Poss. *(nominalizer)-plural (many)-dead (tree),* i.e., ***many dead (trees)*** from Nooksack <s-> *nominalizer* + <C_1eC_2-> *plural, many* + root as in Upriver Halkomelem <s-t’áp-iy> *dead tree,* but AC reported that it may mean *sand flea ridge* (cf. Nooksack (BE:SJ) and Skagit /č’út’əp/ *flea*) – but the sand flea may be a different type of flea from fleas that afflict dogs and people. LT:LG has Nooksack /k’ʷút’ep/ *flea* and PF:GS has /k’ʷót’ap/ *flea,* BE:SJ has /č’út’əp/ but has a comment, “same as Skagit form”; “[t’o/ut’o/uɬǽm] Fr.R. (S.J. rejected as Nk when making tape, altho’ said it earlier as Nk form),” so the Nooksack form is probably <kw’út’ap ~ kw’ót’ap>. *A Stó:lō–Coast Salish Historical Atlas* (Carlson et al. 2001, 137, 150) has T’ept’óp, Ryder Creek and Ryder Lake, translation ‘dead tree.’ The authors got this form from Galloway’s work, however; Galloway heard it from Amy Cooper, and the last vowel rhymes with English “so,” so the Halkomelem version should be corrected to “T’ept’ṓp” in the atlas.

Ryder Cr. is a north tributary entering the Chilliwack R. about 4.2 miles east of the Vedder Crossing bridge.

141. Syenísiy Mt. Slesse and Slesse (Silesia) Creek. **Map 5**

“Sen-éh-sai” ~ “Sen-eh-say” (BS) ~ “Selacee” (Baker 1900, 37), Halkomelem and/or Nooksack [səlísi] /səlís-iy/ <**Selísiy**>, prob. ~ Nooksack <**Syenísiy**> /s-yənís-iy/. Mt. Slesse and Slesse (Silesia) Cr. (spelled “Slesse” in Canada, “Silesia” in the US). Said by Mrs. Amy Cooper to mean ***fang*** in Lhéchelesem (cf. Nooksack /yənís/ *tooth, teeth* + /-iy/ *place,* Upriver Halkomelem [yíl·ɪs] /yə́l·ə́s/ *tooth, teeth*). Said by Gibbs (1857-61) to mean *leaning mountains;* if so, then poss. <**Slelísiy**> [sll̩ísi] /sləlís-iy/ ***leaning-place*** (cf. Halkomelem /s-lalís/ *leaning*). Both descriptions, *fang* and *leaning place*, are quite apt for the tilted jagged range. *A Stó:lō–Coast Salish Historical Atlas* (Carlson et al. 2001,

137, 146) has Selóysi, translation 'fang.' The spelling <Selóysi> is a misspelling for <**Selísiy**>, a Halkomelem pronunciation of the name. Galloway's Upriver Halkomelem dictionary (2009) shows <silís> *(have) sharp teeth, (have) fangs,* from <s-> *nominalizer* or *stative* + < iy ~ éy> *good* + <-elís> *tooth.* Ryder L. is surrounded by Halkomelem-named places and would have to be a substratum survival; Mt. Slesse has Halkomelem-named places east and west of it, but is on the southern border between Halkomelem and Nooksack; there could be both Halkomelem and Nooksack names for Mt. Slesse.

This peak is visible from parts of the upper North Fork Nooksack R. area, but is more easily seen from the Chilliwack area and is located in the Chilliwack R. drainage.

Part 3
Geography, Semantics, and Culture

5
Naming Patterns

Geographic Features Named

THE MOST FREQUENTLY NAMED geographic features are streams (creeks and rivers). Of 85 place names confirmed through linguistic work with Nooksack elders, 24 refer to streams (8 of which also refer to villages). Of 73 unconfirmed place names, primarily from the Northwest Boundary Survey materials, 29 refer to streams. A second frequently named geographic feature is the prairie, including 7 confirmed names (5 of which are also used for villages) and 9 unconfirmed names. A total of 18 confirmed and 3 unconfirmed names refer to villages without also being used to name any significant geographic features. Additional named features include 13 lakes, 13 mountains, and 44 others, such as fishing rocks, marshes, and mountain meadows.

Determination of Modern Locations of Named Places

An important aspect of our study of Nooksack place names consisted of locating and photographing the named places. This was generally easier for obvious geographic features such as streams, lakes, and mountains, as well as for places known to living elders. Even so, minor creeks and small lakes can be confused or misplaced on maps, and over the long lifespans of the elders the sites of well-known villages can change drastically through river washouts, farming activity, and regrowth of forest and brush.

Among the easy and obvious places is <Nuxwsá7aq> /noxʷsǽʔæq/ (place 78), Anderson Creek and the prairie at its mouth, although the process by which this name was extended to the river and the geographic grouping of people is not clear. The name <Nuxw7íyem> /noxʷʔíyəm/ (place 92) for the South Fork Nooksack River is also well known, and with help from the elders we easily located the village site of the same name. Mt. Baker is a dominant geographic feature of the Nooksack area that should be an unquestionable location, yet untangling its many names has been difficult. The name <Kwelshán> /k^{w}əlšǽn/ (place 113) is the Nooksack cognate of the names commonly used for Mt. Baker in Halkomelem and Northern Straits, but to the Nooksack,<Kwelshán> /k^{w}əlšǽn/ referred to the high snow- and brush-free meadows for hunting, while <Kweq' Smánit> /k^{w}ə́q' smǽnit/ (place 114) referred to the snow-covered peak. The Boundary Survey materials include two additional names for Mt. Baker, "Te-kómeh" (discussed under place 115), a Lushootseed name (/təq^{w}úbəʔ/), and "Tuk-we-sallie" (also discussed under place 115), possibly a Thompson name, possibly Nooksack.

To locate many of the sites in the heavily modified lowland area was surprisingly difficult, especially near the Nooksack River, which continually alters its course. Many traditional sites were directly on the river when they were last used and occupied in the 19th century. Most of these locations have been washed away by the river or are no longer near the current riverbed. The village of <Ye<u>x</u>sáy> /yəx̣sǽy/ (place 84) was located on the river at the mouth of a creek of the same name, now called Smith Creek. The village was occupied through the middle of the 19th century, and the location was claimed as an Indian homestead by a leader of the village. The granddaughter of this man lived at the back corner of the property in 1983, away from the river, which has continually eroded it. The location of the traditional village is now on the other side of the river, in an area of frequently flooded gravel bars, and the creek mouth is now a considerable distance from the village site where it was shown on the 1884 Land Survey map (United States General Land Office 1859-90). (See Map 14 on page xx, for details.) The site of the village of <Spálh<u>x</u>en> /spǽɬx̣ən/ (place 80) has also switched sides of the river, but without being washed away. This village, originally located on an island east of the main river channel, was the site of the last standing traditional plank longhouse. Early in the 20th century, the river changed channels and left <Spálh<u>x</u>en> /spǽɬx̣ən/ isolated in the brush to the west of the river. Although it is difficult to reach, the site of the longhouse is marked by a clump of tall cedar trees, and nearby are the remains of an Indian homestead farm where living elders had lived some years ago. (See Map 13 on page 116 for details.)

Somewhat different, and unnatural, river modifications caused difficulties in locating the village site of <Xwkw'ól7oxwey> /(x^{w})k'^{w}ólʔox^{w}iy/ (place 100) on the North Fork at the mouth of Kendall Creek. This village was permanently occupied early in the 19th century but was abandoned in the 1830s following a smallpox epidemic. Intensive seasonal use continued to the end of the 19th century, and one of the "huge smokehouses" was still standing in 1905. This was just prior to the construction of a Washington State Salmon Hatchery, which has greatly modified the area, including extensive grading and filling and riprap of the riverbank. The oral tradition among the hatchery workers places the Indian smokehouse on the first high ground on the east side of the creek, about 500 feet upstream from its present mouth. In contrast, the 1857-62 Boundary Survey manuscript map indicates a village closer to the mouth on the west side. The Land Survey map of 1890 (United States General Land Office 1859-90) shows the riverbank close to the spot described by the hatchery workers, and places the creek mouth to the east of this spot, thus bringing the two sources into agreement. Details are shown on Map 16 (page 136).

In the case of <Sq’éq’ayex̲> /sq’ə́q’æyəx̣/ (place 44), Indian use at the present time (rights to certain fishing spots, for example, this one, were inherited) enabled us to resolve uncertainties about its location. <Sq’éq’ayex̲> /sq’ə́q’æyəx̣/ was the site of a village occupied perhaps 200 years ago and a fishing location in use in the 19th and 20th centuries. This use is documented in historical sources, and the name, importance for fishing, and general area were known to living elders. We were able to determine the location only to within a stretch of river between the end of Northwood Road and the Timon School site, until we saw a Nooksack fisherman heading towards the river in this area. He was fishing a known location and his nets were set near whirlpools or eddies that we assume were the same ones for which the site is named.

The Nooksack people also made extensive use of areas away from the river, especially the so-called natural prairies. One of the most important of these is in an upland area, including much of the present town of Lynden, that would not have stayed clear without regular burning. This area includes three archeological sites of pit houses, one of which is recognized in the ethnographic record and named <Sp’etós> /sp’ətós/ (place 33). The location of the <Sp’etós> /sp’ətós/ pit houses was known to Percival Jeffcott and illustrated in his book (1949, 34), but, unfortunately, the site was bulldozed in the 1950s to fill in the pits. These pit houses were probably last occupied in the early 19th century and were replaced by a plank longhouse that was also called <Sp’etós> /sp’ətós/, although located nearly ½ mile away. This longhouse was occupied until the 1870s, and its remnants were still visible during the youth of living elders (Richardson 1974, 59). In another extension of the name, <Sp’etós> /sp’ətós/ is also applied to an Indian homestead established about 200 yards from the longhouse site.

The exact location of <Méqsen> /mə́qsən/ (place 21) was more difficult to find, although it had been familiar to the elders in earlier years. <Méqsen> /mə́qsən/ is known to the elders as “Stick Peter’s place,” and its general location is clearly marked on maps as Matsqui Indian Reserve No. 4. It is one of many Nooksack place names in British Columbia, but the only definite Nooksack village located in Canada. The Nooksack identity is emphasized by the elders and backed up with statements that Stick Peter spoke "real Nooksack." Our first attempt to locate the site of Stick Peter's house and the traditional village failed because the access road of 50 years ago had completely disappeared. On a later return visit, we went first to the one house now on the south end of the reserve. The gracious Indian woman living there was able to lead us to an abandoned orchard, which was recognized by a Nooksack elder as adjoining Stick Peter's house.

Place names from the 1857-62 Boundary Survey materials resulted in more puzzles, and usually the names were not found elsewhere and even the locations were unfamiliar to the living elders. An area with still unsolved problems is the upper drainage of Fishtrap Creek in British Columbia. The Boundary Survey manuscript map (Series 68) clearly shows and names four source tributaries: "Se(e)t-séh-no-wa" ("Tse-tséh-ne-wun," place 40), "Ko-kwa-ahm" (<Kwokwe7ám> /kʷukʷəʔǽm/, place 41), "Pehp-she" (place 42), and "Seet-le-wheetsh" (<Yilhíxwich> /(s)yəlíxʷič/, place 43). Part of the confusion was resolved when study of Boundary Survey field materials at the US National Archives showed that the first stream (place 40) was mistakenly connected to Fishtrap Creek. Despite this information, the modern locations for the second and third streams are quite uncertain. The drainage patterns on the 1857-62 map do not match up with the current stream locations, nor are they the same as those shown on a 1914 BC Department of Lands map. The area shows evidence of rechannelling of creeks and lack of water in locations that might have had creeks previously. The fourth named creek matches a modern location and the description and name given by Agnes James to Wayne Suttles.

Another puzzle that began with the Boundary Survey map concerned "Kál-kalk-ku" (<Qalqálqx̲w>, place 16). This is a small creek shown on the map as flowing directly into the Nooksack River, but following a channel that defies the topography of the area. The mapping of this creek may have been based on the Indian Nomenclature (Gibbs 1857-61) description of "Kál-kalk-ku" as "first creek running to Nooksack." This creek was named in a sequence following a trail from the Semiahmoo area, and it is the first creek that is within the Nooksack drainage. The modern creek at the location of the trail crossing is a tributary of Bertrand Creek, which then flows to the Nooksack.

The Boundary Survey records contain much detailed information on the mountainous upper North Fork Nooksack drainage, including many names that would otherwise be unknown. Most of these names clearly correspond to known mountains and creeks, which can be verified by the longitude, latitude, and elevations given in Baker 1900, although these have a consistent pattern of error when compared with recent US Geological Survey maps. The name "Tchahko" (place 111) was a puzzle at first. Both the 1857-62 Boundary Survey manuscript map and the published list of elevations (Baker 1900, 46) use it for a small creek entering the North Fork from the south three miles above Glacier Creek. Unfortunately, at or near this location there is no creek large enough to be placed on recent maps. Study of Henry Custer's field notebooks at the US National Archives clearly shows that "Tchahko" is used to name a creek entering the river from the north, now called Maple Creek.

An opposite complication appears with Swamp Creek, which is given two names. This creek is named "Spespaas" (<Spelhpálhx̲>, place 119) on the 1857-62 Boundary Survey manuscript map, but is clearly named "Nuquoichum" (<Nuxwhóchem>, place 120) in the published lists (Baker 1900, 46). On a sketch map by Teosaluk in the Boundary Survey records (Series 69, Map 26), "Spespaas" is placed next to a lake, near a second lake, draining towards the upper Nooksack River. Swamp Creek does drain Twin Lakes, but Custer's field notes clearly apply the name "Spespass" to two open wet areas in the floor of the river valley, and Teosaluk was his guide and the source of most place names in this area. Although complete certainty will never be achieved on the locations of many of the place names, continuing linguistic and ethnohistorical research should reduce the number of unsolved problems.

Semantic Naming Patterns

Analysis of semantic naming patterns looks at place names to discern areas of cultural emphasis and different ways of thinking about and interpreting the world. Northwest Coast Native languages have detailed vocabularies for salmon and the many other animals and plants upon which the speakers depended for food, materials, and medicine. Place names in the Nooksack language provide a sample of this vocabulary, as well as insight into the Nooksack people's view of their world. The naming patterns that we have found in the Nooksack language are summarized in Table 1. There are some overlapping categories in the table; for example, "flora" and "fauna" overlap with "flora/fauna used as food." The percentages are calculated only for each category and thus add up to over 100 percent, all told. The total number used here (117) is for those place names that have etymologies, and excludes those for which we have no etymologies.

We have identified meanings for 117 of the Nooksack places. The greatest number of these (55) are named for environmental features. Fifteen names describe environments in general terms, such as *always has a lake* or *many dead trees,* and four have a root meaning *swamp, bog, marsh,* which can also refer to *Labrador tea* (a plant). Eleven names describe water qualities such as *whirlpool,*

TABLE 1

Patterns for naming places found in the Nooksack language

Place named for	Number of such places	Percentage of the 117 etymologies
Environs, general	15 (+ 4 whose root has such a meaning)	12.8 (+ 3.4)
Environs, water qualities	11	9.4
Environs, land	25	21.4
Salmon	9	7.7
Mammals	4	3.4
Birds	5	4.3
Amphibians (frog)	1	0.9
Mollusks (butter clams)	1	0.9
Fauna	20	17.1
Flora	13	11.1
Manmade items	9	7.7
Activities of Nooksacks	14	12.0
Occurrence in legends	3 (at least)	2.6
People (individuals or groups)	4	3.4
Creek and village at mouth	8 (+ 2 with camp at mouth)	6.8 (+ 1.7)
Village and prairie	5 (at least)	4.3
Flora/fauna used as food	28 (of the 33 flora and fauna)	23.9 (28.2)
Mountain, lake, and creek	1	0.9

getting turbulent, clear water, and *sound of water splashing or dripping fast and hard.* Twenty-five other names describe specific natural features in the environment: *cut ravine, rocky bottom creek, tide goes way out, white face place,* and a rock resembling a person turned to stone. Nine places are named after salmon, four after mammals (beaver and black bear), five after birds, one after butter clams, and one after frogs, for a total of twenty places named after fauna. Thirteen are named after flora, including *black hawthorn berry, tall marsh blueberry plant,* and *bracken fern root.* Nine are named after manmade items (*fence, plank, pit house, slaughter-house, trail to beach,* etc.).

Fourteen places are named after activities of the Nooksack people (*crossing, trading, resting, shooting*), including the following examples (full details on these examples can be found in Chapter 4):

38. Shó̱qwil Trail crossing, fishing site with drying houses, and small prairie area on Fishtrap Creek just south of the International Boundary near Northwood Road.

<**Shó̱qwil**> or <**Sháqwil**> ***Crossing (of water)*** or ***cross (water)-go, come, get*** from Nooksack [šǽq^{w}iˇl] *go across* (LT:LG), cf. also [šx^{w}šǽ·ˇq^{w}il] *bridge, something one goes across on* (LT:LG); Skagit has /šáq^{w}il/ *cross a river or lake;* the Nooksack forms appear to be influenced by both Halkomelem and Skagit.

45. Ey7í7shil7 Location near the mouth of Timon Creek.

<**Ey7í7shil7**>; [ʔé·yʔx^{y}ɪl] (BG) is a Matsqui Halkomelem version of this Nooksack name. The Halkomelem means *bring(ing) a load of food (by canoe) for trade;* Upriver Halkomelem also has /ʔí·x^{y}əl/ *paddling a canoe;* Nooksack has [ʔíšilʔ] /ʔíšilʔ/ *paddle a canoe* and /ʔəy ʔíšilʔ/ ***paddling a canoe*** (BG:SJ).

65. Ch'e7ó̱lesem Village, fishing site, and prairie on Johnson Creek at Clearbrook, Washington, three miles southwest of Sumas, Washington.

<**Ch'e7ó̱lesem**> ***Resting place*** (WS:GS), cf. Halkomelem /c'á·lə́s-əm/ ***turn around***, with /c'/ corresponding to Nooksack /č'/.

113. Kwelshán The high open slopes of Mt. Baker.

<**Kwelshán**>. ***Shooting place*** (WS:GS) or *shoot (with bow and arrow)-(transitivizer)* from Nooksack /k^{w}ə́lə́š/ *to shoot (with bow and arrow) (later with gun)* + /-ǽn/ *place*, or, less likely, instead /-Vn/ *transitive (do on purpose to s-th)*. This is likely the source of the names for Mt. Baker in the neighbouring languages: Halkomelem /k^{w}əlx^{y}-έ·lx^{w}/ (Halkomelem /k^{w}ə́lə́x^{y}/ *to shoot [with bow and arrow, later with gun]*) and Lummi /k^{w}əlšέn/.

At least three places are named after occurrences in legends (although *thunderbird* may have been regarded as a real bird):

89. Leme7ólh Fishing rocks on the east bank of the Nooksack River ½ mile upriver from Deming.

<Leme7ólh>. PJ says it means *taking the salt water away*, from a legend about when salt water extended inland to this point; LG and EF say it may be related to Nooksack /ləməʔ-óɬ/ *kicking* (BG:EF) or perhaps better ***kicked (away) long ago***; also cf. Nooksack [ləməʔ-ǽ·n] *kick something;* poss. /-óc ~ -óʔc/ *edge; (perhaps) mouth,* although *mouth* is usually /-ócin/, so more likely /-óɬ/ (*past tense*).

131. Ch’ínukw’ Toad Lake.

<Ch’ínukw’> *Thunderbird* from Nooksack [čínʊkʷ] *thunderbird* (BG:EF); also cf. Skagit [sč’ídəkʷ] *thunderbird* (BG:LG).

21. Méqsen Village known as “Stick Peter’s place,” Matsqui Indian Reserve No. 4.

<Méqsen> *Nose* because of a story after the time of /x̣ǽ·ls/, the Transformer, about a man sneezing as a sign of coming disaster (WS:AJ). *A Stó:lō–Coast Salish Historical Atlas* (Carlson et al. 2001) has Méqsel (the Upriver Halkomelem pronunciation or form), “significance, ‘large transformer rock in Aldergrove Park, X̱á:ls transformed the nose of a sneezing man as a sign of coming disaster,’ translation ‘nose.’”

Four places are named after people, including the following two groups and one individual:

1. Sq’eláx̱en An area on the southeast bank of the Nooksack River that includes the prairie between Tennant Lake and Barrett Lake.

<Sq’eláx̱en> ***Fenced off*** or ***go around/over the side (e.g., of a log jam).*** The Nooksack word for *fence* is <q’élex̱in ~ q’élax̱en ~ q’élex̱en> (PF:GS), <asq’eláx̱en> *to be fenced off* (PF:GS, file card box 2, card 552, 7 September 1950). Upriver Halkomelem has cognate <q’eléx̱el> *fence,* probably from root <q’el> *go around, go over* + <-ax̣el> *side (of something constructed);* Squamish /q’iáx̣an/ *fence, stockade, fortification;* there were logjams on the river at or near this location that people had to portage or go around, so this may be the origin of the place name rather than

specifically the meaning *fence*. This name also refers to a group of people occupying this area in the early to mid-19th century.

130. X̲achu7ámish Village at the upper, southeast end of Lake Whatcom.

<**X̲achu7ámix**> (Nooksack with Halkomelem accent), unaccented Nooksack prob. <**X̲achu7ámish**>. ***Lake-people*** from /x̣ǽčoʔ/ *lake;* [ǽmixʸ] resembles Halkomelem /-á·məxʸ/ *in appearance,* but the latter is cognate with Nooksack /-ómiš/ as in [qələɬó·mɪš] /qəl-əɬ-ómiš/ *ugly, bad-looking;* Skagit /-ábš/ *people* corresponds to Nooksack /-ǽmiš/, although Nooksack also has /-mixʷ/ *people, person.*

53. Sx̲witl’ Captain John’s place and prairie, across the river from Kwánech.

<**Sx̲witl’**> [sx̣ʷéyƛ’] or [sx̣ʷé·ƛ’], /sx̣ʷíƛ’/, [swé·ƛ’] (PFM). Apparently named after Captain John’s nickname, /sx̣ʷíƛ’/, which in turn means ***bush robin (varied thrush)*** in Nooksack; cf. Halkomelem /sx̣ʷík’/ *bush robin, varied thrush.*

Mt. Baker was important enough to have three different names for the features at different elevations, as well as different names in four Native languages. It is interesting that no names have been identified so far after fish other than salmon (unlike in Halkomelem). Among the places named after flora and fauna, 28 of 30 involve food resources. As in Halkomelem, a creek and a village at its mouth often share the same name (8 cases here, plus 2 of a creek and a camp at its mouth). There are also at least 5 cases of a village and a prairie sharing the same name (very rare in Upriver Halkomelem due to the lack of grassland or prairies). In a few cases, it can be shown that a village gave its name to its creek; in 1 case each, a village took its name from a lake or a creek. In 1 case, it can be shown that a mountain gave its name to a lake and a creek (a common occcurrence in Upriver Halkomelem because of the many mountains upriver); in some cases, it is unclear which was named after which. The Nooksack ethnographic name comes from a creek name, not a village name; the Nooksack language name comes from a village name. So, too, for Halq’méylem and its upriver speakers, the Stó:lō (Galloway 2009).

6
Conclusion

Linguistic Units

To GAIN SOME PERSPECTIVE on the place names in this book in the context of surrounding languages and dialects and village accents, we will discuss these languages, dialects, and village accents here as linguistic units that have influenced each other and that influence the names. This is useful since almost all speakers we worked with and those whom earlier recorders worked with were multilingual, not just in Nooksack and English but also in closely related Salish Indian languages. Multilingual and multi-dialect differences and influences have therefore been taken into account in our study.

Working with the last speakers and partial speakers of Lhéchelesem has revealed a number of interesting facts. All of the last speakers as well as those who have recently learned to speak the language have been at least trilingual. All spoke Lhéchelesem, English, and either Upriver Halkomelem or Skagit (a dialect of Lushootseed). George Adams, who became fluent in Lhéchelesem around 2005, is also fluent in Lummi and English. Brent Galloway, now partially fluent in Nooksack, also speaks English and Upriver Halkomelem. Upriver Halkomelem is one of three dialects of Halkomelem (besides Downriver Halkomelem and Island Halkomelem, each of which has some subdialects). Between the three dialects, there are consistent differences in grammar and sound. Between subdialects of a given dialect, the difference are much, much less, amounting to perhaps 100 words and only one or two minor sound differences. Upriver Halkomelem has a number of subdialects: Tait (called Teltíyt, meaning "from upriver"), Chehalis (spoken on the Harrison River and at the Chehalis Reserve, BC, not related to the Chehalis language in Washington), Pilalt (Pelólhtxw, spoken around Seabird Island, at Chilliwack Landing, and Rosedale, east of Chilliwack, BC), Chilliwack (Ch'elxwíyeqw, spoken at the southern end of the town of Chilliwack, Sardis, and up the old course of the Chilliwack River from Vedder Crossing to Cultus Lake), and Tzeachten (Ch'iyáq'tel, spoken on the reserves east of Sardis, including the Tzeachten reserve). Brent Galloway (1993a) worked with speakers from all these areas and called each variety a subdialect of Upriver Halkomelem.

Of those Lhéchelesem speakers who also spoke Upriver Halkomelem, most spoke the Chilliwack dialect or the Tzeachten dialect; some spoke Pilalt. The rest spoke the Sumas subdialect, which is intermediate between Upriver and Downriver Halkomelem and was spoken at Sumas, at Kilgard, and in a village or camp on the old Sumas Lake. Galloway worked with speakers of this subdialect as well. What made the Sumas subdialect intermediate was the occurrence of glottal stops before other consonants, a feature of Downriver Halkomelem, whereas Upriver Halkomelem replaced all these with phonemic vowel length. Also, while Upriver Halkomelem had replaced all Downriver "n's" with "l's," the Sumas subdialect (spoken by Alice Hunt, for example) had replaced only some of those (see Galloway 1993a, 2009).

The trilingualism of Lhéchelesem speakers came about because of the widespread Coast Salish pattern of village exogamy; that is, most marriages were between members of different communities. Dorothy Kennedy's detailed study of 19th century Coast Salish marriages shows over 75% village exogamy; in about 75% of exogamous marriages, residence was with the husband's group (patrilocality) (Kennedy 2007, 18-19). For the Nooksack people, this often meant marriages to speakers of other languages, in the earlier years mostly the Skagit dialect of Lushootseed and especially Upriver Halkomelem. One example of this was the custom of Nooksack men taking wives from the Chilliwack area or neighbouring areas in BC. This custom began around 1790, according to an elder, Captain John Sualis of Vedder Crossing (see Hill-Tout 1902). The children of such mixed marriages usually picked up some Lhéchelesem from their father and some Upriver Halkomelem (Halq'eméylem) from their mother, or more often one language from one grandparent and the other from another grandparent, since most of the elders interviewed were raised traditionally by grandparents while their parents were establishing careers in fishing, hop picking, and so on.

The resulting Lhéchelesem, since 1790, has had a number of Upriver Halkomelem borrowings; some are also found in the linguistic records as early as those of George Swanaset. Sindick Jimmy, however, spoke English, Lhéchelesem, and Skagit, and only a little Upriver Halkomelem, so his Lhéchelesem is closer to the uninfluenced Lhéchelesem. George Swanaset's Lhéchelesem had strong Upriver Halkomelem influences and was an example of what Galloway calls Lhéchelesem with an Upriver Halkomelem accent.

Place Names, Land Ownership, and Territory

Place names are part of a people's relationship to the land; for indigenous peoples, they can also provide proof of ties to traditional lands. Among the Coast Salish peoples, this relationship is complex due to the nature of traditional society. Specifically, the Central Coast Salish, which includes the Nooksack people, had strong kin groups that directly controlled some of the important resources in conjunction with community ownership of other resources by an entire named group (a cluster of neighbouring villages that share an identifying name and a sense of territory) (see Richardson 1982, 101-2). Another complicating factor is the sharing of the same language by several separate named groups, as in the case of the speakers of Upriver Halkomelem discussed above. Even when a named group has a unique language, as did the Nooksack, the overlapping territories of named groups and frequent sharing of resources introduced under "The Nooksack People" in Chapter 1 add further complexity to the use of place names to define territory. Several questions regarding the Coast Salish relationship to the land are explored in this section.

First, to what extent does the location of named places correspond to areas of land ownership or tribal territories? There might not be a direct match. In this study, we found four quite different names for Mt Baker (places 113 Kwelshán, 114 Kweq' Smánit, 115 Teqwúbe7, and "Tuk-we-sallie" [see under 115]) involving at least two different languages (Nooksack and Lushootseed, and possibly Thompson) with cognate forms known for Halkomelem and Lummi. Clearly, a large number of Native groups had names for Mt. Baker, yet all these groups could not have owned Mt. Baker or even included it in their territories, but the mountain was important to all of them. Different issues are raised by place 132 <Chúkwenet>, Chuckanut Creek and Bay. As detailed in Chapter 4, the Lummi (Northern Straits Salish) form of the name had a slight phonetic difference, and a different etymology has been suggested. The place names evidence would support both Lummi and Nooksack claims to this area, which both groups used in the past and continue to share today. This leads us to a review of Coast Salish concepts of territory and related patterns of access to resources.

Although some specific resource sites were owned by kin groups (Richardson 1982, 101-2), did the Coast Salish have group territories in the sense of bounded areas from which members of other groups were excluded? In his recent work, Brian Thom (2005, 2009) argues that such a view of territory misrepresents Salish concepts and causes harm in the ongoing land claims processes. He states: "The cartographic practice of representing indigenous territories as discrete, mutually exclusive units contrasts starkly with indigenous discourse, which frames the notion of territory within a pervasive ideology of sharing ... What are the epistemological limits of the western notion of 'territorial boundaries' in a world of interlocking kin ties ...?" (2009, 179). To resolve this "paradox of boundaries," Thom proposes a "radical cartography of territory" in which "the Coast Salish world would be represented by lines radiating out from the chosen residence location of each individual" (2009, 199). Strong arguments against an approach to territorial mapping where boundaries and borders would be virtually meaningless are made by Dorothy Kennedy, whose work has focused on social networks based on kin ties. For example: "The expansive social network did not create a regional free-for-all, driven by the moral ethos of kinship and affinity, with an attendant erasure of ownership or 'territory' ... Residential boundaries may have been permeable, and at times elusive, but boundaries of identity and property relations did exist" (Kennedy 2007, 23). To answer the question posed at the beginning of this paragraph, we take the view that group territories were real in the sense of identifiable landscapes, reinforced in many places by place names known from a certain language or dialect, but that the boundaries were not rigid and extensive sharing of resources occurred. The "paradox of boundaries" presented by Thom may be resolved in Kennedy's "two sides of a coin": "Supporting ideology linked people to place, while at the same time the social system permitted the movement of people, information, and goods across a vast landscape" (2007, 6).

To explore issues of territoriality further, let us review some basic features of traditional Coast Salish society. In an article originally published in 1960, Wayne Suttles (1987, 30-31) includes the following features:

1 Communities composed of one or more kin groups firmly identified with their locality by tradition
2 Membership in kin group through bilateral descent, with alternate or even multiple membership possible, making the individual potentially mobile
3 Preference for local exogamy, establishing a network of affinal ties among communities
4 Preference for patrilocal residence, having the result that, within the community, most adult males are native and most adult females outsiders ...
5 Sharing of access to resources among communities through affinal and blood kin ties – possibly leading to some change in residence.

Thus, communities and kin groups were strongly linked to geographic places, individuals were potentially members of several groups, and there was extensive sharing of resources. The links between peoples and places were, and continue to be, grounded in place names, as demonstrated by the importance of this study to the Nooksack Indian Tribe. We share the view of Kennedy and Suttles that this connectedness has deep roots in traditional Coast Salish society.

How were the larger community groups, often referred to as tribes, formed, and in what way did they control territories? "In its common usage, a Central Coast Salish tribe was comprised of a cluster of villages sharing a common name, a shared concept of territory, and occasionally, a common form of speech" (Kennedy 1995, 51). Although Coast Salish groups had concepts of territory, there was often considerable overlap with neighbouring groups. Brian Thom is certainly correct that maps showing group territories with non-overlapping boundaries fail to represent Coast Salish relationships to the land. As discussed under "The Nooksack People" and "Nooksack Linguistic Boundaries" in Chapter 1, Nooksack territory includes joint-use areas and bilingual communities. Even so, the sense of territory is real and is reinforced by places named in the local language or dialect. Also, the ideology of sharing has its limits and "access to territories is not granted to everyone on all occasions, the idiom of kin – directly, through marriage, or through descent reflected in Indian names – provides the rationale through which territories are shared throughout the Coast Salish world" (Thom 2005, 358-59). To conclude, from the evidence of the place names analyzed here, Coast Salish groups, including the Nooksack, had definite territories that often overlapped with the territories of neighbouring groups, and the resources of these territories, including sites owned for specific resources, were shared with members of other groups based on ties of marriage or descent.

Methodological Insights

In carrying out our research, we found a number of works on place names written by authors who were not linguists. Our work here has shown that careful linguistic field work and analysis can provide important methodological rigour for conducting this kind of research. It seems useful to point out some of the insights that we have gained into such work, and to explicate a clear-cut methodology as used by linguists.

In doing field work with speakers, a linguist will often get place names in the language he or she is researching, as examples of either sounds or words, a speaker's personal linguistic history or biography, or something that just happened to pop into an elder's memory. It is important to follow up and document all such information and to keep a separate section of place names in one's research notes. To follow up while doing the interview, it is important to ask whether the speaker knows the literal meaning of the place name, as quite often he or she does. Do this when you first get a place name, since such knowledge is filed in areas connected to the place name in the brain, in either episodic memory or morphological memory.

The literal meaning can be given morpheme by morpheme or as a fluent phrase. Both are helpful. The speaker may not know what a literal meaning is, so just ask whether the place name means anything. Sometimes the meaning will be accurate in later morpheme-by-morpheme analysis, sometimes it may be merely a reflection of facts known about the place name; without linguistic analysis, it is not always possible to tell which.

If a literal or any other meaning is not known for the place name, keep this as a question for other speakers. If you know something about the language, you may be able to analyze the word for its root and/or its affixes. If you can see possibilities, you can ask the speaker whether a given part of the name may mean what the proposed morpheme means elsewhere. Any answers are helpful.

Once a morpheme is identified, it may help identify others. This is especially true if you have an overall meaning or a literal meaning for the place name. Some morphemes are used repeatedly with place names, as we have seen with Nooksack places. This knowledge can help you analyze more place names – for example, to isolate a root or an affix. And so the linguistic detective work continues. Typically, it takes several years to do the maximum possible analysis of a large set of place names, as we have done here, but it is very rewarding because it tells much about the language, the culture, the resources, and the environment of a people. Such rigorous methodology, we argue, is well worth following, for the insights into the language and culture that it provides as well as for the important bridge between generations working towards the revitalization of indigenous languages. It is well worth doing.

As soon as is possible after the first interview, get maps of the area (the best are topographic maps, since these show the geography best and have all the English place names applied in as fine a scale as the map). We obtained topographic maps of the entire Nooksack area, in a few larger-scale maps and in all the smallest-scale maps from the US Geological Survey and Canadian map offices. As we studied these, we could give more correct English names and more exact locations for some of the names. In other cases, we found that we could ask more intelligent questions about the names we had already obtained.

As our work with the elders continued, it became clear that the best approach was to work with as many who had knowledge of indigenous places as we could; by asking questions regarding such places one area at a time, we often got names that we would not have thought to ask about. The best technique, of course, is to tape-record all this information and also transcribe it on the spot, so that the linguist can ask for the name or information to be repeated in order to ensure accurate transcriptions. This is important, since doing a quick transcription of the name and the place it refers to and only partial transcription of the other information, and later relying on a recording to fill in the details, may well backfire if a recording is too poor to transcribe from or if the recorder was still running with no tape left or with noise pollution from passing cars, for example. Such mistakes are easily made by beginning linguists and non-linguists.

Listen to the tapes once before your next interview session to get the maximum benefit and to minimize repeated questions. Keep a record of any questions you need to ask at the next interview in order to follow up on or correct passages in doubt. This is a basic technique of any field work, whether it includes linguistic, anthropological, oral history, or other interviews. If there is no opportunity for work with the same person, these questions can be asked of other speakers or interviewees.

Where multiple informants are used, the information can be evaluated comparatively. If there is agreement, well and good. If there are still questions, they may be resolvable by the next stage of research, study of the literature from any field that might have relevant information. Ideally, one does this first and returns after each interview, but often the opportunity to do interviews may arise before one has done much documentary research or even knows what knowledge the informant has that one will need to research. If there is disagreement between the informants and/or disagreement between them and the documentary evidence, detective work and deduction will be needed to resolve questions. If this does not resolve the disagreement, keep it in mind while carrying out further interviews with new informants or examining new documentary sources. Sometimes, as with our work presented in this book, the answer comes only after 20 or 30 years of research.

Most often we alternated between interviews and documentary research, so that we did the interview, studied the results, connected them with documentary evidence and map study, and then did more interviews.

One of the most useful techniques we utilized, and fairly early in our research on Nooksack places (the fifth year out of 30), was trips to visit the places with as many elders as we could fit in two cars. This provided the best opportunity to find or refine the locations of the named places, and to get information about Nooksack places that were unnamed. The only drawback was that we could not record or write down some of the information while driving, so when there was too much new information to remember until the next stop, we stopped and wrote it down before driving on. We usually met with the elders' group for lunch, then went to a given area for one or two hours, often with topographical maps. Such site visits involved Brent Galloway's taking black-and-white photos and Allan Richardson's taking colour slides, since the black-and-whites could be more easily published and the slides could be used in talks about the place names. With digital storage, which in 1979 we could not have predicted would become so universally available, we can now include the colour slide images in the online Audio and Photo Supplement for this book.

When preserving photos or slides, it is crucial to keep a running record of each shot as it is taken. We used this information in labelling both prints and slides. This labelling should be done as soon after the trip as possible. We found that we remembered additional useful information if we did it promptly, whereas we did not remember as much several months later. We have not yet solved the problem of how to link detailed labels with scanned photos or slides on computer, but each computer image must have a distinct filename. In the online Audio and Photo Supplement, the colour slides are sorted according to the place being shown.

Insights into Language Loss and Rebirth

Under "Linguistic Units" above, we described the dialects and subdialects of the speakers, as we also did when talking about each speaker in the Introduction. Here we need to take a look at the condition of these dialects and subdialects, their health and, for most, their demise. Just as a language may die with the last speaker's death, so may a dialect or subdialect, or even one individual's way of speaking that subdialect (i.e., their idiolect). Fortunately, with tape recordings, digital recordings, and written transcriptions, it is possible to preserve any of these, at least in part. And now, with modern applied linguistic and pedagogical techniques, it is also possible to slow the loss of these and even to revive most of them. Can this be done for a language that has died? As a matter of fact, it can, as the cases of Lhéchelesem and Upriver Halkomelem show.

There are a number of excellent books and articles on language death and language loss, particularly by Nancy Dorian (for example, *Language Death: The Life Cycle of a Scottish Gaelic Dialect* [1981] and *Investigating Obsolescence: Studies in Language Contraction and Death*, a collection of essays that she edited [1989]). Another impressive source is *When Languages Die: The Extinction of the World's Languages and the Erosion of Human Knowledge* by K. David Harrison (2007), which emphasizes the cultural and knowledge loss that occurs with language loss. We did not use these directly in our research, but we have gained some direct experience and insights through Galloway's work with Lhéchelesem and Upriver Halkomelem. When he began work with Upriver Halkomelem in 1970, there were probably about 70-80 speakers among the Stó:lō of the Fraser Valley, British Columbia, and the Nooksack Tribe in Whatcom County, Washington. Galloway 1980 and Galloway 1993a list 60 by name (almost all of them are now deceased), and 10-20 more speakers have come to light or become fluent since. Thanks to ongoing Halkomelem classes in both BC and Washington, about 20 more have become partially fluent. Although the last fluent speaker of Lhéchelesem died in 1977, he was not the last speaker. In 2002, George Adams began transcribing all the extant tapes, now copied onto CDs for the Nooksack Tribe. He also studied the analysis of the language done by Galloway since 1974 and has been fluent since around 2005. Galloway himself has become a partial speaker of Lhéchelesem, as has Catalina Renteria, and Adams has been teaching the language to Nooksacks of all ages in various classes, so there is hope that both Upriver Halkomelem and Nooksack will survive. Nooksack has in fact been reborn as a result of extensive study, subvocalizing, and daily practice, so it was dead only from 1977 to 2001.

How does place names research help? In Upriver Halkomelem territory and, to a lesser extent, in Nooksack territory, many native language place names survive in modern names for topographical features, reserves, roads, and such, most badly misspelled in English orthography, as they were recorded by geographers not fluent in the languages. In a linguistically and ethnographically accurate study of place names (ethnogeography), the misspellings are corrected, as are most of the inaccurate English literal translations of the names' meanings. In addition, most erroneous locations are corrected through careful work with elders who know the locations and the activities that occurred in them.

As the Indian people whose ancestors spoke the language become aware of the proper pronunciation of these place names and the names' meaning and importance in their culture, they can correct erroneous information from the past and carry on their precious traditions. They also become familiar with the sounds of the language and the meanings of roots and affixes found in the names. Since many of these names are of places still travelled through and used, enough of the language is brought to mind to make people who have not been exposed to it before curious to learn more about it. Those who remember hearing the names experience the return of many positive memories and a desire to learn more of the language. And those who are fluent, partially fluent, or even just beginners are able to teach the sounds of the language to friends and relatives through correct pronunciation and the meanings through correct literal interpretations, as presented in this book.

What of the subdialects of Upriver Halkomelem? There are still speakers of Tait, Chehalis, Pilalt, Chilliwack, and Tzeachten. All the first-language speakers of Pilalt and Sumas, and perhaps of Chehalis, Chilliwack, and Tzeachten have died, so the speakers of these subdialects are all second-language speakers of Halkomelem and first-language speakers of English. There have been classes in all the subdialects at various times between 1970 and the present, but we believe that today it is mainly Chehalis, Pilalt, and Chilliwack/Tzeachten that are being actively taught.

The Nooksack Tribe now offers both Upriver Halkomelem classes and Lhéchelesem classes. Both languages have been spoken by tribal members since the 1790s. Why did Lhéchelesem die first? It appears to have suffered the slow loss of speakers for many years; Upriver Halkomelem also lost speakers, but its numbers were maintained into the 1970s by the constant influx of Halkomelem-speaking wives into the Nooksack community as well as by frequent cross-border family ties and visits. Lhéchelesem, on the other hand, never had many speakers living in Canada, with only the small settlement of Méqsen (place 21) occupied in the 19th century, so it lost ground in the Nooksack Tribe compared with Halkomelem. When we began working with the Nooksack elders in 1974, Galloway was hired by the tribe to teach a Halkomelem Workshop, whose goal was language maintenance and revival of Upriver Halkomelem since there was only one Lhéchelesem speaker left. Of the 23 elders in the workshop, all but 6 spoke Upriver Halkomelem. In today's Nooksack elders group, there are one or two Halkomelem speakers.

While we were researching Nooksack place names with the elders group from 1974 to 2002, the discussions of and visits to the named places helped with the revitalization of both Halkomelem and Lhéchelesem, although only to a minor extent compared with the language lessons in each. They did help with language maintenance, since knowledge of even a few names taught elders something new, enabled them to review the sounds and structures of both languages, and stimulated their interest in taking classes. Discussions about our meetings, about new place names, or about details that the elders had learned were held in a number of homes, sparking curiosity and even causing some family members – mainly grandchildren but also a few children and spouses – to enrol in classes. Classes now include great-grandchildren and great-great-grandchildren of elders we worked with.

Another advantage of teaching and learning from place names is that analysis of such names shows them to be more conservative than many other parts of the vocabulary. More Nooksack language morphemes survived in place names than in words spoken by partially fluent tribal members before 2002. These names also sometimes preserve older pronunciations of morphemes, older embedded grammatical structures, and older meanings of some morphemes than is attested in linguistic field notes taken with the last speakers. In some cases, the speakers know this and bring it out; in other cases, they do not know this and it is left to the linguist to discover. When these older layers are uncovered, they can lead students of the language to see language change in process, and can even help restore a number of linguistic features and morphemes that might otherwise be forgotten and never learned by students. Thus, all of these features can be of help in revitalizing language and stimulating curiosity and interest.

The ceremony in 2002, described in Chapter 1, held to present the Nooksack Tribe with boxed CD sets with copies of all extant Nooksack language tapes, had a major effect on efforts to revive the language (see, for example, Galloway 2007, 2008; Galloway et al. 2004a) and also spurred the learning of Lhéchelesem by George Adams and Catalina Renteria, as well as the offering of classes in the language. For cultural reasons, ceremony is often crucial to the effectiveness of new initiatives in the Nooksack Tribe and is the best way to involve the entire tribe in significant events. Two complete sets of the boxed CDs were given to the tribe; another complete set each went to the Canadian Museum of Civilization and the Department of Linguistics of the University of British Columbia; a final complete set was kept by Galloway and now resides with all his research, tapes, and CDs in the Brent Galloway Collection in the Northwest Linguistics Collection of the University of Washington. One of the Nooksack Tribe's copies is kept as an archival copy and the other copy is allowed only limited use, such as by Adams for his study of the language and for language revival. CDs also allow the material to be copied onto computers. The same is true of sets of CDs that contain copies of original field notes of Fetzer, Amoss, Thompson, and Efrat, typed into digital files by Galloway and his research assistants over several years. All these CDs can now be used for computer searches to find Nooksack words, sentences, stories, and analyses.

Bridging Linguistic and Ethnographic Insights

In the years since we began our study of Nooksack place names, there has been increasing interest in the relationship of people to geographic places through culture and language. Perhaps the best known work is Keith Basso's *Wisdom Sits in Places: Landscape and Language among the Western Apache,* published in 1996. Another excellent book combining culture and language is Gary Palmer's *Toward a Theory of Cultural Linguistics* (1996), a very wide-ranging book that covers a vast amount of interdisciplinary work combining language and culture and cognitive linguistics. At the same time, *Senses of Place* (Feld and Basso 1996) brought together the work of several scholars who had studied a range of different cultures. Basso (1996, 69-70) presents the following challenge to scholars studying people and their environment:

> If anthropology stands to benefit from an approach to cultural ecology that attends more closely to the symbolic forms with which human environments are

> perceived and rendered significant, so, too, there is a need for an expanded view of linguistic competence in which beliefs about the world occupy a central place. If it is the meaning of things that we are after – the meanings of words, objects, events and the claims people make about themselves – language and culture must be studied hand in hand. Our knowledge of one can only enhance our knowledge of the other.

We feel that we have met Basso's challenge, even if we began our study almost 20 years before his publication! Basso's own work combines a thorough knowledge of Apache culture and language to reach a deep understanding of the people's relationship to the land. For the Western Apache, cultural knowledge and moral lessons quite literally "sit in places," as stories embodying this knowledge are bound to specific places (see Basso 1996). Although we found stories related to many of the Nooksack places, there were few examples comparable to the extensive Apache use of places to teach moral lessons. More importantly, the naming of places in Lhéchelesem gives the Nooksack people a sense of place.

Another presentation of American Indian sense of place is provided by Bierwert (1999) in *Brushed by Cedar, Living by the River,* a contemporary ethnography of the Stó:lō speakers of Upriver Halkomelem. Chapter 2, "Figures in the Landscape," focuses on one fishing site on the Fraser River and the different ways in which this place can be viewed. Different views of Nooksack places are included in this book, if not explored in the same detail for any one place. One of us has written a detailed study of one place for a legal case (Richardson 1995); the other has written a detailed study of 59 Squamish and Halkomelem place names for a land claims legal case (Galloway 1996a) and a detailed study of Halkomelem words referring to economic activities for a fishing rights case (Galloway 1991). We hope that this book has contributed to the broader understanding of Coast Salish senses of place by combining linguistics and anthropology to document all the places named in the Nooksack language (and a few places without known names) and their cultural and historical significance.

As can be seen from Table 1 on page 194, place names were extremely important in identifying and remembering important features of the Nooksack environment: 55 places are named for features of the environment, either general features, water qualities, or land features; 28 (of the 33 named for flora or fauna and not included in the figures for environment) are named for flora or fauna that are food sources; and 14 are named for cultural activities of the Nooksack. Nine are named after manmade items, mostly constructed with materials at the sites. Only 4 are named after people, either individuals or groups, and 3 are named for their occurrence in legends (but some of those in the previous category of people may also fit here, with the legends being lost). Eight are names applied to a creek and a village at its mouth, 5 places are named for a prairie and a village on the prairie, and there is 1 instance of a mountain, lake, and creek sharing the same name (speakers could always add the word for lake or creek after the name to make the reference explicit).

What does this teach us about how the Nooksack view their environments, food sources, social relationships, myths or legends, and soundscape, and about their poetic feelings regarding these places? Based on the Nooksack place names and their meanings, the Nooksack viewed the environmental factors and the flora and fauna used for food as the most salient in 83 of the 117 places for which we have etymologies. The knowledge of flora and fauna used for food, so important for survival, is preserved in place names. Naming places after some environmental factors also has survival value, as does naming them for descriptive orientation, especially when someone is lost or needs to confirm his or her location. Some of the names that reflect Nooksack activities have survival value, while others serve to remind people of resources used for making things or of places where cultural activities took place. This is one difference from Upriver Halkomelem place names, which include a far greater proportion based on legends, possibly due to the fact that more Halkomelem legends have been recorded or preserved.

As with English place names, some Nooksack place names gain salience and atmosphere through reference to the plants, animals, or activities they are named for. The elders told us that few places were named for sounds or poetic feelings, so these do not appear to be important factors in Nooksack place names. One exception is Whatcom, X̱wó̱tqwem (place 133), which is named for the noise of rushing water (for example, of a waterfall, as found in Whatcom Creek) or water dripping fast.

Several differences between English and Nooksack place names stand out. For example, many English place names refer to people, but almost no Nooksack place names do. On the other hand, many Nooksack place names have direct survival value, whereas most English place names do not. And although many English places are named for positive feelings or value judgments (Pleasanton, California; Happy Valley, Washington) or after places in the Bible (Eden Valley and Goshen in Washington) to encourage settlement, Nooksack places are rarely named in this way.

In summary, the meanings and histories of Nooksack place names provide a valuable understanding of things important to the Nooksack people, and often surprising knowledge about the places themselves and the people to whom these places belong.

References

Books, Articles, and Unpublished Reports and Manuscripts

Adams, George, and Brent Galloway. 2009. Classified Word List for Nooksack. Unpublished manuscript, 370 pp.

Adams, George, Brent Galloway, and Catalina Renteria. 2005. "A Nooksack Story from 1956; How to Become an Indian Doctor." Paper presented at the 40th International Conference on Salishan and Neighboring Languages and published in *University of British Columbia Working Papers in Linguistics* 16: 1-31.

Amoss, Pamela T. 1972. "The Persistence of Aboriginal Beliefs and Practices among the Nooksack Coast Salish." PhD dissertation, University of Washington.

–. 1978. *Coast Salish Spirit Dancing: The Survival of an Ancestral Religion.* Seattle: University of Washington Press.

Baker, Marcus. 1900. "Survey of the Northwestern Boundary of the United States, 1857-1861." *Bulletin of the United States Geological Survey,* no. 174.

Basso, Keith. 1996. *Wisdom Sits in Places: Landscape and Language among the Western Apache.* Albuquerque: University of New Mexico Press.

Bates, Dawn, Thom Hess, and Vi Hilbert. 1994. *Lushootseed Dictionary.* Seattle: University of Washington Press.

Beckey, Fred. 2003. *Range of Glaciers: The Exploration and Survey of the Northern Cascade Range.* Portland: Oregon Historical Society Press.

Bierwert, Crisca. 1999. *Brushed by Cedar, Living by the River.* Tucson: University of Arizona Press.

Boyd, Robert. 1990. "Demographic History, 1774-1874." In *Handbook of North American Indians,* vol. 7, *Northwest Coast,* ed. Wayne Suttles, 135-48. Washington, DC: Smithsonian Institution.

Carlson, Keith Thor, Albert (Sonny) McHalsie, and Jan Perrier. 2001. *A Stó:lō Coast Salish Historical Atlas.* Vancouver: Douglas and McIntyre.

Clark, Ella. 1953. *Indian Legends of the Pacific Northwest.* Berkeley: University of California Press.

Coleman, Edmund. 1869. "Mountaineering on the Pacific in 1868." *Harper's New Monthly Magazine* 39: 793-817.

Collins, June. 1974. *Valley of the Spirits: The Upper Skagit Indians of Western Washington.* Seattle: University of Washington Press.

Curtis, Edward S. 1913. *The North American Indian,* vol. 9. New York: Johnson Reprint Corporation.

Custer, Henry. 1858a. "Report of Henry Custer, Assistant, of His Reconnaissance of the Country between Camp Simiahmoo and Sumass Prairie. Camp Simiahmoo, April 7, 1858." Unpublished field report of the United States Northwest Boundary Survey, US National Archives, RG 76, E 196.

–. 1858b. "Report of Henry Custer of Survey of Shore Line from Camp Simiahmoo to Whatcom and of Reconnaissances of Mouth of Lummi River; Whatcom Lake & Vicinity and Trail Leading Thence to the Nooksahk River: and of Whatcom & Nooksahk Trail. Camp Simiahmoo, July 18, 1858." Unpublished field report of the United States Northwest Boundary Survey, US National Archives, RG 76, E 196.

–. 1859. "Report of Henry Custer of Reconnaissances along the 49th Parallel and Vicinity, between Schweltcha Lake and Senehsay River. Chiloweyuck Depot, July 2 1859." Unpublished field report of the United States Northwest Boundary Survey, US National Archives, RG 76, E 196.

–. 1866. "Report of Henry Custer Assistant of Reconnaissances Made in 1859 over Routes in the Cascade Mountains in the Vicinity of the 49th Parallel. May 1866, Washington, D.C." Unpublished field report of the United States Northwest Boundary Survey, US National Archives, RG 76, E 196.

Dorian, Nancy. 1981. *Language Death: The Life Cycle of a Scottish Gaelic Dialect.* Philadelphia: University of Pennsylvania Press.

–, ed. 1989. *Investigating Obsolescence: Studies in Language Contraction and Death.* Cambridge: Cambridge University Press.

Duff, Wilson. 1952. *The Upper Stalo Indians.* Anthropology in British Columbia, Memoir No. 1. Victoria: BC Provincial Museum.

Edson, Lelah Jackson. 1968. *The Fourth Corner.* Bellingham, WA: Whatcom Museum of History and Art.

Emmons, Richard V. 1952. "An Archaeological Survey of the Lower Nooksack River Valley." *Anthropology in British Columbia, 1952:* 49-56.

Feld, Steven, and Keith Basso, eds. 1996. *Senses of Place.* Santa Fe: School of American Research Press.

Fetzer, Paul S. 1951a. "The First Draft of Some Preliminary Considerations on the Subject of Territory and Sovereignty among the Nooksack and Their Neighbors." Unpublished manuscript dated 7 March.

–. 1951b. "Nooksack Enculturation: A Preliminary Consideration." Unpublished manuscript.

Fitzhugh, E.C. 1856. Fitzhugh to Simmons, letter, 21 September. Records of the Washington Superintendency of Indian Affairs, 1853-74. US National Archives, Microfilm M5, Roll 10.

–. 1858. "No. 135, Bellingham Bay Agency, Washington Territory, June 18, 1857." In *Report of the Commissioner of Indian Affairs, accompanying the Annual Report of the Secretary of the Interior for the Year 1857,* 325-29. Washington, DC.

Galloway, Brent. 1977. "A Grammar of Chilliwack Halkomelem." PhD dissertation, University of California at Berkeley.

–. 1980. *The Structure of Upriver Halq'eméylem: A Grammatical Sketch and Classified Word List for Upriver Halq'eméylem.* Sardis, BC: Coqualeetza Education Training Centre.

–. 1982. "Proto-Central Salish Phonology and Sound Correspondences." Paper presented at the 17th International Conference on Salishan Languages, Portland State University, Portland, OR.

–. 1983a. "A Look at Nooksack Phonology." In *Working Papers of the 18th International Conference on Salishan Languages,* comp. Eugene Hunn and Bill Seaburg, 80-132. Seattle: University of Washington.

–. 1983b. "Nooksack Pronouns, Transitivity, and Control." Paper presented at the 22nd Conference on American Indian Languages, American Anthropological Association, 82nd Annual Meeting, Chicago, 17-20 November.

–. 1984a. "A Look at Nooksack Phonology." *Anthropological Linguistics* 26 (1): 13-41.

–. 1984b. "Nooksack Reduplication." In *Papers of the XIX International Conference on Salishan and Neighboring Languages*, special issue of *Working Papers of the Linguistic Circle, University of Victoria* 4 (2): 81-100.

–. 1985. "The Original Territory of the Nooksack Language." *International Journal of American Linguistics* 51 (4): 416-18.

–. 1987. "Computerized Dictionaries of Halkomelem and Nooksack: Some Discoveries So Far." Paper presented at the 22nd International Conference on Salishan Languages, Victoria, BC.

–. 1988. "Some Proto-Central Salish Sound Correspondences." In *In Honor of Mary Haas, from the Haas Festival Conference on Native American Linguistics*, ed. William Shipley, 293-343. Berlin: Mouton de Gruyter.

–. 1991. "Some Cognate Words to Halkomelem Words on Economy." Exhibits 31 and 32 in *HMQ v. Alfred Hope et al.* fishing rights case.

–. 1992. "Computerized Dictionaries of Upriver Halkomelem and Nooksack" and "3-D Semantics and the Halkomelem Dictionary." In *Amerindia, Revue d'Ethnolinguistique Amerindienne*, numero special 7 (special issue 7), *Amerindian Languages and Informatics: The Pacific Northwest*, ed. Guy Buchholtzer, 47-82. Paris: Association d'ethnolinguistique amérindienne.

–. 1993a. *A Grammar of Upriver Halkomelem*. Publications in Linguistics, vol. 96. Berkeley: University of California Press.

–. 1993b. "Nooksack Reduplication." In *American Indian Linguistics and Ethnography in Honor of Laurence C. Thompson*, ed. Anthony Mattina and Timothy Montler, 93-112. Occasional Papers in Linguistics, no. 10. Missoula: University of Montana.

–. 1996a. "An Etymological Analysis of the 59 Squamish and Halkomelem Place Names in Burrard Inlet Analyzed in Suttles Report of 1996." Material filed in evidence in the land claims cases of *Mathias v. HMQ, Grant, and George; Grant v. HMQ and Matthias,* and *George v. HMQ and Matthias.*

–. 1996b. "A Look at Some Nooksack Stories." Paper presented at the 35th Conference on American Indian Languages, 95th American Anthropological Association Annual Meeting, San Francisco.

–. 1997. "Nooksack Pronouns, Transitivity, and Control." In *Papers for the 32nd International Conference on Salish and Neighboring Languages*, comp. Timothy Montler, 197-243. Port Angeles, WA: Peninsula College.

–. 2007. "Language Revival Programs of the Nooksack Tribe and the Stó:lō Nation." In *Be of Good Mind: Essays on the Coast Salish*, ed. Bruce Granville Miller, 212-33. Vancouver: UBC Press.

–. 2008. "Revival of Amerindian Languages from the Dead: The Case for Nooksack." Paper presented at the 4th International Conference on Indigenous Education: Asia/Pacific [Regions], Vancouver, and published in *Indigenous Education: Asia/Pacific*, ed. Robert Wesley Heber, 297-308. Saskatoon: Indigenous Studies Research Centre, First Nations University of Canada.

–. 2009. *Dictionary of Upriver Halkomelem*. University of California Publications in Linguistics, no. 141, 2 vols. Berkeley: University of California Press.

Galloway, Brent, George Adams, and Catalina Renteria. 2004a. "Bringing Back the Nooksack Language from the Dead." *University of British Columbia Working Papers in Linguistics* 14: 141-48.

–. 2004b. "What a Nooksack Story Can Tell Us about Morphology and Syntax." *University of British Columbia Working Papers in Linguistics* 14: 149-65.

Galloway, Brent, and Allan Richardson. 1983. "Nooksack Place Names: An Ethnohistorical and Linguistic Approach." In *Working Papers of the 18th International Conference on Salishan Languages,* comp. Eugene Hunn and Bill Seaburg, 133-96. Seattle: University of Washington.

Gardner, G. Clinton. 1857a. "Report of G. Clinton Gardner, Assistant Astronomer and Surveyor, of Reconnaissance of Country East of Camp Semiahmoo, Dated Sept. 3, 1857." Unpublished field report of the United States Northwest Boundary Survey. US National Archives, RG 76, E 196.

–. 1857b. "Report of G. Clinton Gardner, Assistant and Surveyor, of Progress of Work, Dated November 20, 1857." Unpublished field report of the United States Northwest Boundary Survey. US National Archives, RG 76, E 196.

Gibbs, George. 1853? "Indian Nomenclature of Localities in Washington and Oregon Territories." Manuscript 714, National Anthropological Archives. Washington, DC: Smithsonian Institution.

–. 1853-58. "George Gibbs Notebooks of Scientific Observations of the Pacific Northwest." Western Americana Collection, Beinecke Rare Book and Manuscript Library, Yale University.

–. 1857-61. "Indian Nomenclature." Records of the United States Northwest Boundary Survey. US National Archives, RG 76, E 223.

–. 1860. Drawings. Microfilm Reel 3, Gibbs Family Papers, 1763-1918. State Historical Society of Wisconsin, Madison.

–. 1863. "Alphabetical Vocabularies of the Clallam and Lummi." Published under the auspices of the Smithsonian Institution. New York: Cramoisy Press.

Grabert, Garland F. 1983. *Ferndale in Prehistory: Archaeological Investigations in the Lower and Middle Nooksack Valley.* Occasional Paper No. 19. Bellingham, WA: Center for Pacific Northwest Studies, Western Washington University.

Harris, Joseph S. 1858. "Report of the Survey of a Guide Line to the Forty-Ninth Parallel of Latitude from Camp Simiahmoo to Camp Sumass Made in April and May 1858, Dated June 21, 1858." Unpublished field report of the United States Northwest Boundary Survey. US National Archives, RG 76, E 196.

Harrison, K. David. 2007. *When Languages Die: The Extinction of the World's Languages and the Erosion of Human Knowledge.* Oxford: Oxford University Press.

Hawley, Robert E. 1971. *Skqee Mus or Pioneer Days on the Nooksack.* Bellingham, WA: Whatcom Museum of History and Art. Originally published in 1945.

Hess, Thom. 1976. *Dictionary of Puget Salish.* Seattle: University of Washington Press.

Hill-Tout, Charles. 1902. "Ethnological Studies of the Mainland Halkomē'lEm, a Division of the Salish of British Columbia." *Report of the British Association for the Advancement of Science* 72: 355-490.

Indian Claims Commission. 1950. Manuscript map submitted in Nooksack claims case, Docket no. 46. US National Archives, RG 279.

Jeffcott, Percival R. 1949. *Nooksack Tales and Trails.* Ferndale, WA: Author.

–. 1964. "The Nooksack Indians: A Brief History of the Tribe." Unpublished manuscript.

Kennedy, Dorothy. 1995. "Looking for Tribes in All the Wrong Places: An Examination of the Central Coast Salish Social Network." MA thesis, Department of Anthropology, University of Victoria.

–. 2007. "Quantifying 'Two Sides of a Coin': A Statistical Examination of Central Coast Salish Social Network." *BC Studies* (153): 3-34.

Kuipers, Aert H. 2002. *Salish Etymological Dictionary.* Occasional Papers in Linguistics, No. 16. Missoula: University of Montana.

Lane, Fredrick F. 1860. "Diary of Gold Prospecting Trip to the South Fork Nooksack River, August 23–September 7, 1860." Jeffcott Collection, Box 8, Folder 121. Center for Pacific Northwest Studies, Western Washington University, Bellingham.

Majors, Harry M. 1984. "Discovery of Mount Shuksan and the Upper Nooksack River June 1859." *Northwest Discovery* 5 (21): 2-84.

Maud, Ralph, Brent Galloway, and Marie Weeden, eds. 1981. "The Oliver Wells Tapes Relating to Salish Indians." Unpublished manuscript.

Nooksack Indian Tribe. 1974. *Nooksack Tribal Planning Project: Phase I Report.* Deming, WA: Nooksack Indian Tribe.

–. 2000. "Nuxwt'íqw'em, Middle Fork Nooksack River Valley." National Register of Historic Places Registration Form, completed on 5 October.

Nooksack Tribe of Indians. 1924. "Petition of Nooksack Indians," submitted by George Swanaset. In *Hearing before the Committee on Indian Affairs, House of Representatives, Sixty-Eighth Congress, First Session, on HR 2694, February 2, 1924,* 52-55. Washington, DC: Government Printing Office.

Nugent, Ann. 1980. *History of Lummi Legal Action against the United States.* Bellingham, WA: Lummi Communications.

Palmer, Gary B. 1996. *Toward a Theory of Cultural Linguistics.* Austin: University of Texas Press.

Richardson, Allan. 1974. "Traditional Fisheries and Traditional Villages, Camps, and Fishing Sites of the Nooksack Indians." In *Nooksack Tribal Planning Project: Phase I Report,* 50-72. Deming, WA: Nooksack Indian Tribe.

–. 1976. "Nooksack Indian Homesteading." Unpublished report prepared for the Nooksack Indian Tribe.

–. 1977. "Nooksack Indian Homesteading: A Study of Settlement Ethnohistory." Unpublished manuscript.

–. 1979. "Longhouses to Homesteads: Nooksack Indian Settlement, 1820-1895." *American Indian Journal* 5, no. 8 (August): 8-12.

–. 1982. "The Control of Productive Resources on the Northwest Coast of North America." In *Resource Managers: North American and Australian Hunter-Gatherers,* ed. Nancy M. Williams and Eugene S. Hunn, 93-112. Boulder, CO: Westview Press.

–. 1995. "Traditional Cultural Practices of the Nooksack Indians in the Vicinity of Warm Creek, Middle Fork Nooksack River." Written expert testimony in *Nooksack Indian Tribe v. State of Washington, Department of Ecology; Whatcom County; and Warm Creek Hydro, Inc.* (SHB No. 95-1 & PCHB No. 94-148).

Richardson, Allan, and Brent Galloway. 2007. "Nooksack Indian Place Names." Unpublished map.

Shaw, George C. 1909. *The Chinook Jargon and How to Use It.* Seattle: Rainier Printing.

Smith, Marian. 1950. "The Nooksack, the Chilliwack, and the Middle Fraser." *Pacific Northwest Quarterly* 41 (October): 330-41.

Stanley, George, ed. 1970. *Mapping the Frontier: Charles Wilson's Diary of the Survey of the 49th Parallel, 1858-1862, while Secretary of the British Boundary Commission.* Seattle: University of Washington Press.

Sullivan, Michael. 1978. "John Tennant's Lake." In *John A. Tennant: Early Pioneer and Preacher.* Bellingham, WA: Fourth Corner Registry.

Suttles, Wayne. 1951. "The Economic Life of the Coast Salish of Haro and Rosario Straits." PhD dissertation, University of Washington.

–. 1954. "Post-Contact Culture Change among the Lummi Indians." *British Columbia Historical Quarterly* 18: 29-102.
–. 1987. *Coast Salish Essays.* Seattle: University of Washington Press.
Teit, James. 1900. "The Thompson Indians of British Columbia," vol. 1, pt. 4 of *Publications of the Jesup North Pacific Expedition.* New York: American Museum of Natural History.
–. 1910-13. "Notes to Explain Maps of Historical Tribal Locations and Trade Routes during 19th Century." Originals held by the American Philosophical Society Library, Philadelphia; Boas Collection, Item 59. Copy available at Provincial Archives of British Columbia, Microfilm A 239.
Thom, Brian. 2005. "Coast Salish Senses of Place: Dwelling, Meaning, Power, Property and Territory in the Coast Salish World." PhD dissertation, McGill University.
–. 2009. "The Paradox of Boundaries in Coast Salish Territories." *Cultural Geographies* 16: 179-205.
United States Congress. 1869. Northwest Boundary Commission. House Ex. Doc. 86, 40th Congress, 3rd Session, 13 February.
United States General Land Office. 1859-90. Land Survey Maps of Townships in Whatcom County, Washington. Copies available at Whatcom County, Department of Public Works, Bellingham, WA.
Wells, Oliver N. 1966. "Interview with Mr. & Mrs. J.W. Kelleher and daughter, Irene, 11 Sept. 1966." Taped interview, Royal British Columbia Museum, Victoria.
–. 1987. *The Chilliwacks and Their Neighbors*, ed. Ralph Maud, Brent Galloway, and Marie Weeden. Vancouver: Talonbooks.

Archival Collections

Foreign Office Correspondence. FO 5/1468, Northwest Boundary (Land), Com. Hawkins and General, 1865 to 1871. Public Record Office, Kew, Richmond, Surrey, UK.
Howard E. Buswell Collection, Center for Pacific Northwest Studies, Western Washington University, Bellingham.
P.R. Jeffcott Collection, Center for Pacific Northwest Studies, Western Washington University, Bellingham.
Records of the United States Northwest Boundary Survey, 1857-62. In Records of Boundary and Claims Commissions and Arbitrations, Record Group 76 (RG 76). Textual records: Entry 196 (E 196), Reports on Surveys, 1857-66; E 201, Topographical Notes, 1857; E 202, Reconnaissance Books, 1857-63; E 223, List of Indian Words, n.d. Cartographic records: Series 66, Maps Signed by United States and British Commissioners, 1857-62; Series 68, Miscellaneous Maps, 1857-63; Series 69, Field Maps, 1857-62. United States National Archives, College Park, MD.

Unpublished Field Materials Relating to Nooksack Language and Culture

The following are listed in chronological order:

Wayne Suttles – ethnographic and linguistic field notes, 1949-52, 1958
Paul S. Fetzer – ethnographic and linguistic field notes, 1950-51
Pamela T. Amoss – Nooksack language field notes and tapes, 1955-56, 1969-70
Laurence C. Thompson – Nooksack language field notes and tapes, 1967, 1969, 1970
Barbara S. Efrat – Nooksack language field notes and tapes, 1970-72, 1974
Brent Galloway – Nooksack language field notes and tapes, 1974-81
Allan Richardson – ethnographic field notes and tapes, 1974-97

Index of Places by Number

In this and the following indexes, the place names are shown in the Nooksack practical orthography, except for Northwest Boundary Survey and Percival Jeffcott spellings, which are enclosed in double quotation marks, and forms for which no Indian-language names are known, such as 2A, the main Nooksack River. In all indices, m = map, p = photograph, and Bold = analysis of name

Index of Places by Nooksack Name

The alphabetical order of the Nooksack alphabet is: a, ch, ch', e, h, i, k, k', kw, kw', l, lh, m, n, o, o̲, p, p', q, q', qw, qw', s, sh, t, t', tl', ts, ts', u, w, x, xw, x̲, x̲w̲, y, 7.

Place names without a Nooksack name or Nooksack orthographic equivalent are alphabetized in English alphabetical order; for example, b, c, etc.

Index of English-Named Locations

Also of Interest

First Nations Languages

The First Nations languages of the world, many of which are renowned for the complexity and richness of their linguistic structure, embody the cumulative cultural knowledge of Aboriginal peoples. This vital linguistic heritage is currently under severe threat of extinction. This series is dedicated to the linguistic study of these languages.

Patricia A. Shaw, a member of the Department of Linguistics at the University of British Columbia and director of the First Nations Languages Program, is general editor of the series.

The Lillooet Language: Phonology, Morphology, Syntax
Jan van Eijk

Musqueam Reference Grammar
Wayne Suttles

When I Was Small – I Wan Kʷikʷs: A Grammatical Analysis of St'at'imc Oral Narrative
Lisa Matthewson, in collaboration with Beverley Frank, Gertrude Ned, Laura Thevarge, and Rose Agnes Whitley

Witsuwit'en Grammar: Phonetics, Phonology, Morphology
Sharon Hargus

Making Wawa: The Genesis of Chinook Jargon
George Lang

First Nations Languages

Printed and bound in Canada by Friesens

Set in Franklin Gothic, Minion, and Charis by Artegraphica Design Co. Ltd.

Copy Editor: Frank Chow

Proofreader: Dianne Tiefensee

Cartographer: Eric Leinberger

ENVIRONMENTAL BENEFITS STATEMENT

UBC Press saved the following resources by printing the pages of this book on chlorine free paper made with 100% post-consumer waste.

TREES	WATER	ENERGY	SOLID WASTE	GREENHOUSE GASES
5 FULLY GROWN	2,452 GALLONS	2 MILLION BTUs	156 POUNDS	544 POUNDS

Environmental impact estimates were made using the Environmental Paper Network Paper Calculator. For more information visit www.papercalculator.org.